D0427028

DEMOCRACY'S MUSE

OTHER BOOKS BY ANDREW BURSTEIN

*Lincoln Dreamt He Died: The Midnight Visions of
Remarkable Americans from Colonial Times to Freud*

Madison and Jefferson (with Nancy Isenberg)

The Original Knickerbocker: The Life of Washington Irving

Jefferson's Secrets: Death and Desire at Monticello

The Passions of Andrew Jackson

*Letters from the Head and Heart: Writings of
Thomas Jefferson*

*America's Jubilee: How in 1826 a Generation
Remembered Fifty Years of Independence*

*Sentimental Democracy: The Evolution of
America's Romantic Self-Image*

The Inner Jefferson: Portrait of a Grieving Optimist

EDITOR

Mortal Remains: Death in Early America (with Nancy Isenberg)

DEMOCRACY'S MUSE

{ How Thomas Jefferson Became an FDR Liberal,

a Reagan Republican, and a Tea Party Fanatic,

All the While Being Dead }

ANDREW BURSTEIN

UNIVERSITY OF VIRGINIA PRESS
CHARLOTTESVILLE AND LONDON

University of Virginia Press
© 2015 by Andrew Burstein
All rights reserved
Printed in the United States of America on acid-free paper
First published 2015

ISBN 978-0-8139-3722-9 (cloth)
ISBN 978-0-8139-3723-6 (ebook)

1 3 5 7 9 8 6 4 2

Library of Congress Cataloging-in-Publication Data
is available from the Library of Congress.

To Matt and Lizzie

CONTENTS

PREFACE

UP CLOSE, he presented an air of reserve, even of shyness. Yet he was well hated at a distance. Thomas Jefferson made and maintained political enemies, while retaining among his friends a reputation for sturdiness and commitment. When he died, and the heat that emanated from the vigorous positions he took in life had time to cool, he gradually became whatever an adoring posterity wanted him to be.

If we were to aggregate the memories of those whose lives span the seven decades since Thomas Jefferson's head was formed from Mount Rushmore, we would see that the essential founder has passively endured several noticeable facelifts. He has been, in that time, freedom's philosopher, racist-in-chief, the champion of liberal government, and the champion of small government; what remained of his ethereal image was most spectacularly compromised after the exposure of his sexual secret keeping. One thing hasn't changed, though: his is the first name Americans associate with representative democracy. He is the one "founding father" whose political sentiments reverberate loudest. Here and around the world, he is democracy's muse.

Politicians gravitate to Jefferson for obvious reasons. His expressions of hope for the future of the republic—and republics abroad—remain integral to Americans' collective sense of purpose. He provides an ennobling vocabulary that elected representatives draw upon when they seek support from the public. A few brief examples will give an adequate taste of what that language sounds like. Jefferson as the inspired peacemaker: "Let us then, fellow citizens, unite with one heart & one mind; let us restore to social intercourse that harmony & affection, without which Liberty, & even Life itself, are but dreary things (First Inaugural Address, March 4, 1801). As a man of the Enlightenment: "For here we are not afraid to follow truth wherever it may lead, nor to tolerate any error so long as reason is left free to combat it" (to English historian William Roscoe, December 27, 1820). Or, as a fair-minded freethinker: "It behoves every man who values liberty of conscience for himself, to resist invasions of it in the case of others" (to Dr. Benjamin Rush of Philadelphia, April 21, 1803).

Jefferson goes far in clarifying the meaning of freedom. His message is one of faith in the human spirit: it can be used to project confidence in the potential of democracy to shape the ideal society or recover a lost virtue. And so, even when they are not seeking partisan advantage, presidents and members of Congress pepper speeches with quotes from Jefferson's personal letters and public documents. The accomplished architect, book collector, natural historian, and linguist generally strikes a modern audience as the most cosmopolitan in taste among the Revolutionary set, and certainly the easiest to universalize. He is ammunition held in reserve; he is moralizing fodder. He is the supremely articulate superego of the American nation.

Problems occur whenever he is abstracted. We know that professional politicians require a serviceable narrative when they run for office and are under pressure to draw lessons from the past. Jefferson is but one victim of their interpretive shortcuts. Professional historians strive to temper the excesses of professional politicians, and yet even they have been known to succumb to the temptation to oversimplify Jefferson. History is not a stable narrative; the compulsion to rewrite it is rarely more than half-conscious. That, in a nutshell, is what this book is about.

The World War II era furnishes a prime example of the unconstrained use of the mindful founder who speaks so volubly to his posterity. Our study begins here, when the United States was simultaneously fighting Nazi and Japanese militarism. On April 13, 1943, the bicentennial of Jefferson's birth, President Franklin Roosevelt dedicated the Thomas Jefferson Memorial in Washington, D.C. The speech he delivered on that carefully chosen day matched Jefferson to his own political faith.

In that dark year, the third president was nothing less than the light at the end of the tunnel. He had bequeathed to a world at war his abiding faith that, as Roosevelt phrased it, "the seeming eclipse of liberty can well be the dawn of more liberty." No one could have projected America's resolve as well as Jefferson when he wrote in 1800: "I have sworn before the altar of God, eternal hostility against every form of tyranny over the mind of man." Those are the words, as Roosevelt forcefully pointed out, that encircle the interior of the domed monument.

We don't officially celebrate Jefferson's birthday anymore. For that matter, Washington's and Lincoln's February birthdays have been stuffed into the all-encompassing Presidents' Day. The nation has revolving rituals, none so lively as the annual Fourth of July, which was the only birthday Jefferson said he cared to celebrate.[1]

I HAD BEEN thinking of taking up this subject for almost a decade, after having stood before a typed paper with handwritten insertions by John F. Kennedy (see page 46). On April 29, 1962, the thirty-fifth president hosted a dinner at the White House for forty-nine Nobel laureates. The *New York Times* reporter who covered the event described this group as "the cream of scientific America." In the shock that followed the Soviets' launch of *Sputnik* in 1957, superpower competition had escalated; increasingly, Americans saw scientific expertise and technical innovation as critical to their nation's standing in the world.

As the distinguished guests assembled, First Lady Jacqueline Bouvier Kennedy adorned the scene, wearing a gown of "sea-foam green" and wedding-style gloves that extended past her elbows. Colonel John H. Glenn Jr., an instant hero as the first U.S. astronaut to orbit the earth, signed autographs for the scientists and their wives, as he chatted easily with Attorney General Robert Kennedy. The popular poet Robert Frost, then eighty-eight years old, was in attendance, too—fifteen months earlier he had recited "The Gift Outright" at the president's inaugural. Noted authors from John Dos Passos to James Baldwin received their invitations. The controversial physicist J. Robert Oppenheimer, instrumental in developing the atom bomb, was on hand; so was the chemist Linus Pauling, a staunch critic of nuclear testing. There were 175 invited guests that evening, plus "Ban the Bomb" picketers hovering outside the gates of the White House.

On the mantle above the fireplace in the room where the guests gathered, a bust of Thomas Jefferson sat prominently. The third president "would have relished the scene," read the caption in a *Life* magazine spread about the event. At the black-tie dinner, President Kennedy spoke words that instantly became iconic: *"I think this is the most extraordinary collection of talent, of human knowledge . . . ever gathered at the White House,"* he intoned, *"with the possible exception of when Thomas Jefferson dined alone."* Inspecting the text from which the president had extemporized, I was transported.[2]

Kennedy was celebrated for his charm, of course, and for his spontaneous wit. Unlike many other politicians' recurrences to Jefferson, Kennedy's prepared quip had to have been original with him. He had orchestrated the Nobel laureates' dinner himself, rather than delegate planning to the First Lady and her staff, as he had done on previous such occasions. Two months earlier, at a press conference, he had sprung a Jefferson quote on reporters when asked about attacks on his method of dealing with Cold War challenges. "What we are anxious to do is to protect our national security," he lit up, and "permit what Thomas Jefferson called 'the disease of liberty' to be caught in areas which are now held by Communists." Candidate Kennedy had tapped the same quote in a campaign speech in New York on the eve of his election in 1960.

It was as a retired ex-president that Jefferson had written those words to an old ally, the Marquis de Lafayette. Trends in Europe appeared to support the forward march of political democracy, and as Spain's colonies in the Americas formed independent republics, Jefferson asserted that "the disease of liberty is catching" and would inevitably raise people "from the prone condition of brutes to the erect attitude of man." President Kennedy must have understood the historical context behind his words to reporters—they were not mere throwaway lines.[3]

There is something sustaining in the evocation of Jefferson that causes America's modern leaders to reference him by name as often as they do. Of the other celebrated individuals associated with the founding era, none but Jefferson is so closely or emotionally linked to the spirit of democracy and to individual freedom. George Washington may loom large, but he remains cold, aloof, and fairly prosaic in the historic imagination. He was not a giant thinker. Benjamin Franklin is as quotable as Jefferson, but the entrepreneurial printer and scientific experimenter descends to us as a role model for industriousness and practicality more than political activism. At the end of his years, as Washington entered the presidency, Franklin was no longer giving shape to the new republic, at least not directly. It is Jefferson who is seen as prodigious, and this is only right—for he is the quintessential, if not earliest, exponent of what modern patriots term "American exceptionalism," a questionable concept we will explore later in the book.

Works about the historical Jefferson continue to roll off the presses. If he appears as a hypocrite as much as a popular hero these days, we understand why: the liberty-loving planter inherited, and occasionally bought and sold, other human beings. Our embarrassed world is always immersed in heated debates over race and ethnicity, baring our collective concern about national belonging. The facts make it impossible to deny that the distant past still causes us trouble today. It is jarring to consider that Jefferson's time was much closer to Shakespeare's than to ours, yet we are far from done fighting the moral battles of yesteryear.

If President Kennedy will forgive the slight correction, it does not appear that Jefferson dined alone very often during his presidency. The point, however, is that we cannot go back and spy on him. He is indirectly felt, and not really known to us. It is always the case that the fate of the past rests in the hands of the present, and so the final verdict on Thomas Jefferson has not yet been read. The prying eyes of history keep scrutinizing him, aiming to establish the meaning of his life to America and the wider world.

DEMOCRACY'S MUSE is a critique of modern politics. I have written elsewhere about Jefferson's life and times. In *Jefferson's Secrets* (2005), I devoted one entire chapter to an ex-president's later years' preoccupation with the role that partisanship would play in shaping his posthumous legacy. Now I get to give him something of an answer, by taking a provocative excursion through "impersonations" of the historical Jefferson over the decades since the dedication of his luminous memorial in Washington, D.C. In pursuing this goal, I build on two related works: the late Merrill D. Peterson's seminal study *The Jefferson Image in the American Mind* (1960); and Francis D. Cogliano's engaging update *Thomas Jefferson: Reputation and Legacy* (2006). Both account for the creative as well as destructive components of historical memory. Both are irreplaceable studies.[4]

As democracy's muse, Thomas Jefferson wavers for one simple reason: democracy is itself volatile. It does not dispense with domination and control, and it does not distribute liberty in equal shares. But because his special literary qualities caused history to anoint him the supreme expositor of America's founding values, Jefferson has been a barometer of political virtue, and, therefore, held to an impossibly high standard. The historian Michal Jan Rozbicki writes emphatically: "Charges of hypocrisy begin to look a bit eerie when we realize that we are applying our ideal fictions to reproach the Founders for getting carried away by their ideal fictions." It may seem obvious, but it is sometimes easy to forget that bad feelings existed in the Era of Good Feelings and irrationality abounded in the Age of Reason.[5]

There are very few general statements we can safely make in comparing the eighteenth century to our day. One is that theirs, like ours, was a time when people across the social spectrum indulged the fantasy of consummate knowledge and set unreachable goals. With a community's self-definition at stake, it has become second nature to remove unsightly warts from the past and shorten the psychological distance between then and now. This book lays down a challenge to the glib assertions of all who would find certainty, or even comfort, in reconstituting Thomas Jefferson.

Because the language of the Declaration of Independence has been granted an almost Scripture-like status, many have been tempted to imagine Jefferson as someone with a modern conscience. He was not, of course, and history is easily falsified. I will occasionally be moved to identify modern misreadings of Jefferson, while seeking (as every historian does) to minimize my own unavoidable ideological bias in pointing out the restrictive ideologies of others. This is especially the case in part 2 of this book, where I analyze the culture wars of the recent past.[6]

We look into darkness when we try to extrapolate from their papers what the founders would have thought if they were alive today. Here I am describing the fallacy of the doctrine of original intent. Isn't it curious, then, that people should have so personal a reaction to Thomas Jefferson, who has been gone for so very long? One of the reasons he continues to resonate is the easy accessibility of Monticello, the mountain dreamworld he designed and redesigned, and which his slaves and other skilled workers built and rebuilt over the course of decades. Millions have visited. To the imaginative eye, Jefferson still steps from room to room, dines with guests, and sits quietly in his "cabinet," or study, surrounded by his several thousand books. As most are aware, the Virginia gentleman was an ingenious architect, an avid collector, a lover of the Greek and Roman example who transformed his mountain home into a neoclassical museum.

Of the first three national monuments erected to celebrated presidents, Washington's, which came first, is physically imposing but pockmarked and aesthetically unimaginative—like Washington, one might say. The second is certainly ennobling, though its pillared opulence in no ways recalls the log cabin simplicity of Abraham Lincoln's formative years. Only the Jefferson Memorial says something historically accurate about the man it honors.

And that is where we begin the conversation.

PART ONE

Political Setting

Cover of the official brochure for the Jefferson Memorial issued at midcentury by the Department of the Interior.

1

"ETERNAL HOSTILITY AGAINST EVERY FORM OF TYRANNY"

Nineteen Forty-Three

THOMAS JEFFERSON arrived at his two-hundredth birthday in the middle of World War II, in the tenth year of Franklin D. Roosevelt's presidency. On that day, the three-term president dedicated the Jefferson Memorial in Washington, D.C. This new noble structure, polished and shining brightly, immediately became a powerful political symbol.

Something else catches the eye. Words set in stone. If Jefferson is heralded for one ability above all, it is his highly engaging and often intoxicating use of American English. The timeless words that wrap around the interior of the dome of his memorial, drawn from a letter to his friend Dr. Benjamin Rush as he sought the presidency in 1800, are vintage Jefferson. In 1943, they stood as an obvious act of defiance to the Nazi menace:

> I HAVE SWORN UPON THE ALTAR OF GOD ETERNAL HOSTILITY
> AGAINST EVERY FORM OF TYRANNY OVER THE MIND OF MAN.

Jefferson's reputation as an American symbol has risen and receded over the years, generally losing ground when a pro-business ethos prevails in the public's imagination. He is most commonly associated with the rights of individuals, and his nemesis, Alexander Hamilton, with the spirit of enterprise and growth. More recently, the Virginian's representative words and actions as a slaveholder have displaced the Jefferson-Hamilton feud as the paramount expression of his symbolism. But however one reflects upon his record, Jefferson was at or near the height of his posthumous popularity in the Age of Roosevelt, when his political image was reshaped in such a way as to complement the New Deal project of humane reform.[1]

That determination was far from automatic. Unlike FDR, Jefferson was a champion of limited government who placed his trust in the wisdom of ordinary people. On the basis of that philosophy, and his pacific temperament, he appealed to the erudite Woodrow Wilson, a former president of Princeton University and the author of books on constitutional government. Wilson was a restrained-government man, a reluctant interventionist who, like Jefferson, projected the day when freedom-loving peoples around the world would refashion their nations along the lines of the American republic.

Roosevelt, though a confirmed Wilsonian, found it necessary as president to depart from the party's inheritance when he resorted to centralized control over a limp economy. Even so, both he and Wilson expressed their profound antipathy to the fixed character of the Hamilton model, which embraced a strong central authority. Hamiltonianism forever invited the government's cozy alliance with a moneyed elite, and expressed an equally deep disdain for the rights and prospects of the hardscrabble farmer or common laborer. It was left to FDR to make Jefferson amenable to unprecedented federal programs designed to lift up the people who were hurting most.

The process actually began years before his assumption of the presidency. A national figure after he ran unsuccessfully for vice president on the Democratic ticket in 1920, Roosevelt began to channel the liberal humanist version of Jefferson, the practical-minded idealist, while his party was in disarray. The crucial moment in his Jeffersonian makeover occurred at the end of 1924, when Republican President Calvin Coolidge was preaching spending cuts and tax breaks for the rich. At that time, Roosevelt penned a noteworthy book review—at once his first and his last—that took the political tone of the 1920s to be an echo of the discordant 1790s. "I have a breathless feeling as I lay down this book," he wrote of the pointedly titled *Jefferson and Hamilton: The Struggle for Democracy in America*. It was for him "a picture of escape after escape which this nation passed through in those first ten years." The competition between Jeffersonian and Hamiltonian philosophies was primal, and it tracked all ongoing division within American society: Who spoke for the people? And who spoke only for the rich? Roosevelt could perceive "the same contending forces" a century and a quarter after President Washington's combative cabinet members first crossed swords. As he momentously concluded his review: "Hamiltons we have today. Is a Jefferson on the horizon?"

The author of the book that so inspired this future president was Claude G. Bowers of Indiana. He was a dyed-in-the-wool Democrat who, soon after the review was printed, made contact with Roosevelt, enjoyed a three-hour lunch with the New Yorker, and rose so quickly in the ranks of the party that he actually delivered the keynote address at the 1928 Democratic National Convention. That's how dramatic an impact Bowers's book had upon leading Democrats. Colonel Edward House, a close confidant of the late Woodrow Wilson, received twelve copies of *Jefferson and Hamilton* at Christmas; the Tennessee congressman Cordell Hull, FDR's soon-to-be secretary of state, called the book "a godsend to democrats and to our country."[2]

Bowers divided his co-subjects according to their driving spirit and personal disposition as much as their political principles. The elitist Hamilton had only to "snap his fingers," and the wealthy merchants came to him. He openly proclaimed his distaste for the simple farmers and city dwellers with no property and no vote who, until Jefferson arose, had no voice in the halls of government; they were a "scattered mass of unimportant, inarticulate individuals." What they lacked in social prestige, they made up for in personal industry.

According to the author, Jefferson tapped into a yearning for democracy that already permeated the land: "The country was really democratic before there was a party of democracy." Bowers's Jefferson was self-aware, a cautious observer of men and manners, a "philosopher-politician" with a "mild eye" who "teemed with ideas"; beyond that, he was an astute organizer who identified problems and went on to conceive solutions. Without ego, yet with full confidence, he rounded up the most talented political personalities from around the states and formed a political party, the Democratic-Republicans. It suited this "tireless" thinker and actor to have his worthy followers described in energetic terms: "virile," "daring," "able," "resourceful"—and only "fanatical" in their hatred of artificial privilege.

And their combative enemy? The hard-charging Hamilton had no room for the ideas of others: "One may search in vain through the letters of Hamilton for expressions other than those of contemptuous belittlement of his political foes." Jefferson maintained a wry admiration for Hamilton's canniness, but only because he was even-tempered. His natural modesty explained how he became a magnet for all who rejected Hamilton's cynicism.

Jefferson and Hamilton is a political morality tale on the order of *The Adventures of Robin Hood*, dotted with martial metaphors defining the grand battle the two supreme party leaders fought. Hamilton, "ardent and dictatorial," was always galloping ahead like a cavalry officer, "booted and spurred, and riding hard toward the realization of his conception of government." Jefferson "set out to arouse the masses, mobilize, drill, and lead them." Both protagonists had their "lieutenants" who helped them carry out their plans. But, in the end, it was "democracy triumphant," with Jefferson maintaining his vaunted serenity, and Hamiltonian "hot-heads" shamed into accepting the people's choice.[3]

Jefferson mania gripped the out-of-power Democrats. Shortly before Roosevelt gave the nominating speech on behalf of his fellow New Yorker Al Smith, who was to challenge Herbert Hoover in the 1928 general election, Bowers, a practiced, spellbinding orator, proclaimed before his eighteen thousand listeners at the Houston convention—and to a receptive radio audience of millions across the continent—that "there is not a major evil of which the American people are complaining now that is not due to the triumph of the Hamiltonian conception of the state." The enemy, he decreed, was the two-headed force of "privilege and pillage" whom the "American Democracy" would defeat. The packed crowd of delegates cheered at length the attack on the Republican power elite.[4]

National politics is never as simple as campaign rhetoric suggests, of course. A few years earlier, in advance of the sesquicentennial of the Declaration of Independence (July 4, 1926), President Calvin Coolidge determinedly established "American Independence Week," and appointed the Democrat Bowers to the Sesquicentennial Commission that planned the celebration. Noting that the day was also the centennial of Jefferson's death, Coolidge reminded citizens that the author of the Declaration "gave a vivid interpretation of the rightful and universal aspirations of the masses of mankind." It was Jefferson's "insistence" that the Constitution include the Bill of Rights that had made it possible for "the fundamental rights and liberties of the citizen, no matter how humble," to oppose any threat from any oppressor. Coolidge, himself born on the Fourth of July (1872), did not think it necessary to credit the many other politicians of Jefferson's day who had clamored for a bill of rights: nothing was to detract from the nation's affirmative association of its most patriotic moment with Thomas Jefferson. He declared that he would personally initiate "American Independence Week" by ringing a bell in Washington on Monday, June 28. Governors and mayors would follow his lead, signaling bells to be rung in the schools of every town at 11:11 a.m.—the day, and the moment, to be known as the "Echo of the Liberty Bell."

The remainder of the holiday week would unfold gradually:

- Tuesday, June 29, "Universal Education Day." Jefferson to be remembered as champion of "the great American tradition of free education."
- Wednesday, June 30, celebrants to read a "roll call" of the founders. (Washington, Jefferson, and Franklin were the three who were initially named, but it was presumed that others would be added.)
- Thursday, July 1, on "Greater America Day," Jefferson's Louisiana Purchase is singularly honored, under the direction of local bankers, real estate offices, and chambers of commerce—not exactly the gang the populist Jefferson would have chosen to ring in the holiday.
- Friday, July 2, "Signers Day," when descendants of the signers of the Declaration were to lead patriotic gatherings.
- Saturday, July 3, "Monticello Day." Charlottesville was meant to be in the thoughts of paraders across the nation, as every participating town telegraphed its sentiments to Jefferson's home. Monticello had recently opened to the public as a "patriotic shrine for the children of America," operated by the Thomas Jefferson Memorial Foundation. The price of admission was fifty cents.
- Finally, on Sunday the Fourth, "Jefferson Centennial Day," public services were scheduled at the Monticello graveyard, Jefferson's final resting place. Nationwide, churches of all denominations would pay tribute to the patriot's memory.[5]

And so the hallowed day went forward, under Republican auspices.

IF JEFFERSON'S twentieth-century makeover was not wholly Democratic, it was, most assuredly, Democrats who "owned" him. When Al Smith accepted the nomination in 1928, he said he would maintain "direct contact with the people," in keeping with the principles of his party. "I shall strive to make the nation's policy the true reflection of the nation's ideals," he promised. "Because I believe in the idealism of the party of Jefferson, Cleveland, and Wilson, my administration will be rooted in liberty under the law . . . , that equality of opportunity which lays the foundation for wholesome family life and opens up the outlook for the betterment of the lives of our children." Jefferson had come to mean "wholesome" liberty, fundamental human rights, and, theoretically, at least, equal opportunity for all. In terms of a partisan inheritance, Herbert Hoover's Republicans were, Democrats charged, answerable to big business. They might claim Jefferson as a universal American, but Democrats would not agree to loan him to them. When

Hoover defeated Smith, Claude Bowers griped that "the fool people have taken plutocracy to its heart." He and his friend Roosevelt would have to wait four years—four painful years for most Americans.[6]

The man who had placed Al Smith's name in nomination succeeded him as New York's governor. Republicans' fortunes sank along with the stock market, and Roosevelt was comfortably reelected as the state's executive when he opened his campaign for president. At the 1932 Democratic National Convention in Chicago, he was ceremoniously reintroduced to voters as "the incarnation of Thomas Jefferson." Speaking before the nonpartisan Commonwealth Club of San Francisco that September, he began in a lugubrious tone and described the mood of the country as one of "depression, of dire and weary depression." Then he launched into a bright, Jefferson-accented song that replayed Bowers's dramatic narrative. In so doing, FDR imitated the message and the cadence of a famous letter Jefferson wrote, just after his 1801 inauguration, to the liberal theologian and scientist Joseph Priestley.

Jefferson: "We can no longer say there is nothing new under the sun. For this whole chapter in the history of man is new. The great experiment of our republic is new. Its sparse habitation is new. The mighty wave of public opinion which has rolled over it is new." (The third president's point was that the American people were poised to conquer the continent in the name of republican good.)

Roosevelt in 1932: "America is new. It is in the process of change and development. It has the great potentialities of youth and particularly this is true of the great West, and of this coast, and of California."

His rehearsal of Bowers directly followed: "The issue of government has always been whether men and women will have to serve some system of government or economics, or whether a system of government and economics exists to serve individual men and women."

Returning to the era of the American Revolution, the "Jeffersonian" candidate Roosevelt offered a brief history lesson. He pointed out the importance of the shift from a dull acceptance of arbitrary rule to a lively thirst for popular rule. Then, he explained, though independence had been won, an experience with wartime "confusion" left many well-intentioned people with a notion that popular government was "essentially dangerous and unworkable." Those who had lived through the struggle with Great Britain openly worried about a descent into anarchy.

Parties formed on the basis of whether one was hopeful or fearful. Because Jefferson was of a hopeful cast, he saw energetic individuals with their futures before them. In Roosevelt's reading, "Government to him was a means to an end, not an end in itself." For the time being, the laboring classes of America were protected and without need of government assistance. He quoted Jefferson, writing in 1814: "We have no paupers," because the working people of America "exact from the rich and the competent such prices as enable them to feed abundantly, clothe above mere decency, to labor moderately and raise their families." Self-delusion aside, so promising a picture of social interaction could only be short-lived.

As he began to characterize those other early Americans who were mainly directed by their fears, Roosevelt abruptly changed gears: "The most brilliant, honest, and able exponent of this point of view was Hamilton . . . [who] believed that the safety of the republic lay in the autocratic strength of its government, that the destiny of individuals was to serve that government, and that fundamentally a great and strong group of central institutions, guided by a small group of able and public spirited citizens, could best direct all government." This was as Bowers had written: Hamilton spoke for big money, Jefferson for all who did not possess a direct connection to the powerful.

Clawing his way to the present, Roosevelt decried modern Republicans for demanding unequal access to government. He found a serious ethical problem in their currying favor with Washington officials for self-interested purposes. There was a time in the nineteenth century, he allowed, when government gave special breaks to corporations in order to develop infant industries that would bring benefits to everyone in America. But that sort of collusion was no longer appropriate, because by the end of the last century, "industrial combinations had become uncontrolled and irresponsible units of power within the state." The antitrust movement came about to restrain the new "feudal" lords, and to protect the "freedom of individuals" to earn a living wage. "The function of government," Roosevelt asserted, "must be to favor no small group at the expense of its duty to protect the rights of personal freedom and of private property of all its citizens."

Jefferson and Hamilton's "honest" argument was at the heart of everything, he restated, and the people of America won that argument in 1801, when Jefferson took office: "So began, in America, the new day, the day of the individual against the system." Whenever there was hope, there was a "new dream," and Roosevelt repeated the word *dream* several times more as he refocused on the lure of the West, pre-industrial and present-industrial. The simpler options that applied to hardworking citizens past no longer kept the national economy growing on a continent so vast, and so government had to adapt. "Even Jefferson realized," FDR proclaimed, "that the government must intervene, . . . not to destroy individualism, but to protect it."[7]

Rexford Tugwell, a key member of the president's "Brain Trust" in the first years of the New Deal, identified "Jeffersonianism" in candidate Roosevelt's sharp opinions in the crisis years of 1929–30. As political beings, Hoover and Roosevelt were classic opposites, but their opposition was magnified after the stock market crash. "To Hoover it was a cross to be borne, one he had not deserved," said Tugwell. To Roosevelt, of course, the economic disaster was "a challenge to action."

According to the economist Tugwell, FDR possessed a rare combination of instincts that only Jefferson and Theodore Roosevelt, among his predecessors, exhibited to a comparable degree—and that was (a) political savvy, and (b) an engineering capacity. The first defined Roosevelt's and Jefferson's electability; the second enabled them to orchestrate their transformative policies. A number of presidents possessed one or the other quality, but in Roosevelt (perhaps even more than Jefferson), they were "almost ideally combined." In that respect, what made Franklin D. Roosevelt Jeffersonian was a certain similarity between the elections of 1800 and 1932. In both, a watershed change in party control was in the offing, existential fears were raised, and insensitivity to the concerns of non-elites harmed the enervated party on the outs. In the transition that occurred after the election, the incoming presidents anticipated government reorganization on a large scale.[8]

As FDR entered the White House in 1933, Cordell Hull, his secretary of state for the next eleven years, wrote: "I have seen numerous Presidents inaugurated, but no one took the oath in a firmer tone, and with more solemn demeanor than Franklin D. Roosevelt." Hull had "preached the doctrines" of Jefferson from early youth, he recorded, at least those that were "apt for quotation." And in complimenting FDR, the man responsible for carrying out the president's foreign policy drew this comparison: "No President since Jefferson and the Adamses had a wider knowledge of people and conditions abroad."[9]

Hull provides insight into the conversion that took place in the minds of longtime Democrats, whose party platform had always been—until the Age of Roosevelt, that is—married to federal nonintervention. Revisiting the themes contained in Roosevelt's San Francisco campaign address, he conveyed his slow acceptance of what he labeled the "paternalism" that his fellow Tennesseans, former Confederates, had decried ever since he could remember: "When Franklin D.

Roosevelt came to the White House in 1933, the crisis was extraordinary, and called for extraordinary remedies. I was therefore willing to see a broader interpretation of the principle of no paternalism at least for the period of the emergency, although I did not hesitate to call to the President's attention my belief that at times he was adopting cures too sweeping for the disease."[10]

As the New Deal moved forward, Roosevelt expanded his definition of Jeffersonianism as he laid out the trajectory of American democracy in progressive terms. Speaking at Monticello on July 4, 1936, and lauding his "host," he polished his own credentials by blurring the meaning of class. The New York patrician said of the Virginia patriarch and political architect: "He was a great gentleman. He was a great commoner. The two are not incompatible." Then, speaking to the real and present issues of political fairness and economic opportunity, he assured that the standard set by Jefferson's generation was by no means irretrievable: "The world has never had as much human ability as it needs; and a modern democracy in particular needs, above all things, the continuance of the spirit of youth. Our problems of 1936 call as greatly for the continuation of imagination and energy and capacity for responsibility as did the age of Thomas Jefferson and his fellows." With his accustomed verve, he resolved: "It is not beyond our power to relight that sacred fire."[11]

The animated president was a Jeffersonian optimist. He found consistency over time in the impulse toward greater democracy—this, he said, is what directed the mind of a Democratic president, Andrew Jackson, and Republicans Abraham Lincoln and Theodore Roosevelt. Speaking at the Jackson Day Dinner in Washington, D.C., in 1938, FDR explained his thought process as he bade his audience's indulgence: "Let me talk history."

He had won a landslide victory in the election of 1936, besting Governor Alf Landon of Kansas, who captured only eight electoral votes. Brimming with confidence, Roosevelt spoke easily about national unity, defining the greatness of presidents on the basis of the "constructive battles" they fought, "not merely battles against things temporarily evil but battles for things permanently good—battles for the basic morals of democracy." What all great presidents understood, he said, was this simple dictum: "The majority often makes mistakes. But . . . rule by a small minority class unfailingly makes worse mistakes—for rule by class takes counsel from itself." To maintain the "moral integrity of democracy" required steadfast scrutiny.

The Jackson Day Dinner served as a Democratic-accented history lecture. George Washington had unfortunately resolved that government would be "most safely conducted by the minority of education and wealth," said Roosevelt. He listened to Hamilton. "But Jefferson saw that this control, if long exercised by a minority, would be destructive of a sound, representative democratic system." He wished to expand the electorate. Jackson fought "the same evil" as Jefferson; Lincoln, "scorned for his uncouthness, his simplicity, his homely stories and his solicitude for the simple man, . . . fought for the morals of democracy" against Wall Street speculators who placed personal gain above "the boys at the front"—those who unmistakably put the Union first. Cousin Theodore, too, took a moral stand, and "challenged again the small minority that claimed vested rights to power."

Roosevelt's ecstatic celebration of American history was deeply felt, but from a twenty-first-century perspective, deeply flawed. As for the man he honored on that day, General Jackson, FDR saw what he wanted to see: a moral exemplar, not the limited thinker nor, for that matter, the political pugilist who embraced no concrete program. Jackson declared for the people, but he ruled according to his intuitive sense of all-knowingness. He preferred sycophants to a "Brain Trust." Roosevelt also conveniently left out of his speech any acknowledgment of Jackson's knee-jerk resort to violence against Indians and his all-too-avid engagement with the institution of slavery—exhibiting none of Jefferson's mixed feelings about the effects of the system on the morals of the master class. There was also Jackson's long and arbitrary enemies list. The Whig Party to which Congressman Abraham Lincoln belonged arose in reaction to Jackson's imperiousness and unthinking behavior.

More concretely, Roosevelt may have believed that Jackson, as president, assailed the power of bankers on behalf of common folks; but the seventh president's minimal knowledge of economic forces resulted in a credit crisis and national panic. It is true that interpreters of the American past were years from concentrating their study on race enslavement and greedy land grabs. It is perfectly understandable that FDR was not to be dissuaded as he chose his heroic models: Andrew Jackson had descended to him as a good Democrat, "fighting for the integrity of the morals of democracy."[12]

But it was not the frontier fighter who stole the spotlight in the neighborhood of the National Mall. It was the thinking man's founder, the more reserved personality whose glorious words gave birth to the nation. Thomas Jefferson's call to resist tyranny continued to capture the national spirit, encompassing the drama of generations beyond his own. Roosevelt had made sure, over the course of two decades, that the third president's incomparable role in forging an American identity would be memorialized—literally set in stone—to loom large, to inspire awe, to be broadly cherished.

THE FEDERAL government first began looking at the Tidal Basin as a potential location for a national monument in 1901. This was done at the instigation of President William McKinley, and only awaited a figure all could agree warranted commemoration. In 1913, the House of Representatives recognized "a persistent and growing demand" for national memorials to both Jefferson and his political nemesis Hamilton. Then World War I intervened.

Theodore Roosevelt died in 1919. Soon thereafter, Republicans began clamoring for a monument to him on the Tidal Basin. The idea failed to take root. A host of public commentators took issue with all the TR mythmaking and hagiography, and a consensus formed that it was too soon for his historical legacy to be thoroughly established. The Washington monument was not completed until eighty-five years after the national father's death; the Lincoln Memorial had only opened to the public in 1922. Besides, along with Washington, Jefferson, and Lincoln, TR was being sculpted out of fine granite on Mount Rushmore, in South Dakota. He would not suffer for a lack of posthumous visibility.[13]

At a press conference in 1938, FDR revealed that, back in Wilson's day, he had thought it "a sort of funny thing" that Jefferson lacked a major monument; and it seemed fairly clear to him that in the 1920s the ruling Republicans refused to admit that they had reservations about memorializing the first Democrat, and so deliberately dragged their feet. He, therefore, was intent on getting the job done from the day he took office in 1933.

Congress established the Thomas Jefferson Memorial Commission in June 1934, a time, we should note, when the president refused to speak at a Jefferson Day dinner because he was trying to reach out to Republicans on issues of economic recovery. "Much as we love Thomas Jefferson," he wrote to Colonel House, "we should not celebrate him in a partisan way."[14]

There were twelve members on the Memorial Commission. John J. Boylan, an Irish Catholic Democrat from New York City, served as its chairman. Formerly a Manhattan real estate operator, he had entered Congress in 1923, and lodged a protest in 1926 when TR came close to supplanting TJ on the south bank of the Tidal Basin. While a confirmed Jefferson lover, Boylan was no expert in landscape architecture.

The commissioners met multiple times during 1934. In April 1935, the chairman of the government's Fine Arts Commission weighed in, insisting that the monument must make a grand impression. To "perfect" the District's rigorous plan of development, he said, it should be "vitally related" to Pierre Charles L'Enfant's original layout of the federal city (1790); and finally, it had to be effectively set apart from all government and commercial business.

The message was heard. In early 1936, with no time to lose and a price tag (set by Congress) not to exceed $3 million, the commission enlisted as its architect John Russell Pope, who had won the competition to build the abortive TR Memorial. Pope had gone on to design the stately National Archives Building, where the much-faded original of the Declaration of Independence remains on display to this day.

His "Pantheon design" of the memorial attested to Jefferson's love of the classical form—most visibly symbolized by the stately Rotunda on the Lawn of the University of Virginia, the construction of which Jefferson oversaw in his last years. The marble dome of the new memorial would be approximately 103 feet high at its center point. A "heroic-size statue" of Jefferson (nineteen feet high when completed) was to look out from under the dome, encircled by "a suitable inscription" from Jefferson's writings. Of the three inscriptions submitted by the commissioners, the first was the expressive quotation drawn from the 1800 letter to Dr. Rush.[15]

The architectural historian Fiske Kimball, director of the Philadelphia Museum of Art since 1925, was an active member of the commission. In his 1928 book *American Architecture,* he had written about the university's Rotunda, "the perfect model" of what Jefferson called "spherical architecture." Combined with the gently sloping Lawn and "temple-like" Pavilions where the first classes were taught, Jefferson's aesthetic had produced something magical: "Ordered, calm, serene it stirs our blood." Upon his appointment to the commission, Kimball accompanied Congressman Boylan to early meetings with outside experts, leading to the selection of Pope. At one point, Kimball, Pope, and Boylan went to the White House and spread their plans across the floor so that Roosevelt could inspect them. The president mulled over the options presented and personally selected the Rotunda design.

Kimball was one-half of a Jeffersonian "power couple"; his wife, Marie, was shortly to become a celebrated Jefferson biographer. Her timely book *Jefferson: The Road to Glory* (1943) was the first of an eventual three volumes, and took its protagonist up to 1776. It was a painstakingly researched book that highlighted Jefferson's deliberative manner, his intellectual honesty, and his outstanding humanity. Shortly after publication, Marie Kimball was hired as Monticello's first curator, a position she held until the end of her life. So the Kimballs were, indeed, a power couple, and Jefferson study a permanent part of their life together. Their Virginia home, which, like Monticello, took in a view of the Blue Ridge Mountains, borrowed freely from Jefferson's preferred geometry, down to its octagonal dining room, wood moldings, and windows.

Fiske Kimball's modern biographer calls him "America's first true restoration architect," an estimable label, indeed. He was the meticulous, self-confident organizer the Jefferson Memorial Commission sorely needed. Nevertheless, there were those who considered the $3 million cost extravagant, and others, such as the Daughters of the American Revolution, who protested the plan to dig up a sizable number of Japanese cherry trees along the Tidal Basin, and who made their strong feelings known. Even Frank Lloyd Wright complained to FDR that the memorial design was a "world-famous miscarriage of grace." Fiske Kimball wrote to Jack Pope: "There will be squawks . . . but let them yell!"[16]

The commission persisted despite losses. Congressman Boylan died in 1938, at the age of sixty, and would never see the Jefferson Memorial realized. Nor did the architect Pope, who predeceased Boylan by a year.

Of the twelve appointees to the commission, Thomas Jefferson Coolidge III is of particular interest because of his genealogy. A noted philanthropist, he was the great-grandson of Ellen Wayles Randolph Coolidge, Jefferson's favorite granddaughter. In 1825, she had married Joseph Coolidge, a businessman with global interests, at Monticello, and removed to her husband's hometown of Boston. The commission's Coolidge, born in 1893, had served as FDR's undersecretary of the treasury during the first years of the New Deal, resigning because of his fiscal conservatism. He was averse to so much centralization, so much federal spending. Yet he did not turn on the president; he was too genteel for that, too reserved in temperament.

T. Jefferson Coolidge (which was how he recorded his name) kept a curious scrapbook filled with quotes pertaining to the virtues of small government. One from a different namesake, Calvin Coolidge, went: "No method of procedure has ever been devised by which liberty could be divorced from local self-government." A good number of the quotes, not surprisingly, were from his ancestor, the third president, and emphasized the need to limit government spending. To wit: "If we can prevent the government from wasting the labours of the people, under the pretence of taking caring of them, they must become happy."[17]

In the lineup of commission members, we should not underrate the forgotten Elbert Thomas either. He was a Democratic senator from Utah, an accomplished scholar-politician whom we could call Jeffersonian by dint of his wide-ranging studies, even without knowing how strong of an emotional connection to the founder he felt. The liberal Utah senator played a significant role not just in promoting (and he was possibly the one to suggest) the "sworn upon the altar of God" quote, but also in advancing a new, more modern Jefferson image by way of his 1942 book *Thomas Jefferson, World Citizen*. It was published on April 13, the 199th anniversary of Jefferson's birth, and included an appendix, "Jefferson and Architecture," composed by Fiske Kimball.

Thomas would turn sixty in 1943. He had been a Mormon missionary in Japan before World War I, an instructor in Greek and Latin at the University of Utah, and then a professor of political science at that institution until his election to the United States Senate, when he was swept into office along with FDR, in 1932. His acknowledged dream ten years later, as remote as it must have seemed in the dark days of World War II, was something he called "world unity."

In Elbert Thomas's crusade to realize that vision, his universal savior Jefferson received as many superlatives as Claude Bowers had applied to Jefferson's moral purposes. The preeminent founder was, he wrote, "in terms of world significance, the greatest champion of freedom of the individual that ever existed." He had rebelled against "the bigotry and intolerance of his day," and, echoing the New Deal mantra: "Much as Jefferson feared the centralization of power, he realized the need of a strong government and of prompt action by the executive under certain conditions." As a practical man, Jefferson was "willing to make every other consideration secondary to the welfare of the nation." His principles were adaptable.[18]

"His progressive philosophy is designed for a world of free, cooperative men," Senator Thomas wrote approvingly. "His is a message to all mankind." Dictatorships around the world were bound to fall, and a "Jeffersonian gospel" would arise in their place to "lead the world to freedom and happiness." His was, of course, a different Jefferson than had ever existed before. "Jefferson was not only an American," the author insisted. "He expected all the benefits of good government . . . to spread throughout the world." He stood against ignorance and oppression; he stood for free people, and for sympathies that were universal. He was, in sum, nothing short of a prophet who saw the world as a social unit with familial characteristics.

The final sentiment in Elbert Thomas's book poses the largely rhetorical question, "What is the motive power behind America, if it is not the fulfillment of the social and political ideals accepted by the fathers?" The very last line of the book contains the words that encircle the shaded interior of the Jefferson Memorial: "I have sworn upon the Altar of God, eternal hostility against every form of tyranny over the mind of man."[19]

Thomas Jefferson, World Citizen is a literary relic, a rare snapshot of the American mind trapped in the grim urgency of that first year of military mobilization, when Hitler was on the move in Europe and the United States had not yet begun to turn back the Japanese. "The world needs a rededication to democracy," Senator Thomas stated in the opening paragraph of his preface, after heralding the impending dedication of the Jefferson Memorial. His was a unique perspective on world affairs: his ten years in Japan had taught him to admire Asian culture and to cherish his own. As acting chairman of the Military Affairs Committee, he went on short-wave radio after Pearl Harbor to address the Japanese people in their own language.

At that very moment, from uncertain sanctuary in the Chinese city of Kunming, Yunnan Province, Liu Zuochang (1921–2006) was attending Southwest Associated University, fervently hoping for an end to the Japanese occupation of his country. In Kunming, he wrote his graduate thesis, and called it "The New Deal of Franklin Roosevelt." Once he was able to get his hands on Elbert Thomas's book, he never cast aside his fascination with Revolutionary America or his profound admiration for Thomas Jefferson. Committed to the study of history as a moral enterprise, Liu embarked on a long career teaching U.S. history in northern China at Shandong Teachers College.

What made the only Jefferson specialist in Mao Zedong's China a thorough admirer of Elbert Thomas? It certainly did not hurt that before writing *Thomas Jefferson, World Citizen*, the well-traveled professor and U.S. senator had authored a book called *Chinese Political Thought* (1927), and constantly saw in Jefferson's philosophy of life as many Chinese as European characteristics. Liu's combined engagement with Chinese and American history—his father was a schoolteacher—led him to believe that the humane democratic principles of Jefferson were the principles that would one day transform his own country from the despotic society it had been for thousands of years into a place where personal freedoms were guaranteed. Liu took his first tentative step in 1980, with an article in China's premier historical journal, which he titled "Thomas Jefferson's Ideas of Democracy." He published a single-volume Chinese-language Jefferson biography in 1990, and went on to complete a remarkable two-volume, 1,700-page version, issued the year before his death. In the early twenty-first century, he was still copiously citing Claude Bowers's work as well as Thomas's.

The fact that Professor Liu held on to his Elbert Thomas for more than a half century, through the bloody and vindictive Cultural Revolution of the late 1960s, and into the era of Chinese-American rapprochement, is of greater significance than anything Senator Thomas could claim to have accomplished at home. If, beginning with U.S. historiography of the 1960s, the New Deal's Jefferson became a flawed slave owner and a man of contradictions, for China's lone Jeffersonian, FDR's Jefferson remained on his pedestal, impervious to criticism.

In the 1980s, as Liu Zuochang set about writing his biography of Jefferson, China had just begun its shift from a strictly Marxist interpretation of history. Then came the 1989 massacre of hundreds of young protesters in Beijing's Tiananmen Square, which served as a cynical reminder of how far that nation had yet to go to build a civil society. So Liu could not afford the luxury of treating Jefferson and his imperfect democracy with the nuance Westerners applied. His magnum opus of 2005 thus repeated, again and again, how the historical Jefferson was a moral exemplar who always gazed into a brighter future, who resisted the "brutal form of individualism" (personal greed) Hamilton so easily countenanced, while preserving peace and freedom for the national community. "Like Confucius," Liu wrote, "Jefferson exhibited a spirit of kindness toward the people and a kindness to all nature."[20]

IN MODERNIZING Jefferson, Roosevelt altered him, to be sure. Between 1933 and 1939, a minimalist Jeffersonianism was succeeded by the "Jeffersonian" welfare state, a highly regulated system of government. A Kentucky congressman who detested the New Deal's centralizing policies called one FDR program "a stench in the nostrils of those who cherish the ideals of Thomas Jefferson." The Jefferson he knew had been hijacked. Jefferson the organized, control-oriented experimenter became, through New Deal reinvention, an ingenious, flexible problem solver. He could in this way sign on to a program of centrally generated economic recovery.[21]

We should always be cautious about the facile drawing of historical parallels, but just as Jefferson held on to his presidency of the American Philosophical Society during two terms as president of the United States, Roosevelt, as the nation's chief executive, retained a position that meant something to him: He continued to serve, as he had since 1930, on the Board of Governors of Monticello. He named Claude Bowers, the Democrats' darling, as his ambassador to Spain, and later to Chile. In 1937, not inconsequentially, he personally saw to it that Jefferson's image was placed on the three-cent (first-class) stamp; and in 1938, the familiar Jefferson nickel was first minted. In 1939, the president laid the cornerstone of the Jefferson Memorial, speaking to the founder's "many-sidedness," his influence on "the American application of classic art to homes and public buildings," and his memorable conviction that "the average opinion of mankind is in the long run superior to the dictates of the self-chosen." In short, once again, Jefferson was democracy's muse.[22]

FDR's seizure of Jefferson had a real impact. By 1940, when another Indiana-born politico, Wendell Willkie, ran as a Republican businessman against the two-term incumbent, he was careful to describe himself as a longtime liberal. Recalling the business monopolies of an earlier era, the GOP standard-bearer spoke out against private concentrations of power. "We all know that such concentration of power must be checked," he comfortably intoned in accepting the Republican nomination. And then: "Thomas Jefferson disliked regulation, yet he said that the prime purpose of government in a democracy is to keep men from injuring each other."

Willkie felt that the third president had bequeathed a moral imperative to his posterity. "We know from our own experience that the less fortunate or less skillful among us must be protected from encroachment," the candidate continued. "That is why we support what is known as the liberal point of view." He was fine with federal regulation; he only protested that the New Deal had spent too much money, and promised to do as much for less. It was not enough to unseat FDR, who then embarked on an unprecedented third term as president.[23]

In February 1941, as the Jefferson Memorial was nearing completion, President Roosevelt appointed a commission to stage a celebration of the bicentennial of Jefferson's birth. He named himself as its honorary chairman and the long-serving Virginia senator Carter Glass as official chairman. Only one of the commission members was concurrently on the Jefferson Memorial committee, and that was the museum director and architectural historian Fiske Kimball. The program was set up along similar lines to the Coolidge initiative of 1926, and the George Washington bicentennial of 1932, with activities centered in Washington, D.C., and Charlottesville, Philadelphia (in connection with the Declaration of Independence) and St. Louis (in connection with the Lewis and Clark expedition). Public schools across the country would encourage student involvement. The two celebratory scripts would be complementary, as birthday honors coincided with the official unveiling of the Jefferson Memorial.[24]

Then came the Japanese attack on Pearl Harbor. And while most references to Thomas Jefferson in the New Deal era drew from the founder's Enlightenment background and beliefs, this did not mean that Jefferson's pacifistic script was all there was to him. In the months leading up to America's official entry in World War II, the president delivered a fireside chat in which he invoked Jefferson's decision to dispatch U.S. Navy vessels to the Mediterranean. "Freedom of the seas" meant to FDR what "free trade" had meant to his remote, but always relevant, presidential predecessor. German submarines were attacking U.S. vessels on the high seas in 1941, as North African corsairs had done in 1801; FDR would follow Jefferson's example in stepping up patrols to protect the nation's commerce.

His approach to the problem was as reminiscent of Lincoln as it was of Jefferson. His tone carried with it the language of rights, with an appeal to moral justice and a reliance on sound conviction: "My obligation as president is historic," he told his radio audience. "It is clear. It is inescapable." To stand up to an autocrat's bullying was to observe "the necessities of a bold defense"; we would stand our ground against every assault upon "democracy," "sovereignty," and "freedom." Nothing so obviously vibrated with the crisp, sonorous notes of a Jeffersonian vocabulary as Roosevelt's "Four Freedoms," delineated in January 1941. All the world's people were entitled to freedom of speech, freedom of worship, freedom from want, freedom from fear. It was of a piece, too, with Elbert Thomas's Jefferson as "world citizen."

Claude Bowers painted Jefferson as an internationalist when he wrote of his prescience, as early as 1787, in contemplating a Panama Canal. But, Bowers also attested, "He hated all wars of conquest. He hated all wars not waged for the protection of human rights." We should mention, too, that Jefferson had written trenchantly to John Jay in 1785, when the latter was secretary for foreign affairs in the Confederation Congress: "Weakness provokes insult & injury." The record contains nearly as many Jefferson statements about the sources of national pride as Jefferson's better-known pronouncements on rights of conscience and political liberty.[25]

In the lead up to April 13, 1943, Jefferson's two-hundredth birthday, the national press reminded that the Jefferson Memorial was only the third such monument to grace the federal city, after Washington's and Lincoln's. (Indeed, it would be the last such monument to a president until the Roosevelt Memorial was dedicated, across the Tidal Basin, in 1997.) The Associated Press described the new memorial as a dazzling vision: "sparkling white amid the flowering cherry trees, a domed and columned shrine." The tall statue of Jefferson inside the $3 million project would be of plaster until the war ended and it was cast in bronze.[26]

The April 12 cover of *Life* magazine featured a splendid photograph of the stately memorial taken from across the water; interior pages contained thirty-seven separate photos and illustrations pertaining to Jefferson's life and legacy. The bicentennial commission issued the *Thomas Jefferson Quiz Book,* with ninety-one questions and answers relating to the founder. Demonstrating Jefferson's humility, it quoted him stating, "The only birthday I recognize is that of my country's liberties."

On Broadway, Sidney Kingsley's drama *The Patriots* was being performed. It starred actors playing Jefferson and Hamilton, and covered events of the 1790s, which was, as Claude Bowers held, the most politically charged decade before the approach of the Civil War. "Told against a background of dissension on the home front and turmoil abroad," wrote *Life*'s drama critic, "the play has overtones that reach into the newspaper headlines of today. Filled with strong and eloquent talk, *The Patriots* is well-written, but its dramatic force comes from history itself." It won the New York Drama Critics Circle Award for best play that year.[27]

Thousands gathered on April 13 to witness as the president formally opened the Jefferson Memorial to the public. "Today, in the midst of a great war for freedom, we dedicate a shrine to freedom," he began. "To Thomas Jefferson, Apostle of Freedom, we are paying a debt long overdue." Right away, historical analogies flowed: "He faced the fact that men who will not fight for liberty can lose it. We, too, have faced that fact." And, "Generations which understand each other across the distances of history are the generations united by a common experience and a common cause." Roosevelt collapsed all distance in recalling what Jefferson did to rescue liberty 150 years earlier, at the height of his contest with Hamilton: the Jefferson of 1793 was "closer by much to living men" than most of the politicians and presidents who came in between.

There was more to Jefferson than an abstract love of liberty, Roosevelt held. He, like his famous Declaration, "called for the abandonment of privileges." Jefferson was a pragmatist, a first-rate thinker who did more than simply dream. He led with actions, with deeds. "I like to think that this was so because he thought in terms of the morrow as well as the day—and this was why he was hated or feared by those who thought in terms of the day and the yesterday."

One might argue that autobiography mingled with historical interpretation in this section of Roosevelt's dedication speech. But the speaker would not be constrained. "Exponent of planning for the future," Jefferson aimed to establish "the permanent integrity of the republic." He was the most forward-thinking of the founders. He spoke to the present.

Then came the truly grandiose:

> Thomas Jefferson believed, as we believe, in man. He believed, as we believe, that men are capable of their own government, and that no king, no tyrant, no dictator can govern for them as well as they can govern for themselves.

Offering encouragement at a moment when untold numbers of young Americans were abroad fighting for their country, and for the freedom of other countries, FDR reminded his audience that Jefferson's life "proved that the seeming eclipse of liberty can well be the dawn of more liberty." At that, he ended his prepared remarks with the soul-stirring refrain that so many visitors to the memorial have since looked up at: "The words which we have chosen," he said, "speak Jefferson's noblest and most urgent meaning; and we are proud indeed to understand it and share it: 'I have sworn before the altar of God, eternal hostility against every form of tyranny over the mind of man.'"

In his massive biography of Jefferson, Liu Zuochang translated "mind of man" as *xinling,* which means "heart and spirit," and is also the Chinese word for the elusive concept of "soul." It seems as good a translation as any that we might come up with in an attempt to recover an eighteenth-century thinker's frame of reference.

SOME MONTHS after Roosevelt was inaugurated for the third time, but before Pearl Harbor, an editorial writer for *Life* magazine took the pulse of partisanship in America. Likening FDR to the most famous of his predecessors, he put in print what the president's enemies were saying about him. Starting with the current century and moving backward, he was: "as weasel-wordy as Woodrow Wilson," "as contemptuous of Constitutional barriers as Abraham Lincoln," "as bullheaded as Andrew Jackson," and "as slippery as Thomas Jefferson." The sitting president's friends made gentler historical comparisons: "as adroit as Lincoln, as resolute as Wilson, as firm as Jackson, and as wise as Jefferson." Regardless of the adjectives chosen, it was good company to be in while still breathing. And by all accounts, FDR loved being compared to Jefferson.[28]

Historic memory is a powerful drug in every generation, and a malleable, mind-altering one at that. Woodrow Wilson, the brainy southern Democrat who steered the United States through the First World War, was posthumously viewed in much the same way that the twenty-first century tends to depict another brainy southern Democrat, Georgia's Jimmy Carter. To some, he was admirably guided by morals, yet unable to guide events; to others, he was a stubborn moralist, and misguided, too. *Life*'s "bullheaded" Jackson, highly popular, if dangerously undereducated, descended through history to the 1940s as the epitome of a man of unrelenting ardor; the martyred Lincoln was still remembered (much more than now) as one who had played fast and loose with the Constitution during the Civil War.

With or without the Roosevelt magic, Jefferson was indisputably thought great on the eve of World War II. But he was, at the same time, regarded as a comparatively "slippery" figure. This Jefferson image worked to Roosevelt's detriment as he brought Jefferson up to date. The era's political liberals found Jefferson as "wise" as he was humane, of course; but if FDR was to claim him, he would find his own reputation still attached to surviving reminders of Jefferson's political canniness. These reminders came courtesy of the renowned Henry Adams, scion of presidents, whose creditable, nine-volume work on the administrations of Thomas Jefferson and James Madison, first published in 1889–91, continued to resonate. This Adams's Jefferson was deserving of acclaim, but also a man of fungible principles, whose ideas were somehow doomed; there was a bit of smoke and mirrors amid all the lofty pronouncements.[29]

Like Jefferson, Franklin Delano Roosevelt was destined to become an enduring symbol of societal transformation. Both men willfully embraced social experiment. Iconic photographs of FDR, and the various ways in which his voice and image were captured for all time, stand as concrete reminders of the longest-serving president, his cockiness and self-command, his winning manner and clever repartee. But Roosevelt's legacy is debated in terms of solutions tried, and of the evolving nature of the social contract, more than so fundamental a question as, "Who was he, really?"

But that is how we most often greet Jefferson. He exists largely on the page, and in paintings and engravings that say more about the artist than the subject. This simple fact makes him, despite (or, perhaps, because of) his tenacity, a bewildering historical actor. We can try to reconstruct the moral boundaries within which he lived and encounter him there, but we can never truly know him. Historians have quibbled about "the real Jefferson" for the better part of two centuries. The polymath has been recast and reconstituted so often that we are bound to exaggerate his traits and focus on his contradictions. Yes, "slippery" is a most appropriate word.

That was not how Claude Bowers saw the third president, however. With his barnstorming *Jefferson and Hamilton,* he did more than any conventional politician to end the reign of pro-Hamilton business types as interpreters of the founders' collective legacy. He presented to his fellow liberals what we might call a blueprint for didactic democracy. It was Roosevelt, though, who went the extra mile, giving Jefferson a monument worthy of his enormity, worthy of the universality that the likes of Elbert Thomas and Liu Zuochang perceived. A half century after the fact, Professor Liu was still writing of this Jefferson, because China had stood still in terms of human rights thinking, while the West (and its Jefferson image) was fast evolving.

Writing retrospectively at the end of his own political career, Hubert H. Humphrey of Minnesota, the son of a druggist, reflected on a political education that had begun in the 1930s as a political science major and ended after he nearly won the popular vote in a bid to be president of the United States in 1968. "The New Deal found historical support in the supreme individualist Thomas Jefferson," wrote the Democratic mainstay. Any constitutionally questionable powers Roosevelt took on in combating a national economic emergency were powers Jefferson would have "condoned," because they were "conferred by the people." "To lose our country by a scrupulous adherence to written law would be to lose the law itself," said Humphrey: as conditions changed, the nation had to adapt. The Jeffersonian premise was clear to the senator from Minnesota and Lyndon Johnson's vice president, in quoting Jefferson word for word: "No society can make a perpetual constitution, or even a perpetual law."

According to Humphrey, the New Deal could always be defended by analogy to the founding generation, and Roosevelt, the greatest Democrat of the twentieth century, knew this. Getting the federal government involved in reducing abuses by business interests, promoting "a more equitable distribution of wealth" were social ideals first advocated by Thomas Jefferson, and later advanced by Theodore Roosevelt and Woodrow Wilson. (Humphrey left out Lincoln.) Government bore a responsibility to provide for the general welfare. This was the liberal credo.[30]

JEFFERSON WAS ostensibly in Franklin Roosevelt's thoughts on June 6, 1944. He had chosen to wait for news of D-Day in Charlottesville, at the home of his dear friend Edwin "Pa" Watson. Watson, a West Point graduate and military advisor to the president, lived on property once owned by Jefferson, literally across the road from Monticello. FDR's fondness for the place was brought out in a *Life* magazine feature a few years earlier. Eight months after D-Day, while accompanying Roosevelt on the return voyage from the Yalta Conference, Watson died of a brain hemorrhage. The sixty-two-year-old president, who attended his friend's funeral at Arlington National Cemetery, would meet the same fate not long thereafter.[31]

It was nearly two years to the day after the dedication of the Jefferson Memorial, in fact, April 12, 1945, that Roosevelt put the finishing touches on an address he planned to give in honor of Thomas Jefferson's birthday. Though he did not live long enough to deliver it, his widow prized it and would continue to quote from it. In this tribute, the loftiest of the founders was to be remembered as "the greatest of all democrats"—and here, Roosevelt carefully indicated that he meant to spell "democrat" with a lowercase "d."

"The once powerful, malignant Nazi state is crumbling," Roosevelt wrote eagerly. "But the mere conquest of our enemies is not enough." To honor Thomas Jefferson's spirit, it was now necessary to unite nations in, as Jefferson put it, the "brotherly spirit of science," and to "cultivate the science of human relationships" so as to avoid a third world war. "I ask you to keep up your faith," wrote Roosevelt. "Let us move forward with strong and active faith." Those were his last words intended for the American public. He suffered a massive stroke on the afternoon before Jefferson's birthday.[32]

FRANKLIN ROOSEVELT certainly put his imprint on the age, but not everyone operated on the same premise who witnessed Jefferson's transformation into a knowing, unjaundiced modern. Not everyone liked his "look" in 1943, as he turned two hundred. In spite of the visible grandeur of the Jefferson Memorial to which the president had lent a strong hand in bringing to life, some New Deal era aesthetes complained that the structure's classicism was passé; they expressed their wish for a sportier, more modish monument to the likable liberal.

No one is saying that anymore. Mr. Jefferson continues to have his ups and downs; he has been reviled in the intervening years in some quarters. But the memorial has proven, over the raw and rowdy decades since its erection, to be beyond criticism.

2

"HIS MIND LIBERAL AND ACCOMMODATING"

When John F. Kennedy Dined in Company

ALBERT A. GORE, a native of Jackson County, Tennessee, traced his ancestry back to a Revolutionary soldier. First elected to Congress in 1938, Gore traveled to Ohio in 1946 to campaign on behalf of fellow Democrats running for House seats. Speaking in Akron to a gathering of women, he stressed the need to uphold progressive principles, observing that the Republicans' message of limited government and lower taxes was out of step, even confusing. To get his partisan point across, he quoted from one of the panels inside the Jefferson Memorial: "Laws and institutions must go hand in hand with the progress of the human mind. As that becomes more developed, more enlightened, . . . institutions must advance also, and keep pace with the times."[1]

Jefferson had put these thoughts to paper in 1816, in a letter to a Virginia attorney named Samuel Kercheval, who in later years authored a frontier history of the Shenandoah region. The rest of the quotation reveals Jefferson's wit in wordplay, as he pointed out the shortsightedness in ignoring social growth and resisting change: "We might as well require a man to wear still the coat which fitted him when a boy as civilized society to remain ever under the regimen of their barbarous ancestors."[2]

Jefferson's devotees often came from less obvious places, and less predictable professions, than Senator Gore's. One such enthusiast was Nathan Schachner, a science fiction writer who did many things well, and who turned to founders' biography midcareer. Incredibly, the author of *Emissaries of Space* and a slew of similar titles, though trained as a chemist, wrote successful biographies of Burr (1937) and Hamilton (1946) before his deeply researched *Thomas Jefferson* appeared in

1951. This remarkably astute popularizer of American history kept the eminently quotable New Deal humanist Jefferson alive. In the foreword to his two-volume Jefferson treatment, he wrote: "In an era of complex and many-sided men, he was without doubt the most complex and many-sided of them all." (On laying the cornerstone of the Jefferson Memorial, Roosevelt had called Jefferson a "many-sided" leader.) When it came to the founding itself, Schachner added, "No man contributed more"; and here he was privileging the power of the word over all else in birthing and steadying the nation: "Phrases tipped with immortality rolled happily from his pen. The *mot juste,* the pregnant apothegm and the ringing affirmation may be culled from every page." The key to Schachner's Jefferson was the permanence of his power over the collective mind: "Without a close study of the man . . . , no proper understanding of America as it was and as it is today can be arrived at."[3]

Democrats were holding fast to their Jefferson: the global citizen, the believer in progress. Upon publication of *Thomas Jefferson's Farm Book* in the early 1950s, Henry A. Wallace of Iowa, secretary of agriculture from 1933 to 1940, and vice president from 1941 to 1945, wrote of a self-disciplined optimist: "Jefferson in a way was the whole future of the United States in embryo. He was by instinct and temperament as much a manufacturer as a farmer. . . . Our nation must be forever grateful that Jefferson in a practical way guided us from the very start in the appreciation of scientific agriculture, education, and democracy." When she spoke at the Democratic National Convention in Chicago, on July 22, 1952, Eleanor Roosevelt quoted from the Jefferson's birthday speech her late husband had been planning to give at the time of his sudden death. It went: "Thomas Jefferson, himself a distinguished scientist, once spoke of the 'brotherly spirit of science, which unites into one family all its votaries . . . throughout the different corners of the globe.'" These were words Jefferson wrote after having been elected to the Institute of France for his achievements in agricultural science, and FDR had intended the quote as a reminder that science should ally itself to the cause of world peace.[4]

AS A SPEECH maker, Harry Truman did not do much to keep Jefferson's name in the news, though he stated after his retirement from the presidency that Jefferson was his "favorite character in history." He claimed unabashedly, when speaking before fellow Democrats, that their party had been the "party of the people" ever since Jefferson. He said he believed that when modern editions of the papers of Presidents

Jefferson, Lincoln, Wilson, and Franklin Roosevelt became widely available through the nation's libraries, future Americans would know why the Democratic Party could never die: it expressed the great aims of the mass of citizens. Truman did not explain his fondness for the first Republican president, however, until he was interviewed years later and remarked of Lincoln: "He was a Jefferson Democrat and didn't know it."[5]

It has always been the case that no American's official or unofficial writings have been so carefully dissected and publicly shared as those of Thomas Jefferson. In 1950, Princeton University Press published the first installment of the (as yet unfinished) *Papers of Thomas Jefferson*. In a formal gathering at the Library of Congress, the president of Princeton presented a copy of volume 1 to the president of the United States. The founding editor of the series, the Princeton librarian Julian P. Boyd, had governed the project since 1943, when Congress authorized it. Once he had obtained needed financial support from the *New York Times,* he and his team proceeded to collect microfilmed copies of every known letter to and from Jefferson that existed—some 50,000—with, he hoped, no meaningful scrap left out. As of 1949, 423 different sources had been identified and an impressive number of documents filmed. Under Boyd's direction, Jefferson's original spellings were retained, his mannerisms preserved, and a truer sense of history revealed.[6]

Accepting the inaugural volume, President Truman declared: "This edition will be of lasting value to our nation for generations to come." In prepared remarks, he reinforced the Franklin Roosevelt/Elbert Thomas mode of interpreting Jefferson to the world. First there was the quintessential struggle of good versus evil: "Throughout his life, Jefferson waged an uncompromising fight against tyranny. The search for human liberty was a goal which he pursued with burning zeal. The spirit of democracy shines through everything he ever wrote." Then there was America's modern role in informing the world of its Jeffersonian values: "Today, when democracy is facing the greatest challenge in its history, the spirit which Jefferson expressed in his battle against tyranny, and in his search for human liberty, stands out as a beacon of inspiration for free peoples throughout the world."

Truman's Jefferson had lived at a time when the new nation first attempted "to establish itself as a democracy of free men." Jefferson's original mission was being expanded in the postwar world of Harry Truman; it was now being "waged over the whole world, not merely in our own country," to establish a community of nations in which "free men can create for themselves a good society, in which they live together at peace."

To the "Man from Independence" (Missouri), the lesson left by Jefferson was simply one of combining democratic thought with democratic action: "When freedom is at stake, we need to draw upon every source of strength we can. Jefferson thought deeply about how to make liberty a living part of our society, and he proved the rightness of his thinking by practical demonstration." And as for the value of publishing his papers at length, Truman considered the cause an obvious one, a partisan one, and echoed Jefferson's pet peeve with regard to the knee-jerk ideologues who consistently lied about his beliefs and his public record: "History can be fairly written only when all the facts are on record," said Truman. "Jefferson has suffered at the hands of unscrupulous biographers and biased partisans ever since his death. The publication of his papers should correct the mistakes that have been made about him and should help prevent misinterpretations in the future."[7]

Truman's concern, shared by Jefferson, recalls the purpose of the present study. We know that political movements and rival ideologies have produced Jeffersons with vastly different emphases. In the Truman years, though, when Jefferson biographies were so very positive, the New Deal version of Jefferson had very little competition.[8]

SO, HOW did Jefferson fare under McCarthyism? It is not a simple question to answer. When the House Committee on Un American Activities (HUAC) convened in 1947, its examination of alleged Communist influence in Hollywood not surprisingly perked up many ears around the nation. Testifying before the headline-stealing committee, Ronald Reagan, as president of the Screen Actors Guild, did his level best to supply satisfactory answers. When the committee's chief investigator, Robert Stripling, asked what might be done to "rid the motion picture industry of any Communist influences," Reagan had a Jefferson quote—or at least paraphrase—at the ready.

"Well, sir, ninety-nine percent of us are pretty well aware of what's going on. . . . I believe that, as Thomas Jefferson put it, if all the American people know all the facts they will never make a mistake. Whether the [Communist] Party should be outlawed, that is a matter for the government to decide. As a citizen, I would hesitate to see any political party outlawed on the basis of its political ideology." As long as no direct ties to a foreign enemy were uncovered, he felt, democracy was sufficiently strong to withstand obnoxious opinions.

This was vintage Jefferson. The committee's Republican chairman, Parnell Thomas of New Jersey (no relation to Elbert Thomas of Utah), took special interest in the actor's reference. Jefferson was "just why this committee was created," he said. "Once the American people are acquainted with the facts . . . , [they will] make America just as pure as we can possibly make it." Seeing how the congressman had twisted his meaning, Reagan (at this point in his career a Democrat) clarified a second time that while he personally loathed the Communist Party, he would never "compromise with our democratic principles through that fear or resentment." Purity was an unreasonable expectation, and uniformity impossible in a democracy. It became known much later, during his presidency, that in spite of public eloquence that would suggest a profile in courage, Reagan had in some form or other suggested the names of Communist sympathizers. Meanwhile, the "pure American" proponent Parnell Thomas went to prison in 1950 after being found guilty of corruption.[9]

Senator Joseph McCarthy was able to steal the limelight beyond anything Congressman Thomas of New Jersey could have hoped for. Elected to the Senate in 1946, he began his infamous witch hunt in February 1950. That June, as the Korean War began, the Wisconsin Republican stepped up his attacks on supposed Red sympathizers in government. Secretary of State Dean Acheson, one of his primary targets, came to describe this moment in history as a "shameful and nihilistic orgy."

The Connecticut-born son of an Episcopal bishop, and a Harvard Law School graduate, Acheson was contemptuous of McCarthy, denoting him "a lazy, small-town bully, without sustaining purpose." On Secretary Acheson's birthday in 1951, some friends gave him an engraving: an extended excerpt from a letter of 1805 written by President Jefferson to Judge James Sullivan of Massachusetts, a political ally living and somehow thriving in unfriendly Federalist territory. Meant to reflect Acheson's recent political trials, it began: "You have indeed received the federal unction of lying and slandering. But who has not? Who will ever come again into eminent office, unanointed by this chrism? It seems to be fixed that falsehood and calumny are to be their ordinary engines of opposition; engines which will not entirely be without effect." It went on to urge reliance on the ultimate justice of public opinion: it was Jefferson's habit never to see politically generated hatred as permanent, or a downturn in fortunes as irrevocable. In the republic of his eager imagination, liars never prospered long.[10]

Jefferson's name kept coming up in the context of Harry Truman's quest for justice from the writers of history. In his administration's final days, he publicly lauded Acheson as "among the very greatest secretaries of state this country has had," asserting that, among his illustrious predecessors neither Jefferson (the first to hold the office) nor William H. Seward (Lincoln's right hand) "showed more cool courage and steadfast judgment." This can be read as Truman's projecting onto Acheson the positive endorsement he himself hoped to receive eventually.[11]

They were mutual admirers who carried on a friendly correspondence throughout the Eisenhower years. Acheson obliged Truman to read the post-presidential correspondence between Adams and Jefferson—their model. The latter two were, in Acheson's words, "robust old codgers." Truman grimly anticipated, as Jefferson had, the opposition ideologues who would write his history poorly. "I don't want a pack of lying historians to do to Roosevelt and to me what the New Englanders did to Jefferson and Jackson," he said.

Nearly a decade of handwritten letters later, Truman addressed his friend Acheson with a pointed plea to be rescued from an eternity of bad press. "Now articles are coming out, along with books, showing I could never make a decision unless some smart boy told me how to make it." He was deeply disturbed by the retrospective treatment of his presidency, fearing, he said, that he was be lumped together with the likes of Andrew Johnson, Rutherford B. Hayes, Grover Cleveland, and Calvin Coolidge. Truman was old enough to recall Cleveland, and perceived a downfall in Cleveland's reputation as the result of his having strayed from Jeffersonian liberalism in an embrace of big business in his second term. To be a Democrat, Truman said, was to show commitment to "welfare of all the people and not just a few." This was, he insisted, the principle in Jefferson's contest with Hamilton, which revived with Jackson, and reasserted itself with Wilson and then FDR— "the greatest of all liberals in the whole history of the country."[12]

Truman did not hold back. Given the fears he expressed to Acheson, he would be ecstatic to know how he fares today, as a president praised by hard-headed Republicans and Democrats alike, his refreshing directness contrasted with the intellectual dishonesty of meek, chameleon-like men who labor for lobbyists and are unashamed when they make contradictory statements (sometimes on the same day) about their supposedly core beliefs. While his "Give-em-Hell-Harry" persona contrasts with Jefferson's reputation for soft-spokenness and measured reserve, the two shared a visceral desire to see their detractors chastised for wrongheadedness; more positively, Truman and Jefferson expressed what was, for their respective times, an easy identification with common folks. Truman described as "the Jefferson theory" their similarly derived principle that "the common people, if they'd be instructed, as they should be, could make just as good administrators . . . [as the] patrician class."[13]

Young Robert F. Kennedy, as a law student at the University of Virginia, was a member of the audience in 1951, when Senator McCarthy launched into one of his notorious tirades. In the question-and-answer period that followed, Kennedy rose to confront the senator. A woman who was present recalled many years later:

> He wasn't argumentative in the least, he was very quiet, very dignified, but very sincere; you could hear this in his voice. And he said— I shall never forget it—"Senator McCarthy, will you, standing on this rostrum made sacred to liberty and freedom by our founder Thomas Jefferson, and waiving your congressional immunity, publicly state that General George Marshall is now or has ever been a member of the Communist Party?" Well suddenly, the impact of that question struck him in the face, you know, he was just astounded and he realized what the impact was, so he turned red as a beet and stamped his foot and stomped off the stage. And, it was a fantastic moment. The whole audience rose simultaneously and booed, which they seldom do in a place like Charlottesville.[14]

Unbeknownst to the woman, it was Bobby Kennedy who had invited McCarthy to speak, just as he had invited his congressman brother Jack and their father, Roosevelt's one-time ambassador to Great Britain. As president of the Student Legal Forum, he used his connections to score prominent speakers. Bobby was not exhibiting vitriol so much as theatricality when he confronted the senator; he saw McCarthy to his bed that night once the alcoholic pol got sloshed at the after-party.[15]

At midcentury, there was no more dignified statesman, no more highly esteemed patriot, than General George Catlett Marshall. As chief of staff of the U.S. Army, he had mapped out America's successful course in World War II, and then launched the economic recovery plan in Europe that bears his name (and for which he won the Nobel Peace Prize). He served as secretary of state under Truman until ill health led him to step aside in 1949, making way for Dean Acheson. The next year, Marshall returned to Washington to help guide military policy in the Korean War, only to be attacked by McCarthy in mid-1951 for supposedly being soft on communism.

McCarthy knew what he was getting into, though, and eventually wrote an entire book on Marshall's political errors. In *Retreat from Victory,* McCarthy asserted that Truman's team had "lost" China to the Reds by pretending that "Chinese Communists were moderate reformers, simple agrarians in the style of Thomas Jefferson." This was really the only Jefferson whom McCarthy recognized at the height of his inquisitorial career—not the philosopher of democracy. He certainly didn't see Jefferson as one who rose above the other founders, in the Roosevelt-Truman mode.[16]

As Dwight D. Eisenhower took occupancy of the Oval Office in 1953, the walls of the White House Cabinet Room changed. Theodore Roosevelt's portrait replaced Woodrow Wilson's over the fireplace; William Howard Taft replaced James Madison; and George Washington took the place of Thomas Jefferson. That same week, Elbert Thomas died. Beyond the walls of the White House, the abrasive McCarthy remained vocal but declined in relevance, slowly supplanted by a new, less reckless, more businesslike breed of Cold War Republican.

Adlai Stevenson, the Democrat Eisenhower had defeated, figured he knew what the election meant for the domestic economy: government by business leaders, a return to the Coolidge-Hoover mind-set. Speaking at the Jefferson-Jackson Day Dinner at the Waldorf-Astoria in Manhattan, the Illinois senator asserted that the struggle between Democrats and Republicans remained, as ever, an extension of the primordial Jeffersonian-Hamiltonian conflict. "There is always the tendency to mistake the particular interest for the general interest," said Stevenson, hastening to condemn the business-knows-best model. At the event, Lyndon Baines Johnson of Texas, Senate minority leader, avowed that the Democrats' job was now to "solve the problems of America, not just to obstruct the majority party." Voters would take heed, and "place their confidence in a party which seeks honestly to serve them." That vote of confidence in an educable public sounded mighty Jeffersonian.[17]

McCarthy's star faded after the Soviet leader Josef Stalin died in 1953, and then, in 1954, it momentously exploded after the unrepentant senator claimed to have unearthed subversives in the U.S. Army. Until that happened, though, all who questioned him came in for a drubbing. In March 1954, with the televised Army-McCarthy hearings about to begin, Senator Mike Monroney, Democrat of Oklahoma, identified Jefferson and Lincoln with the political Left when he braved the bluster of his bullying colleague. Monroney, who was to remain in the Senate until 1969, dared to criticize McCarthy openly, and was immediately berated as a mere "water-boy for the left-wingers"; even more dismissively, he became "your little Lord Fauntleroy," a reference to the prim, all-too-innocent, velvet-suited American boy, heir to an English title, in the David O. Selznick film of 1936.

Monroney's dramatic retort to McCarthy's name-calling was meant to sting as Bobby Kennedy's taunt as a law student had done: "I expect Senator McCarthy feels anybody so old-fashioned as to still believe in the Bill of Rights and the Constitution may be a Fauntleroy," he said, "and those still old-fashioned enough to believe in trial by jury and presumption of innocence, may be as dangerously left-wing as Thomas Jefferson and Abraham Lincoln." The designation of Lincoln as a latter-day Jefferson continued to resonate with Democrats.[18]

On television, *Hallmark Hall of Fame* ran an allegorical drama meant as an exposé of McCarthyism and the hyperbolic language used by conservatives who believed that education in America was falling prey to dangerous leftist influence. The episode, written by Helene Hanff, was called "The Ordeal of Thomas Jefferson." The "ordeal" referred to the Alien and Sedition Laws of 1798–1800. As vice president under John Adams, the honorable Jefferson was branded a traitor who would impose a "government by rabble" simply for upholding the First Amendment and disagreeing with the jailing of newspaper editors who stood up to an abusive regime. In a letter to a friendly politician in 1798, Jefferson referred to their time as "the reign of witches," and confidently predicted that it would soon end, with "the people" reawakened to the need to pursue right and recognize the delirium for what it was.[19]

Early in his retirement, Harry Truman had been quick to invoke the Alien and Sedition Acts, when "hysteria," as he framed it, was overtaking the Republican press. The Federalist Party had lost power, he reminded, because of its prosecution of pro-Jefferson editors. "I hope somebody will learn a lesson from that," Truman bellowed. "In all I did, when I was president, to combat communism, I always sought to preserve the rights of the individual. I always tried to hold in check those ugly passions of intolerance and hate which can be so easily manipulated by unscrupulous demagogues."[20]

There was every indication (timelessly so, one imagines) that politics and politicians were irrationally driven. Making sense of the red-baiting of the 1950s is beyond the scope of this book. Yet one vignette is too irresistible to ignore: After his Senate colleagues finally censured him, McCarthy reported provocatively to the *Milwaukee Journal* that he had been reading Thomas Jefferson's writings, and was convinced, as a result, that no one deserved to be persecuted for his beliefs, no matter how radical they were. How literal he intended to be when he invoked Jefferson hardly matters, though McCarthy's momentary engagement with the symbolic protector of public speech and private conscience does not appear to have been completely invented. Still, what might have been a national news story before no longer attracted notice outside of Wisconsin.[21]

The Kennedy legacy is complicated by the family's intimacy with Joe McCarthy. Power flowed from the patriarch, Joseph P. Kennedy, who warmly embraced his fellow Irish Catholic, and even encouraged McCarthy to date two of his daughters. This was how young Bobby Kennedy went from the outwardly fearless legal apprentice of 1951 to assistant legal counsel on McCarthy's investigative committee two years later. Through an arrangement made between his father and the Wisconsin senator, Bobby ended up working for McCarthy for six months. Whatever political distance eventually developed between the Kennedys and the sinking senator in 1954, it did not greatly diminish the personal affection Bobby retained for McCarthy. No Kennedy wanted to appear soft on communism. Indeed, no Kennedy was.[22]

How, then, did Jeffersonian ideals match up with the intense anticommunism espoused in the 1950s? Would a Republican decade undo all the work of FDR and his successor to monopolize the Jefferson mystique? A partial explanation comes in the form of a book review, and ultimately in a question posed by the University of Virginia history professor Thomas Perkins Abernethy.

Evaluating the newly published *Jefferson Reader* for the *New York Times,* early in the Eisenhower administration, Abernethy first remarked that the country, at midcentury, placed Jefferson above party in accepting him as "the chief spokesman for those who love freedom." That meant he attached to virulent anticommunists as well as lifelong liberals. Abernethy next observed that "some New Dealers have distorted Jefferson's beliefs to bolster their own philosophy and theories"; but at the same time he appeared to doubt whether the Democrats' hold on Jefferson could ever be weakened.

Jefferson, he said, was not so naive as to believe, in the Jacksonian remodel, that all men were equally fit ("physically, mentally, or morally") to govern. If the Virginian's "immortality" lay, as Virginia-born Woodrow Wilson put it, "in his attitude toward mankind," then Americans of the 1950s were left to mull over what kind of Cold Warrior this liberal idealist who governed as a pragmatist was. True, he was easier to envision as a liberal, but he was not exclusively one thing or another. The reviewer's ultimate equivocation is manifest in the questions with which he ended his piece: "Will the Republican victory dilute his resuscitated popularity?" the professor wondered. "Will the chameleon mood return him to the twilight?"[23]

Other giants of liberal America kept Jefferson in play in the 1950s. With the Soviet launch of Sputnik in 1957, Associate Justice William O. Douglas warned that the space race was not just about weaponry: "Our thinking has been too military—as a general and not as a Thomas Jefferson or an Abraham Lincoln." Alarmed that the nation's foreign policy was solely directed at displays of power, the jurist proposed doing more to advance the political values Jefferson taught. At this stage, he feared, the United States was "losing the contest for the minds of men."[24]

Around the same time, Eleanor Roosevelt spoke about Sputnik as a wake-up call for national education policy: "We need to change the attitude in our country toward learning and knowledge, its value, and the respect due to those who take the trouble to learn." An embarrassing percentage of students recently tested had shown no understanding of the Bill of Rights. She urged a hike in teacher salaries and greater recognition for the work of educators: "We should remember Thomas Jefferson's admonition that democracy, which we have discovered through the years to be one of the most difficult forms of government, cannot function except with an educated electorate."[25]

THE PRESIDENTIAL contest of 1960 came to define an entire generation. The Harvard historian Arthur Schlesinger Jr., a friend of Jack Kennedy's, produced a short book meant to clarify the issues of the campaign—especially the character issues. *Kennedy or Nixon: Does It Make Any Difference?* noted a "superficial resemblance" between the candidates. Both were war veterans, and both took "a cool, professional pleasure in politics for its own sake"; but the similarities ended there.

In describing the political paternity of the contenders, Schlesinger associated JFK with FDR, the latter of whom he credited as the same kind of leader Jefferson was in the eyes of his contemporaries: "a man of immense tactical agility, with marked and deplorable talents for evasion and dissimulation." As a creature of politics, he was not without imperfections, "but both his friends and his foes knew that at bottom he had a sense of historic direction." The line from Jefferson to Roosevelt to Kennedy was fairly direct, then. In contrast, Schlesinger continued, Richard Milhous Nixon was notoriously hard to gauge:

"Mention Nixon," he wrote, and "no coherent viewpoint comes to mind." With an "almost disembodied alertness and intelligence," he adapted his behavior to suit the moment. Nixon had an ability to take the pulse of the electorate, but he did not reflect clear political values. Kennedy was more knowable: "He has a sense of history, he cares about issues."

The historian doubled down from here, hinting that Nixon was biting off more than he could chew. With his inaccurate sense of scale, the small-town California boy had taken pains to wrap himself in an American Dream that allowed him to rise from extremely modest roots and to stand before the nation beside a true hero, the architect of D-Day. In associating himself with the fatherly president under whom he had served two terms, Vice President Nixon actually boasted that theirs was "the best eight-year record in the history of the country." Schlesinger took Nixon's claim to mean: better than Washington, Jefferson, and Jackson. "This is an astonishing judgment," he chided, as he pointed to history's ironies: "Alexander Hamilton and Herbert Hoover came from poverty; Thomas Jefferson and Franklin Roosevelt from affluence." Projecting the American Dream onto himself, then, Nixon was selling an inverted perspective on actual historical experience, misrepresenting the founders' political bequest.

Schlesinger unabashedly pronounced that the election of 1960 was about which candidate would prove most capable of "showing the world that the American Revolution is not dead in the land of its birth." It was the energetic Democrat, not the morbid Republican, who would "put American idealism to work." History had abundantly demonstrated that conservatives aligned themselves with a "single interest," generally the "business community"; that's what Eisenhower and Nixon had done. Those able to praise a President Jefferson for retaining open-minded Federalists in government jobs were as likely to assign to the liberal tradition (exclusively) a willingness to hear contrasting voices; presidents such as Roosevelt were happy to appoint to high positions one like—and Schlesinger mentioned him by name—Jefferson descendant T. Jefferson Coolidge, a fiscal conservative. Liberals supported "businessmen of good will," embracing a multiplicity of interests. The reader/voter was left to mull over the differences between two who carried with them the partisan baggage of history.[26]

In another sense, the election of 1960 was about two versions of the historical Jefferson. In his July nomination acceptance speech in Chicago, Nixon was anything but the grim and gloomy caricature in Schlesinger's admittedly biased assessment. He made his message about freedom and fairness, repeatedly saying that his vision of America ("a proud example of freedom for all the world") was nothing new: "It is as old as America and as young as America, because America will never grow old." Quoting Jefferson first—"We act not for ourselves alone, but for the whole human race"—and then quoting, in turn, Lincoln, the first Roosevelt, and Wilson, candidate Nixon stuck to the theme that the "forces of freedom" were to be marshaled in fulfilling a bright destiny.[27]

For his part, candidate Kennedy found in Jefferson more than one lesson to be learned. The man who oversaw his campaign in the battleground state of Virginia was William C. Battle, the son of a former governor, who recalled in a later interview what took place at a campaign event in Norfolk. As they fought their way toward the rostrum through the large crowd, Kennedy realized that he had gotten separated from the aide who was carrying his prepared speech. "What must I talk about?" he asked Battle, who joked back: "It's a Virginia audience, and you just praise Jefferson and damn Nixon and you'll be all right."

Two weeks earlier, Nixon had acted the part of a Virginia Democrat in a speech in nearby Richmond. So Kennedy got up before the crowd and opened his extemporaneous remarks by saying that he understood his opponent had been by recently, and had gone around claiming Jefferson for himself. Battle described what happened next, and how Kennedy let the hammer drop:

> Of course, he was a great student of Jefferson. He said that a contemporary of Jefferson's had once written that at the age of twenty-nine—and I am not sure I am accurate on these various dates—that Jefferson was a master statesman, master politician, accomplished violinist, he could dance the minuet, he could survey a field, he could plot an eclipse. Then in his Massachusetts tones, he said, "Now what, what has Richard Nixon in common with Thomas Jefferson?"[28]

A *New York Times* contributor took the time to speculate on which of the talked-about candidates were likely to woo the home audience most effectively. (This was some months before the nominating conventions had even met and long before the now-famous Kennedy-Nixon television debate.) Kennedy was deemed "too handsome on TV, too youthful in appearance" to do well—especially given his accent. Nixon was, hands down, the perfect TV politician: "He knows the emotions of an audience and how to stir them. . . . He knows how to be entertaining. He appears to be relaxed."

Lingering on the lighter side for a moment or two, the writer, a historian of campaign oratory, wondered how different history would have been if America's early leaders had been obliged to campaign in the television age. Washington had "ill-fitting false teeth" that produced a whistling sound, and his face bore the after-effects of smallpox. Lincoln's features were too "heavy." Jefferson, the writer said, was "frequently described as having 'shifty eyes.'" (He provides no source for this questionable statement.) For us, the irony is all too obvious in that the televised Kennedy-Nixon debate prompted many to give Kennedy the edge based on his calm, communicative manner. It was Nixon who was widely described as "shifty-eyed" in this most critical performance of the 1960 campaign. Thus, in a perverse way, he did get to claim a "Jeffersonian" quality.[29]

How could "too handsome on TV, too youthful in appearance" have been seen as detrimental? Before Kennedy had captured his party's nomination, the irrepressible Harry Truman went on TV and said that the senator from Massachusetts lacked the "maturity and experience" to be president in this time of global crisis. Kennedy, greatly perturbed, countered with a quip that Truman's "maturity" requirement "would have kept Jefferson from writing the Declaration of Independence."[30]

Nearing Election Day, the occasionally cheeky campaigner attended the National Conference on Civil Rights in Harlem, where he once more invoked Jefferson. Standing on a rostrum alongside the popular, mixed-race Adam Clayton Powell, the first African American congressman from New York, Kennedy mouthed an obligatory anticommunist crack, noting that there were no children in Africa named after Marx or Lenin. Upon which, he lit up: *But there are children called Thomas Jefferson!* A pregnant pause, and then: "There may be a couple called Adam Clayton Powell." From behind, Powell spoke in a loud whisper: "Careful, Jack." The congressman was alluding to his own reputation, for certain. Perhaps Kennedy's, too. And perhaps Jefferson's, as men who had possibly fathered children of one hue or another out of wedlock.[31]

JOHN F. KENNEDY'S inaugural address is remembered for its call to service, "Ask not what your country can do for you. . . ." Having as yet made no mark on the country, the newly sworn-in president had doubts that the historic speech, being among the shortest of its genre, would make any real impression on the national audience. As news commentators weighed in, offering their pros and cons, he specifically told his wife, Jackie, that he did not believe his inaugural address to be the equal of Jefferson's.

As he came into office, writes the historian Robert Dallek, Kennedy "intended to measure himself" against the third president, marveling at what Jefferson brought to the English language. Though his poise, articulation, and Harvard credentials helped him to exude a kind of mastery over audiences that few politicians can boast, Jack Kennedy, a less than diligent scholar when young, apparently felt that there could be only one Jefferson.

That admiration for Jefferson went beyond political considerations. Kennedy's Jefferson had an irreproducible style and saw the world in a unique way. According to his close aide Theodore Sorensen, the president "delighted" in a letter Jefferson had written requesting White House gardeners who could double as musicians after dinner—a measure Kennedy jokingly said he would try as he looked for cost-cutting solutions at the Executive Mansion. And speaking of Jefferson's green thumb, according to Caroline Kennedy her father kept Jefferson's *Garden Book* on the nightstand beside his bed in the White House.[32]

Though Inauguration Day in January was a day for heavy overcoats, the young president had taken the oath of office without his on, shedding upon Washington a picture of vigorous masculinity. The Kennedy administration promptly assembled a new version of FDR's "Brain Trust," as it promoted an attractive, thirty-one-year-old First Lady with a particular eye for the historical aesthetic. For her redesign of the White House, Jacqueline Bouvier Kennedy called on Julian Boyd, editor of the *Papers of Thomas Jefferson* at Princeton, the first several volumes of which series had been regularly and admiringly reviewed in the *New York Times* during the 1950s. Boyd responded to Mrs. Kennedy's request with book recommendations on the founders and their successors, to supplant the Agatha Christie mysteries in the White House library. She confirmed: "Jefferson is the president with whom I have the most affinity, but Lincoln is the one I love."

Jackie's affinity for Jefferson was indefinable, more about his cultural sophistication—the French immersion and architectural focus—than his political persona. Her greater love for Lincoln probably had something to do with the more tangible reality expressed in photographs, the humanity conveyed in his features, which no painted portrait of an eighteenth-century founder could quite capture. Neither was there a Jefferson bedroom to help conjure the Revolutionary spirit. The First Lady said she greatly enjoyed sitting in the Lincoln bedroom and reflecting on the Kennedy family's place in history. (It was not actually Lincoln's bedroom, but it contained many items he owned.) "To touch something I knew he had touched was a real link with him," she said.[33]

Her restoration of the White House was a true labor of love, aimed at authenticity and offering tactile reminders of her husband's predecessors. Each room reflected a presidential era. The Louis XVI style had adorned the President's House for the "Virginia Dynasty" of presidents, Jefferson, Madison, and Monroe; and so the Green Room featured the furniture they knew. The Blue Room was decorated in the Empire style, which the Monroes put in place in the rebuilding that followed the fire of 1814; the Red Room had a Jacksonian flair; the Lincoln sitting room and Lincoln bedroom were Victorian. Also, as Jefferson had done, the Kennedys hired a French chef, René Verdon, for the White House. Esther Peters, chair of "Women for Kennedy" in West Virginia, put it this way: "President and Mrs. Kennedy brought a dignity and culture to the White House that hadn't been there since the days of Thomas Jefferson."[34]

A symbolic rehanging of presidential portraits took place in the White House Cabinet Room, as ultra-Democrat Andrew Jackson now faced Jefferson, and William Howard Taft came down. The first year of the Kennedy administration did not delight everyone equally, of course. *Time* ran a feature about young conservatives, showing that increasing numbers were rebelling against their parents' sympathies—to them, liberalism was "ironbound conformity." Unimpressed with the legacy of FDR, they had turned to Ayn Rand's *Atlas Shrugged*.[35]

Along these lines, the best-selling book in college towns in 1961 was, in fact, Barry Goldwater's *The Conscience of a Conservative*. The editor of the University of Michigan's student newspaper said: "The signs point to a revival of interest in individualism and decentralization of power—principles espoused by John Locke and Thomas Jefferson, and rekindled by Barry Goldwater." A young Texan named Karl Rove who was given a copy later recalled, "It was a rip-roaring good read."[36]

The Goldwater phenomenon was so striking that Eisenhower, as a lame-duck president, had taken notice. In October 1960, he wrote a confidential letter to the editor of the *Atlanta Constitution* (never sent), scanning the partisan landscape. "The people who nowadays proclaim themselves liberals either directly or indirectly support centralization of power in Washington," he observed. "This is the very antithesis of what Jefferson believed and taught, yet we think of Jefferson as a liberal." The foregoing made him think of Goldwater: "Regardless of my complete disagreement with some of his beliefs, he does follow Jefferson in his championship of the authority of the several subdivisions of government—that is 'States' Rights.'"

Eisenhower's resurrection of the "states' rights" Jefferson may not have found its way into print, but the appearance of Goldwater's book was evidence that the Jefferson who feared consolidated government might be staging a comeback. In notes recorded as he was planning *The Conscience of a Conservative,* the Arizona senator associated Jefferson's Declaration with the ultimate guarantee of personal freedom, adding his own rich commentary: "government cannot be the provider without being the master."[37]

If he feared a Goldwater challenge in 1964, President Kennedy continued to bring up the liberal humanist Jefferson. In a message to Congress on February 6, 1962, he addressed the same education deficit that Eleanor Roosevelt had warned against four years earlier, after the launch of Sputnik. Kennedy called for federal aid to the arts, a war on adult illiteracy, the use of television for educational purposes, and increased teacher salaries to bring more talent into the classrooms of America. In concluding remarks, he returned to the source, to the republic's earliest champion of education: "'If a nation,' wrote Thomas Jefferson in 1816, 'expects to be ignorant and free, in a state of civilization, it expects what never was and never will be.' That statement is even truer today than it was 146 years ago." Intuiting the best Jefferson he knew, the president explained the theory behind his new policy: "The education of our people is a national investment. It yields tangible returns in economic growth, an improved citizenry and higher standards of living. But even more importantly, free men and women value education as a personal experience and opportunity—as a basic benefit of a free and democratic civilization." This was the Jeffersonian call to arms of which Kennedy never tired, and he would recycle the same quote on more than one occasion in 1963.[38]

Here's what's odd about that lovely sentiment of Jefferson's: it was written to a Virginia state legislator when the ex-president was seventy-two years old and gravely concerned that New England (Harvard and Yale, in particular) was where a young Virginia scholar would go for a superior education; the graduate would then return south tainted by New England ideas, and with "fanaticism & indifferentism to their own state." As Jefferson took the first steps toward establishing the University of Virginia, he wanted state legislators to recognize what would happen if they failed to give financial support to his project. He felt that improving the educational system was the only viable way to "rescue" the future of his southern community.[39]

In 1962, on the Sunday before Jefferson's birthday, the *New York Times* commissioned Saul Padover, politics professor at the New School for Social Research, to celebrate the founder in print. The lengthy article he wrote highlighted Jefferson's world-transformative message and growing reputation abroad. Emerging peoples, as well as western Europeans, now saw him as "the American philosopher of democracy par excellence," "champion of the universal ideal of freedom." His birthday was, by this time, a public holiday in only three states, the professor noted, but elsewhere in the world, his ideas about self-government were catching fire.

When Professor Padover had taught at the Sorbonne in 1949, he learned that even the most educated of the French were only vaguely aware of Jefferson, despite the fact that he had served as U.S. minister to their country as the French Revolution took shape. A 1956 biography with the subtitle *Un militant de la liberté* promoted Jefferson as one whose ideas were as historically influential as Leonardo da Vinci's—he was a kind of "philosopher king" in the cause of freedom. Jefferson may have written to Lafayette that "the disease of liberty is catching"; but, as Hungary's abortive attempt to break free of the Soviet hold in 1957 reminded—to quote Jefferson again—"The ground of liberty is to be gained by inches." To Padover, then, Jeffersonianism was marked by resilience, by perseverance.[40]

Just as Padover's *Times* piece appeared in print, the White House was gearing up for a very special event: forty-nine Nobel Prize winners would be honored at a gala banquet. Generally, the First Lady's staff took care of such programs. But the president was intent on orchestrating the Nobel dinner, and deputed Arthur Schlesinger Jr. to draw up the guest list. According to the housekeeper of the Executive Mansion, who knew the official schedule as well as anyone, the president "took more interest in that party than any other." He became impatient with Schlesinger when the historian was too slow in getting the list to the president for review; afterward, when the evening proved a giant success, Kennedy took pride in what he had done. His private secretary, Anne Lincoln, said he called her excitedly when the next issue of *Life* magazine reached his desk, greatly pleased that twenty pages (it was actually ten) were devoted to the Nobel dinner, with photos of the receiving line and a group portrait with each laureate identified by number. "It's just wonderful," she quoted him as having said into the phone, as he put the issue aside to show the First Lady on her return from an outing.[41]

THE HEADLINE in *Life* read: "Cognoscenti Come to Call." Just above, in a smaller font: "A brilliant night to remember at the White House." The widow of the late George C. Marshall was seated beside the president; the poet Robert Frost had the First Lady's ear. As the Air Force string orchestra played, scientists danced. The president, in black tie, regaled his guests with good-humored drollery, opening his comments with a joke borrowed from a Canadian journalist: that the April evening marked the White House "Easter egghead roll." The smiling guests were gathered around nineteen tables, forming the largest group to date that the Kennedy White House had hosted.

It was this nearly surreal atmosphere that *Life* captured. Its story began with excerpts from the president's remarks at dinner:

> I think this is the most extraordinary collection of talent, of human knowledge . . . ever gathered at the White House, with the possible exception of when Thomas Jefferson dined alone," said President John F. Kennedy to 175 dinner guests last week. There in Jefferson's "President's Palace" were laureates of achievement in the pursuit of peace, literature, and science.[42]

Iconic language can be original, even when it is not entirely unprecedented. The same was true for Jefferson's foundational "life, liberty, and the pursuit of happiness," which he openly borrowed from the English philosopher John Locke, who had introduced a "pursuit of happiness" into his *Essay Concerning the Human Understanding* fourscore and six years earlier. Jefferson's amplification of the phrase instantly took on Revolutionary import after July 4, 1776, and was copied into state constitutions in seven of the former British colonies, including Virginia, New York, and Massachusetts. By Jefferson's own account, the words he had drawn from a seventeenth-century Englishman were never meant to do more than express the collective mind and combined political will of American patriots.

Just as his presidential forebear had recast Locke, Kennedy was not the first to accord Jefferson his singularity as America's most inventive and multifaceted founder. Something similar had come from the lips of the celebrated architect Frank Lloyd Wright not long before. In a magazine interview conducted in 1959 at Taliesin West (near Phoenix), Wright reacted to being called the greatest architect in the world.

The President
Remarks
Nobel Prize Dinner
April 29, 1962

I am proud to welcome to the White House the winners of the
Nobel Prize in the Western Hemisphere. I doubt whether in the long
history of this house we have ever had on a single occasion such
a concentration of genius and achievement as we have tonight.

The Nobel Prize, of course, is intended for humanity in
general. It knows no geographical or political frontiers. With
brisk disregard for his fellow countrymen Alfred Nobel even
took care to specify in his will, "I declare it to be my express
desire that, in the awarding of prizes, no consideration whatever
be paid to the nationality of the candidates, that is to say, that
the most desrving be awarded the prize, whether he or she be a
Scandanavian or not...".

Nobel's passion was to honor men and women who served
mankind in the fields of science and in literature and in the
cause of peace. His faith was that the spirit of inquiry and
the extension of knowledge would best guarantee the freedom and
welfare of humanity. "Knowledge", said Plato, "is the food of the
soul". We must all agree with Nobel that the free and disinterested
pursuit of knowledge has always been-- and always will be-- the
mainspring of human Progress.

Excerpt from the text used by President Kennedy when he ad-libbed remarks to a distinguished group of Nobel laureates at the White House, describing them as "the most extraordinary collection of talent, of human knowledge . . . with the possible exception of when Thomas Jefferson dined alone." The single-word reminder "Jefferson" appears above the text; "when Jefferson was here," crossed out, is visible in the left margin. (Courtesy of John F. Kennedy Presidential Library)

He had visited Monticello, he said, and had marveled at its designer's mind. At a dinner of history's greats, he told his interviewer, Jefferson would have to be seated "at the head of the table."[43]

Jefferson continued to occupy a special position in the liberal imagination. It was not purely a leftover of FDR's obsession, nor a function of the publicity generated by one epigram about a president dining alone; but while no one political interest could completely co-opt Jefferson, liberals were particularly adept at portraying his most attractive, most human side. Their Jefferson was open to new ideas, open to the world, open to honest dialogue. A *New York Times* editorial of July 4, 1962, assured its readers that "life, liberty, and the pursuit of happiness" contained no ambiguity. One, "unalienable" rights were given in equal measure to all. Two, "governments were the designated agents of the people." Jefferson's seven-word phrase was secure, and only buoyed by the Rooseveltian amendment that "freedom may now lie in interdependence rather than in independence." However conceived, "consent of the governed" was as self-evident in the American society of the 1960s as it had been at any time previous, going back to 1776. With this editorial rendering of the *Times'* corporate credo, the newspaper of record sought to cement Jefferson's liberal reputation.[44]

At Christmas in 1962, White House Press Secretary Pierre Salinger gave the president a gift: a framed facsimile of an 1807 letter from Thomas Jefferson to a young man and future newspaper editor, John Norvell. The document exposed the third president's mixed feelings about the press of his day. "The man who never looks into a newspaper is better informed than he whose mind is filled with falsehoods and errors," wrote Jefferson. "Any time you get mad at the press, just remember Jefferson got madder," wrote Salinger on the matte bordering the modern reproduction.[45]

Though better known for crafting uplifting sentiments, Jefferson proves, in the Norvell letter, to have been equally adept at metaphorical swordplay. In language that could be consumed in our century without a single word being altered, he wrote of the contagion spread by sensational editorializing, and railed against "the demoralizing practice of feeding the public mind habitually on slander, & the depravity of taste which this nauseous ailment induces." Jefferson fed Norvell bitter irony: "Perhaps an editor might begin a reformation in some such way as this. Divide his paper into 4 chapters, heading the 1st Truths. 2d Probabilities. 3d Possibilities. 4th Lies. The 1st chapter would be very short."

In closing the letter, a tired, besieged president implored his correspondent to keep to himself the confidences contained in their communications, all too aware that, as he put it, "political enemies torture every sentence from me into meanings imagined by their own wickedness only." Politics brought out the bad side in too many people, requiring a leader to adopt a smooth public persona and constantly jump hurdles. Jefferson knew, Truman knew, the victims of Joe McCarthy knew, and Jack Kennedy knew, too, that critics in the opposition press hung on their every word, always looking for some slip-up.[46]

DURING HIS June 1963 visit to Berlin, President Kennedy famously declared himself "ein Berliner." But he also renewed his focus on education, telling the faculty and students of the Free University in that city that he, like Jefferson, considered scholarship essential to a free society. Benjamin Franklin, James Madison, and Thomas Jefferson saw the role of science as integral to the spirit of social progress. "It is not enough to mark time, to adhere to a status quo, while awaiting a change for the better." That same month, at a Chicago symposium titled "Challenges to Democracy," the physicist Robert Oppenheimer— one of those present at the Nobel laureates' gathering—invoked Franklin and Jefferson as well. "Reading Jefferson today," he said, "we do owe a surprising measure of our own democratic institutions to him, to his life, to his time. He expected that these institutions would change rather more than they have; but he articulated the connection between a free society and the growth of knowledge and its application to the alleviation of illness, hunger, tyranny, and superstition." In short, the Jefferson whose "informed citizenry" was the republic's ultimate protection played a lead role in defining the optimistic prescriptions of the Kennedy era.[47]

Yet the conservative prescription for the country had its votaries, too. Writing in the *Chicago Tribune*, Washington bureau chief Walter Trohan observed that Democrats from the president down to the precinct level regularly gave "mouth honor" to the putative founder of their party, but helped their cause more when they quoted the first Republican president, Lincoln, who was the superior liberal. "Jefferson opposed centralization of power," Trohan explained, and promptly supplied four strong pieces of evidence from his cache of Jefferson quotes:

In questions of power let no more be heard of confidence in man,
but bind him down from mischief by the chains of the Constitution.

I have never been able to conceive how any rational being could propose happiness to himself from the exercise of power over others.

It is the old practice of despots to use a part of the people to keep the rest in order.

I think we have more machinery in government than is necessary, too many parasites living on the labor of the industrious.

The columnist went on to say that as Jefferson did not believe in "entrenched power," he would not have seen tyranny in the way the Democrats imagined he did. Instead, he upheld what Trohan called "industrial freedom" (the free enterprise system), which meant resisting government that was too busy. Beyond that, "Jefferson could hardly be quoted to support the foreign aid dole"; he wanted "entangling alliances" with no foreign nation, "honest friendship" and regular commerce with all nations. Jefferson, Trohan ended the piece, "was not a man who sighed for power."[48]

Trohan's assessment of Jefferson (and modern Democrats) was compelling up to the final pronouncement, where he fell to idealizing the founder as a selfless public servant. For to call Jefferson a man without ambition is either naive or a gross lapse in historical judgment. As a Virginia planter and one of the most land-rich men in Albemarle County, Thomas Jefferson felt his privilege every day. When moved by an issue, he could become a bright visionary. On certain days a justice-seeking populist, he showed himself, on other days, to be a stern political pragmatist. As Trohan does not define the "entrenched power" he says Jefferson resisted, we can at least say that if Jefferson did not himself, in preserving the Virginia Dynasty of presidents, court *entrenched* power, he absolutely saw the viability of preserving executive power. He was a take-charge president.

The Kennedy brothers' Jefferson connection was certainly more than sporadic and beyond the merely anecdotal. The astronaut and later U.S. senator John Glenn, a close friend, said that Bobby Kennedy was an eager student of Jefferson's writings: "He'd quite often quote Thomas Jefferson who said that if our democracy was to work, every man must have his voice heard in some council of government." It mattered to Bobby how ordinary people felt about their government. On the campaign trail with him in Nebraska in 1968, Glenn observed Bobby's romance with the wide-open fields, and his genuine affinity with the farmers he met. Another friend said that Bobby deeply empathized with the American farmer, perceiving him as a less obvious example of the "forgotten and alienated" toward whom he felt he wanted to commit himself. There is something of Jefferson's romance with the storied yeoman in this image of Bobby Kennedy; for Jefferson had warmly referred to the nation's cultivators as "the chosen people of God."[49]

When, near the end of his life, Jefferson was shopping around for professors to appoint to the brand new University of Virginia—his brainchild—he took pains to identify men of "clear and sound ideas," as he put it to his old friend James Madison. Of a candidate for the professorship in law and politics, he remarked: "His character is perfectly correct, his mind liberal and accommodating, yet firm." Liberal and accommodating, yet firm. This was the political standard with which the Kennedy brothers identified, and the way they perceived the historical Jefferson, too.[50]

3

"WE CONFIDE IN OUR OWN STRENGTH"

The Reagan Revolution(ary)

IN THE 1960s, Jefferson's script was translated into the dominant liberal concepts of tolerance for difference, a free and eager pursuit of knowledge, and heightened awareness of individualism. These were seen as quintessentially American traits. So when, as president, the conservative convert Ronald Reagan lent his support to the cause of prayer in public schools, he was really embracing what he had subscribed to as an old-time liberal: tolerance. To outlaw prayer was to be intolerant.[1]

Reagan was by no means a simple man, though some part of him did find in conventional wisdom, in proverbs and words of inspiration, a simple means of getting across a high-minded message. Like Jefferson, he was adored and despised, but rarely anything in between. Reagan may have seemed heartless to the working men and women who were hurt by the economic policies of the 1980s, when real wages fell, but he was wholly convinced that he was acting to improve conditions, and it is true that the U.S. economy, in general, performed well during his presidency. Whatever may be said about him, Ronald Reagan did more than learn his lines; he savored the opportunity to remake America.

As one who constantly honed his communication skills, Reagan kept notecards, the twentieth-century equivalent of the eighteenth-century commonplace book that Jefferson and his peers maintained. On one of those cards, the actor-turned-politician penned the words of Learned Hand, an oft-quoted New York judge: "Nothing which is morally wrong can ever be politically right." This pithy line captures the basic moral philosophy of both Ronald Wilson Reagan and

Thomas Jefferson. Reagan always tried to sound conciliatory, which was Jefferson's modus operandi, too.[2]

The disheveled look of America in the decade and a half between President Kennedy's assassination and the red-white-and-blue assertiveness of President Reagan has been chronicled in many places. But the meaning of "Jeffersonian democracy" to those restless Americans is less well understood. The nation Lyndon Johnson presided over with his somber drawl, the nation an ungainly Richard Nixon misused, did not much engage with the Jefferson symbol. Does that mean Jefferson served politics only when the jauntiest leaders tapped his invigorating prose? Perhaps. But it would be too simple to leave it at that.

IN ONE sense, Leonard Levy's 1963 *Jefferson and Civil Liberties: The Darker Side* captured the coming malaise. Levy's Jefferson enjoyed power a little too much and found ways around the Constitution. A "pliability of principle" (in John Quincy Adams's keen rendering) marked his legacy no less than a firm *rhetorical* commitment to liberty. Professor Levy, a First Amendment scholar trained at Columbia, agreed with the second Adams. "The saintly vapors that veil the real Jefferson clear away," he wrote, revealing a man whose "failings" were "plentiful," and whose outward actions did not match the tender emotions contained in his private letters. Taking aim at the Jefferson Memorial's beautiful inscription—"eternal hostility against every form of tyranny"—Levy noted a problem with Jefferson and consistency: "The sentiment was a noble one, poetically true," he said. "But it was not the whole historical truth."

Levy didn't believe that Thomas Jefferson had even once risked his career to speak out against civil wrongs. He quoted FDR's adulatory speech at the 1943 dedication, but only to challenge its underlying assumption that Jefferson adhered to his stated values. The ends justified the means for him, according to Levy. When Jefferson felt it politically necessary, he abridged people's liberties: he tampered with the federal judiciary, he interfered with Aaron Burr's trial, and he imposed a belt-tightening embargo on the entire nation. He lacked any self-critical capacity. "Whose happiness did Jefferson's trademark pursuit leave out?" seemed to be the central question underlying the unhinged, hyperactive 1960s and all their discontent and public dissent.[3]

Levy's book notwithstanding, Jefferson's modern protectors stood strong. The most authoritative source for all things Jefferson remained Julian Boyd of Princeton, the unofficial dean of Jefferson studies ever since 1950, when he unveiled the first volume of the *Papers of Thomas*

Jefferson. The cognoscenti's newspaper, the *New York Times,* relied on Boyd's every word. This was certainly the case in 1964, when, as president of the American Historical Association, Boyd announced his finding that in 1790, Jefferson's chief antagonist, Alexander Hamilton, had revealed the substance of secret cabinet meetings to the British "intelligence agent" Major George Beckwith. It was "almost the gravest offense of which a cabinet officer can be guilty," Boyd proclaimed, stopping just short of calling Hamilton a traitor. As secretary of state under President Washington, Jefferson ostensibly directed foreign policy; yet Hamilton sought to undermine Jefferson (who wished to stand up to British might), and to spearhead U.S. foreign relations as well as direct its domestic economic programs.[4]

Whether as an advisor to Jacqueline Kennedy on her redesign of the White House, or as an expert on loan to the *Times,* Boyd made it easy to love Jefferson. He helped to make the author of the Declaration of Independence the all-purpose founder: inspired philosopher, beacon of knowledge, a Renaissance man who got most things right. Knowing the dangers of hyperbole, Leonard Levy scoffed at Boyd's calling Jefferson "a figure of universal dimensions, wholly committed to the rights of man."

Levy's criticism never quite got through. The Jefferson Memorial, having by this time stood solid for twenty years, was so much a fixture of the Washington landscape that to attempt to diminish the nineteen-foot-tall giant of democratic thought who peered out from under the dome was akin to sacrilege. The Tidal Basin shrine would shine through the night, from this moment forward, thanks to a massive lighting project. "Thomas Jefferson never again will be left in the dark," the *Washington Post* reported.[5]

It had been one year since the Kennedy assassination. In honoring the slain leader, President Johnson transitioned from the obvious Lincoln comparison ("Now he belongs to the ages") so as to emphasize JFK's Jefferson-like quality: "Never did nature and fortune combine more perfectly to make a man great, and to place him in everlasting remembrance." How fitting to repeat Jefferson's words in eulogizing George Washington. "He saw the world and its problems in all their fantastic complexity," Johnson added, making his predecessor sound that much more like the broad-minded and expansive third president.[6]

Elected in his own right, Johnson included Jefferson in his State of the Union address on January 5, 1965: "Every child must have the best education our nation can provide. Thomas Jefferson said no nation can be both ignorant and free. Today no nation can be both ignorant and great." It is hard to know precisely what LBJ meant by greatness here, or how he might have imagined himself a successor in spirit to the New Deal's Jefferson. One easily reads FDR in Lyndon Johnson's social programs, but the Texan's presidency seems to have produced no more direct communication of the Jeffersonianism previous Democratic administrations embraced.

Among popular treatments, *The Shackles of Power,* by John Dos Passos, represented the last gasp of a superior Jefferson—for a while anyway. Here was a major name in American letters, a man respected by Julian Boyd, who stood with those bent on reclaiming the narrative Leonard Levy had muddied. Dos Passos (1896–1970) was a literary artist who thrived on controversy. A 1916 Harvard graduate, he made waves early on with searing portraits of contemporary American society. Ernest Hemingway and Jean-Paul Sartre were among his fans. But there's a twist: A left-wing radical litterateur in the 1920s, Dos Passos had turned arch-conservative by the 1960s; still, he was among the distinguished guests invited to the April 1962 Nobel laureates dinner at the Kennedy White House. A Jefferson lover going back decades, the author underwent a political transformation that provided a foretaste of the Reaganite Jefferson.

In his formative years, Dos Passos recorded, he was taught that "private enterprise had lost its usefulness in the world," and that the socialized state held out greater promise. Hamilton's vision of "money men" running a stable republic modeled on Britain had proven unsuccessful by the end of the prior century, with "the Jeffersonian side," however it might be described, offering the best, and only, counterpoint. An undated scrap of yellow lined paper in his private papers has Dos Passos ruminating: "How does the medium independent man whom Jefferson depended on to govern himself live today."

After spending time in Stalinist Russia, "Dos" soured on communism. He eventually went on to write, with extreme satisfaction, for William F. Buckley and the *National Review,* and threw his support behind Barry Goldwater in 1964. In between, he found in Jefferson an instrument for understanding his own political path. The door opened, in a way, at the end of World War II, when Dos Passos was egged on by Democratic mainstay Claude Bowers, who sent him his most recent book, *The Young Jefferson* (1945), and each new Jefferson book he could lay his hands on. As the recipient of this largesse, the famed author of the trilogy *U.S.A.* was inspired by a visit to Monticello and the University of Virginia, and set aside a fiction project in order to tackle Jefferson.

His first attempt at Jefferson biography, *The Head and Heart of Thomas Jefferson* (1954), though it took him the better part of a decade to bring to life, was widely panned by specialists: Marie Kimball called it "a blustery, slangy series of yarns." *The Shackles of Power: Three Jeffersonian Decades* (1966) was a better-researched if still deficient popular history, and it completed its author's storied, if inconstant, career as a chronicler of the American experience. The book found Jefferson and his Virginia-bred successors as president to be an embattled but resilient tribe, and all eager to make republican government function efficiently. To Dos Passos, who had seen two world wars up close, Jeffersonian America was a fresh, hopeful canvas, and Jefferson, above all, a creditable political moralist and ruminative champion of education. As president, he fought for a wise, judicious, discerning citizenry, and in retirement he devoted "every spark of influence he had left" to building a great university. Over the course of the twentieth century's first five decades, then, Dos Passos lost faith in government's capacity to arrive at humane solutions; but he never lost his faith in Thomas Jefferson as a guide.[7]

WITH THE 1960s, the era of the equivocal Jefferson opened. As youth protest magnified, the name of Jefferson was bandied about, but more as a convenient mascot than as a serious philosopher of individual freedom. There was no logic beyond wordplay in the christening of "Jefferson Airplane," the popular rock band. (It was most likely the legendary blues singer "Blind" Lemon Jefferson, rather than the third president, who inspired the name.) Jefferson had greater meaning, of course, at the University of Virginia, where, in 1965, a student demonstrator expressing support for civil rights activity in Selma, Alabama, bore a sign that read: "All eyes are opening to the rights of man," a Jefferson quote taken from a letter of 1826, the last important communication from the founder before his death.

At the Selma support rally, the Jefferson scholar Merrill D. Peterson took a chance when he spoke from the University Rotunda that Jefferson had designed. He said that the university ought not to be thought of as a place apart from the "actions and passions of the time," nor "an artificial, walled-in atmosphere." Selma mattered, because "the struggle there involves what is taught here: truth, honesty, justice, compassion, the rights and freedom of all men in a democratic society." Professor Peterson, author of *The Jefferson Image in the American Mind* (1960), recalled Jefferson's insistent opinion that "the earth belongs to the living," adding that "the dark Jeffersonian shadow of state rights" needed to yield to "the bright Jeffersonian day of human rights." Though a great Jefferson lover, he recognized where Jefferson's legacy was weak, and where it was strong.[8]

The Free Speech Movement at the University of California at Berkeley was larger and more menacing in appearance than anything students and liberal professors could muster in Charlottesville. In late 1964 and early 1965, Berkeley grabbed national headlines. Students politicized the campus in defiance of state university policy, and were cast as "antic anarchists" by the political Right. "Jefferson stood for violent resistance to tyranny," said one of the defiant students. "He believed in rebellion as the answer to oppression." The language was hardly more radical than Peterson's, but reaction from above was different. A state education administrator reminded readers of the *Los Angeles Times* that the Declaration of Independence described a people's acquiescence to war only after their "repeated petitions" in "the most humble terms" had been rebuffed. The California Board of Regents had received no petitions, he said, because the students were insincere, and without justification for a misguided protest that consisted of bashing in police cars. Ronald Reagan's election as governor the following year is generally linked to his hard-line opposition to campus activism.[9]

Jefferson entered a second of LBJ's State of the Union addresses, that of January 10, 1967. This time, in invoking Jefferson, the president did not refer to civil rights or freedom in the abstract. Instead, explaining his escalation of the war in Vietnam, he offered—without providing any actual context—Jefferson's rationalization for the War of 1812. In his second term as president, Jefferson had resorted to an ill-fated, self-destructive trade embargo in the hope of gaining from Great Britain the shift in policy he wanted, without resort to war. As an ex-president, writing to his one-time private secretary, the diplomat William Short, he applied a surgical metaphor to the eventuality that his friend Madison had been forced to confront as president. Sometimes, said Jefferson, one had to give a limb when risk to life presented; and so, war made sense because the risk of a thorough "submission" to London's will appeared very real.

Was that what Vietnam was? LBJ universalized a phrase plucked from Jefferson's letter to Short, invoking "the melancholy law of human societies to be compelled sometimes to choose a great evil in order to ward off a greater." Had the president or his speechwriters looked more carefully, they would have understood Jefferson's point to favor the antiwar community: it was only because the "great majority of the nation" clamored for war that war was declared in 1812.

Jefferson reminded Short that America was compelled into war as a consequence of insolent provocations ordered by "ravenous" authorities in London, redirecting the attention of a nation of producers, minding its own business, while pursuing free trade on the high seas: "Our enemy has indeed the consolation of Satan on removing our first parents from Paradise: from a peaceable and agricultural nation, he makes us a military and manufacturing one. We shall indeed survive the conflict. . . . We shall retain our country, and rapid advances in the art of war will soon enable us to beat our enemy, and probably drive him from the continent." America had felt directly threatened. Not so in Southeast Asia. And of course, the Vietnam War was undeclared. It was not the best use of Jefferson.[10]

LIKE LBJ, Richard M. Nixon did not, in any significant way, exhibit interest in modeling his thought or action on the exalted Jefferson whom historians of the mid-twentieth century had promoted. In the pages of *Time* magazine, the reporter Brock Brower exemplified the problem when he lamented the decline of "real leadership" in American political life. In a long, discursive, deeply pessimistic article near the midpoint of Nixon's presidency, he ascribed to the "Jeffersonian ideal" the "free ascension of moral and able leaders"—a result that only occurred when the republic functioned according to its Revolutionary design. With a population seventy times larger than that of 1770, there ought to have been "about 800 Jeffersons," the journalist calculated. But as the 1970s began, America was mired in Vietnam, lies poured from officials, and "political sleight of hand" substituted for political eloquence. The president, a withdrawn figure, had created an atmosphere that militated against any improvement in mood. "There are no neat, well-adjusted leaders," a White House source told the reporter. "They cannot be humble men. They have to be to some extent monomaniacs."[11]

Nixon quoted Jefferson sparingly. To judge by the reflection of the president's top foreign policy advisor, Henry Kissinger, Nixon is best identified with negative Jefferson qualities. He shared Jefferson's reputation among contemporaries for contradictory values, for slipperiness. "There was no true Nixon," said Kissinger, but "several warring personalities"; one was "reflective" and "philosophical," another "impulsive" and "erratic." When Kissinger informed the president of Soviet leader Leonid Brezhnev's nervous complaints, Nixon wrote at the bottom of the memo: "And Jefferson complained of 'headaches' every afternoon in his last 3 years as President!" It is true that Jefferson's "periodical headaches," as he described them in letters, ended upon his retirement from politics, but one wonders where Nixon came up with his "every afternoon" for three years.[12]

In one of his post-presidential memoirs, Nixon joined Jefferson's name to that of John Locke, Baron de Montesquieu, and Alexander Hamilton, and cast them in opposition to Marx and Lenin, which suggests that it was as a political thinker that Nixon principally saw Jefferson—comfortably close to Hamilton only in the polarized world of free versus communist. The opposing party leaders' contest was, he wrote, a "squabble over interest in power," not a world-transformative conflict over "the destiny of man." In a different, more philosophic memoir, Nixon spoke to the ideals that the American nation embodied, as he embraced (ironically, one must acknowledge) the enduring optimism of his fellow citizens. "Thomas Jefferson said, 'We act not just for ourselves but for all mankind,'" wrote Nixon, repeating what has been called his "favorite" Jefferson quote. Righteous in his prose, the incriminated ex-president assured that: "We were the only great power in history to make its entrance on the world stage not by the force of arms but by the force of its ideas." And, Nixon concluded, "we have stayed true to our ideals," as a force for good.[13]

James "Scotty" Reston of the New York Times titled one of his weekly columns "Mr. Nixon and Mr. Jefferson." He opened with the spirited refrain at the heart of Jefferson's first inaugural address, which called for a bipartisan restoration of "that harmony and affection without which liberty and even life itself are but dreary things." Reston agreed with the distinguished historian Henry Steele Commager, who had lately urged that the same principle should animate America "in the days ahead." While Nixon's divisiveness had "brought the Democrats back from the grave," voters had short memories, and there was still time for the president to stop exploiting the climate of fear, and to do something to change the morbid tone. He should stop blaming Democrats and the press for the sour state of affairs, and instead start communicating better, to "restore Mr. Jefferson's ideal of 'harmony and affection.'"[14]

Amid the Watergate scandal that brought down Nixon's presidency, the besieged second-termer resorted to a Jeffersonian move. But it was not one of Jefferson's shining moments that Nixon imitated but rather a slick legal maneuver. In 1807, during the treason trial of Aaron Burr, his former vice president, Jefferson improperly associated with the prosecution, refusing to maintain his distance from the proceedings. More to the point, he invoked "executive privilege" to deny the court access to a letter that had been subpoenaed from him. Nixon invoked the same privilege in refusing to turn over those Oval Office audio-tapes that would eventually expose his participation in the cover-up of a crime. In the opinion of U.S. District Judge John Sirica, who had ordered Nixon to turn over the tapes, the president convinced himself that he represented the supreme authority in this matter, that national well-being required him to resist the judge. Quoting Jefferson directly, Nixon affected concern with his "higher obligation" to country. "To lose our country by a scrupulous adherence to written law," the third president had said, "would be to lose the law itself." Nixon seized upon that quote. (In his memoir, he likened his situation to Lincoln's sus-pension of habeas corpus as well—never mind that Watergate was far removed from the kind of domestic crisis the Civil War presented.) Nixon's appropriation of Jefferson was, Sirica wrote, "false, arrogant, and near-sighted."[15]

In August 1973, shortly after the existence of the Oval Office tapes was made public, and while the president's role in the scandal remained under intense scrutiny, *Time*'s Washington Bureau chief, Stanley Cloud, authored a fantasy conversation between Jefferson and Hamilton over the meaning of Watergate. Their two apparitions were lounging beside the Washington Monument, trying to make sense of the current state of affairs. They naturally drew comparisons to the days when the two of them had debated whether the central func-tion of government was to protect ordinary citizens or to cultivate the big money men who promised growth and stability in a dangerous world. "The country is everything I always knew it would be: powerful and rich," proffered Hamilton. "The country is bigger and richer and more powerful—not greater," returned Jefferson. Hamilton defended Nixon: "If there is distance between him and the people, well, so much the better." Jefferson, predictably, decried rampant corruption in poli-tics and saw Nixon as one who remained tolerant (at the very least) of the White House conspirators while they did whatever was required to secure their man's election. To Jefferson, this behavior smacked of monarchy, not republicanism. He therefore credited his adversary with ultimate victory in their long war for the soul of America—Hamilton's soulless government had won. "You are the most deserving of the title 'Founding Father' in 1973," said the ghost of Thomas Jefferson.[16]

The Jefferson-Hamilton dichotomy has long stood for essential differences in domestic policy prescriptions. It captures, first and fore-most, the issue of state, local, and individual independence versus cen-tral control of the economy; but it also extends from a written rec-ord in which Jefferson expresses a tolerant populism, and Hamilton a studied cynicism. That said, it is just as true that there are modern dissenters who cry out for fairness from a cynical place; and defenders of patriarchal power who take refuge in Norman Rockwell images of a glorified traditional home life. The Nixon years were muddied in that way.

Cynicism was overt and widespread from the beginning to the end of Nixon's presidency. In what had to be a first of its kind, a coalition of student groups at the University of Virginia staged a protest on Jefferson's birthday in 1969, refusing to celebrate with the customary procession until black students were accorded greater rights. While the *Washington Post* reported the story without indicating what rights had been withheld, the paper did note that the student coalition had decided to give an "Alexander Hamilton award" to the university administrator who "has done the most to thwart Jeffersonian ideals."[17]

In 1974, with Nixon's climactic resignation, odd reminiscences and sober reassessments were aired. Hugh Sidey's column in *Time* compared the lavish lifestyle Nixon indulged while in office to the modesty he imagined of Jefferson: "Men like Thomas Jefferson appreciated what money could do," he wrote, "but they designed the presidency to protect it from the corruptive influence of wealth, and their years of service were marked by a modesty that they felt important to democracy." In a second column, Sidey elaborated:

> For Jefferson and his contemporaries, power was never the final joy. The ultimate pleasure was to be back among the places and people they loved. Jefferson's reward for service was not cheers or ceremonies but the opportunity to perfect his thoughts, use the language well, design a graceful structure, plan a garden ("No occupation is so delightful to me as the culture of the earth, and no culture comparable to that of the garden").

> How far we have drifted. Almost all of our national political leaders are totally consumed by the pursuit and exercise of power. Few of them ultimately translate their efforts into the small increments that give life the special depth that Jefferson perceived. One wonders about the Watergate criminals and whether things would have been different had these men had other interests with which to soften and better interpret the purpose of power.[18]

Hugh Sidey, a native of Iowa, was a presidential insider for decades, trusted by men who trusted few. For him, Jefferson had come to represent the leader who did not abuse power. The scholarly Leonard

Levy disagreed with that assessment: the Louisiana Purchase was, as Jefferson recognized, unconstitutional, but it was also, he felt, expedient, necessary, and irresistible. And Jefferson's treatment of Aaron Burr was an even more egregious episode in abuse of power in a life-or-death trial. But in comparison to Nixon—in 1974, at least—all past presidential land grabs and legal niceties appeared unexceptional.

Roger Morris, one-time member of the National Security Council, examined Nixon from a different angle. He wrote a biography of his former boss, focusing closely on the formative years, and afterward gave a paper describing the task he had confronted. He remarked upon a key difference between Richard Nixon and other notable presidents as they had emerged in standard biographies: Franklin Roosevelt was associated with aristocratic Hyde Park; Dwight Eisenhower with dusty Abilene, Kansas; and Thomas Jefferson with a particular spot in Virginia. Nixon, in the national imagination, lacked a real "native soil," a place to assign to his roots. That is what he sought to accomplish in tackling Nixon; in Morris's words, "to repatriate an alien."[19]

The Jefferson of FDR, Truman, and Kennedy was secure. He still had his Tidal Basin monument (a new first-class stamp was issued in

In 1947, four years after President Franklin D. Roosevelt formally dedicated the Jefferson Memorial, Congressman Richard M. Nixon, wife Patricia, and daughter Tricia pose under the cherry blossoms across from the Jefferson Memorial. (Courtesy of the National Archives/Nixon Library)

December 1973 that featured the Jefferson Memorial) and an exquisite mountaintop home that described his attachment to the land. He was no less respected than before, though he was, for the moment, less widely and less passionately embraced in the media, or by the White House, as a man of democratic wisdom. His character in the 1972 film version of *1776* was vulgarized, to the dismay of those movie critics who actually noticed. The color had been drained from him, or so it appeared. As if to dramatize the point, a piece published on July 4, 1973, began by stating that "American tourists began vandalizing Monticello" almost from the day of Jefferson's death. Describing his tour of the estate, the writer explained his detachment from the political beliefs of the architect, feeling, he said, like the female guides who spoke as if Mr. Jefferson was to be found in the next room on the tour. The Jefferson they were talking about was the violinist, gadget collector, horseman, "practical farmer," and polymath—but not politician. Here was where an enlightened man who once lived lay buried. Monticello was where one came to "feel," where intimacy was experienced.[20]

It fell to the UCLA historian Fawn M. Brodie to humanize Jefferson for the greatest numbers of Americans. In her wildly popular 1974 biography *Thomas Jefferson: An Intimate History*, she listened well for Jefferson's heartbeat, probed his psyche, and highlighted his epicurean side. But the real impact of her ambitious book lay in the purposeful connection she made between the third president and his house servant, a biracial slave he had inherited: the "beautiful quadroon" Sally Hemings.

Brodie contended that theirs was a decades-long affair, a love match. Her interpretation reversed the trajectory of all previous mainstream Jefferson biographies, which either stuck to his political legacy or added just so much spice to his personal life as to make him a man attractive to women—yet his primary role at home was always that of a loving father and grandfather. His wife, Patty, had left him a widower at thirty-nine. Crushed, he chose not to marry again, and family lore had it that he promised his dying wife that their girls would not have an unfeeling stepmother. Presumably, after that, the moral Jefferson invested his manly fire in building democracy.

Brodie's psychologically enriched critique was impatient with this whitewashed inheritance. The author clearly overreached in believing herself able to detect hidden meaning in Jefferson's word selection; but she surely launched an industry when she undermined the cadre of white male historians who had dominated the field for eons. Who were these unresisting obsessives (her word) who became lifelong students of Jefferson? Brodie queried. What were they really looking for? Her answer was aggressive: "There is always a danger that the biographer will exaggerate in the life of the man he writes about those problems from which he himself suffers." Her predecessors in Jefferson biography wanted him to be "a somewhat monkish, abstemious . . . passionless president." Freud, she reminded, had warned of biographers who "devote themselves to a work of idealization" in order to re-create "their infantile conceptions of the father." So much for the reigning experts, Brodie taunted. If Jefferson had a "pervasive, lifelong secrecy about his private life," she would penetrate the facade.

Her method was not subtle in the least. Even the nonsexualized in her book was converted into decisive language. For instance, Jefferson's debt situation was framed by "ill health and grinding anxieties," "chronic optimism," "leechlike relatives," "great inner conflict," and princely indulgence. He had imbibed all this as a youngster, because his father and mother looked upon him as "heir apparent." The child prodigy, grown, was "an aristocrat of the spirit" who "could not himself bear the thought of being held an ungenerous parent, either in love or in money." And so forth. Brodie thrived on all-embracing, interlocking pathologies.

This new Jefferson image caught on. He became more than a thinker, more than a public figure. He was now an affectionate man, "innocently seductive" in family letters, yet drawn to forbidden women. The acclaim that Brodie's biography received invited a new, lively presumption about Jefferson that would affect a wave of Jefferson scholars and swarms of breathless popularizers—a multifaceted Jefferson who possessed neurotic character traits easily relatable to the modern condition. Fawn Brodie's commercial success proved that Jefferson biography could be lucrative if done arrestingly. Jefferson was back.[21]

AS THE United States marked the bicentennial of its birth, it was only natural that the author of the Declaration of Independence would receive his due as a part of the summer celebration. On March 4, Congress designated the Library of Congress Annex as the Thomas Jefferson Building. Later that month, the House of Representatives declared April 13, 1976, the third president's 233rd birthday, to be "Thomas Jefferson Day." In keeping with earlier ritual, President Gerald R. Ford gave a short address at the Jefferson Memorial that morning, drawing heavily on Jefferson's first inaugural address, with its call for national harmony. Meanwhile, citizens were treated to a number of museum exhibitions about the Revolution that presented Jefferson as a superior thinker. Notable among these was *The Eye of Thomas Jefferson,* at the National Gallery in Washington, D.C., which tapped the "mind and imagination" of the man of letters. Further demonstrating Jefferson's reach, the Islamic Republic of Pakistan issued a commemorative stamp in honor of the American bicentennial, casting the Jefferson Memorial against a blue background.[22]

With great fanfare, the two-dollar bill with Jefferson's image returned to circulation on Thomas Jefferson Day. It was last in circulation ten years earlier, when the Bureau of Engraving and Printing determined that the only people who really liked it were collectors. In 1976, 400 million new two-dollar bills were distributed, meant to replace one-half of the 1.6 billion one-dollar bills in circulation—which, if it had come to pass, would have saved the government $7–8 billion annually.

Banks were urged to give the two in change to customers until they became accustomed to it. The Texas Commerce Bank in Houston reported people waiting in line all day just to get their hands on the new bills. "It was like a run on the bank," said one bank executive. A single branch sold some $20,000–$30,000 in "deuces" in the first five hours. Senator Harry Byrd Jr., whose ancestry extended to the planter elite of Jefferson's day, and who often confessed his love of Jefferson, spontaneously quipped: "If the government does not do something about inflation, I am afraid that my fellow Virginian George Washington [e.g., the one-dollar bill] is going to be an extinct species." The craze soon died down, though it should be said that Jefferson's reputation did not suffer from the truncated career of "the deuce."[23]

In Congress on that day, April 13, 1976, a number of Jefferson-coded speeches were heard. Democrat Joseph Karth, a Minnesota representative nearing the end of his eighteen-year career in Washington, reflected on the unraveling of Nixon's presidency by offering his interpretation of a series of Jefferson quips relating to the role of a free press in a democracy. "The history of the 1970s has proved the enormous power of the press and of investigative reporting," Karth observed. As president, Jefferson had complained in 1807: "Nothing can now be believed which is seen in a newspaper." On an earlier occasion, he had written: "Our citizens may be deceived for a while, but as long as the presses can be protected, we may trust them for light." The congressman's point in presenting Jefferson's criticism of the press alongside his praise of it when it worked was to seek "truth and fairness" through the appointment of ombudsmen as "a self-policing conscience" within the nation's newspapers.[24]

Senator Claiborne Pell, the Rhode Island Democrat best known for his sponsorship of the student-aid grants that bear his name, addressed Jefferson's educational legacy: "When Thomas Jefferson warned that no nation should expect to be ignorant and remain free, he raised education to top rank among national priorities. Economically and politically, this self-governing nation depends for its strength and resiliency on an educated electorate."

Harry Byrd of Virginia took a decidedly different tack. As a conservative southern Democrat in the Jefferson mold, he spoke about the balance of power between the central government and the states: "Our first Presidents were leaders of a nation truly diverse in character. State and local governments vigorously asserted their autonomy." He recognized, he said, that local autonomy in the past was in some measure a function of the poor network of roads and communications. But, he added, "Jefferson foresaw the consequences of future concentration of power. He articulated belief—and it is central to our whole history—that power concentrated, sooner or later, becomes power abused."

Senator Byrd warned of a heavy-handed federal government that "has spun a giant web of regulation that reaches every aspect of business and industry and the lives of all our citizens." Byrd was a Democrat before 1970 and an independent thereafter, and his choice reminds us that the now well-defined difference between modern Democrats (decrying concentrated business power) and Republicans (fearing concentrated government power) worked itself out over time. To Byrd, Americans wanted to return to Jefferson's "wise and frugal government." He affirmed what he considered most Jeffersonian: "faith in individual liberty—the faith which created our country." One of the senator's more vocal supporters was the Jefferson lover John Dos Passos, who had swung from Left to Right.[25]

The Jefferson Day festivities in Washington, D.C., were led by House Majority Leader Thomas "Tip" O'Neill of Massachusetts. Julian Boyd, still at the helm of the *Papers of Thomas Jefferson,* was once more in the thick of things. He opened his presentation with a favorite quote from Jefferson upon his retirement from politics: "Nature intended me for the tranquil pursuits of science by rendering them my supreme delight. But the enormities of the times in which I have lived have forced me to take a part in resisting them, and to commit myself on the boisterous ocean of political passions." For the protective editor, any negative valuation of Jefferson had to have been "invented" by political enemies: for, when Jefferson spoke for himself, he gave posterity an accurate picture. Boyd concluded his speech by asserting that Jefferson "added luster and honor to every public trust bestowed upon him by a people in whose good sense and decency he had an unshakable confidence. He was our first and still is our greatest philosopher-statesman." The simple message from Boyd to mainstream Democrats was that Jefferson was their man, more philosopher-scientist than politician. Boyd was stuck on JFK's Jefferson. And he refused to give a second thought to that woman Fawn Brodie.[26]

ON THE Fourth of July 1976, as a flotilla of tall ships from around the globe sailed up and down the Hudson River, along the shore of Manhattan, President Ford was onstage at Monticello for the swearing in of 105 new American citizens from twenty-three countries, a duty performed that day by Lewis F. Powell, associate justice of the Supreme Court. "Unfettered by ancient hates, the people of the young United States really believed that 'all men are created equal,'" Ford said, more wishful than historical. He noted the "blind spots" of the Revolutionary generation in failing to consider the rights of blacks and women, which led him to suggest: "This is not the day, however, to deplore our shortcomings." It was the last of six speeches by the unelected president at various bicentennial locales. Afterward, Ford stood alone outside the graveyard gate where Jefferson lay buried, and paid his respects. A few days later, Queen Elizabeth II stood at the same site—she, the direct descendant of King George III, whom Jefferson most famously accused of ignoring the just demands of his American kin.[27]

Not surprisingly, Jefferson's triad, "life, liberty, and the pursuit of happiness," was the subject of published commentary. William V. Shannon, a member of the editorial board of the *New York Times*, wrote an op-ed titled "What Is Happiness?" to coincide with the bicentennial: "When he used the word happiness, Jefferson had in mind something nobler and more difficult than mere pleasure-getting or status seeking. He wrote in terms of the philosophical conception of happiness deriving from the ancient Greeks. Happiness is 'a life well lived or a good life as a whole.'" Shannon's version was arguably the best, most concise understanding made accessible to the public. He was probing the interior dimension of Americans' uncertainty at the end of the Vietnam decade, making allusions to Hugh Hefner's "empty" *Playboy* philosophy, the cloistered lives of some of the super-rich, and the notion that family had come to be "the human equivalent of the disposable diaper." Shannon concluded pertly: "Only by our moral performance as a people can we make good on our political promises to ourselves."[28]

Perhaps the finest expression of the Jeffersonian spirit uttered during that bicentennial weekend was that of Maine Democrat Edmund Muskie, who rose in the Senate and pronounced: "We would betray our Revolutionary predecessors if we did not ask ourselves the question that they posed themselves as they embarked upon history's great adventure: What is the substance of a nation?" The answers he gave were virtually indistinguishable from sentiments Jefferson had expressed over the decades in his familiar letters to family and friends. First, said Muskie, Americans needed to appreciate that wealth is transitory. Money had "a certain mortality attached to it." Yet each generation offered, in its turn, "new claimants to the national being." Intentionally or not, Muskie was echoing Jefferson's famous proposition put to the more pragmatic Madison, an idealized refrain that he stuck to through life: the dead hand of the prior generation should not be able to hold its successor hostage.

According to Muskie, the second element comprising a nation's substance was "its intention toward its people, how it presumes to attend to their prosperity or despair." Reiterating the Jeffersonian generational focus: "Each era judges government in the light of how it deals with its people." The bicentennial seemed an appropriate moment for the respected senator (then the presumed front-runner in pursuit of his party's presidential nomination) to reflect on history's judgment. He warned of government's growing remoteness from its people, and took solace in the fact that partisan discord was at low ebb—absent of demagogic candidates "who postulate lethal simplicities" when mature discussion was called for.

The senator ended the relatively short speech with his one direct Jefferson reference: "Just as Jefferson warned us that slavery was a firebell in the night, so poverty and the cruelty that it inflicts and breeds, is the firebell in this particular American evening." Muskie seems not to have understood that Jefferson was on the wrong side of history when he took the states'-rights position on the issue of slavery and its extension west. The firebell represented a problem with no easy solution, and to Jefferson in 1819, Congress had no right to draw a line dividing slave from free. He wanted planters to have the means to rid themselves of "surplus" slaves profitably. He wanted, in short, to preserve the interests of white southerners. Nevertheless, the senator's allusion to the "firebell"—a crisis that a compassionate republic should not ignore—was entirely proper.[29]

How far should the federal government go to manage the private concerns of dependent individuals?, Muskie pondered aloud. This was to be a critical—perhaps *the* critical—question in the years to come, conditioning both Democrats' and Republicans' claims to Jefferson. Had the New Deal forgotten the small-government Jefferson, or was it Jefferson's empathetic vocabulary that needed to be applied to the issues of justice and equality that confronted America in the third century of its independence?

IT IS HARD to know what to say about Jimmy Carter and his White House in terms of a Jefferson identity. He did not use Jefferson as a model statesman as his Democratic predecessors had done. Carter's ancestors had fought as patriots during the American Revolution and on the side of the Confederacy fourscore years later. Trained as an engineer, he was the fresh face among old hands on the campaign trail in 1976. During the waning days of the Nixon administration, while serving as governor of Georgia, the political moralist said: "I can't imagine somebody like Thomas Jefferson tiptoeing through a minefield on the technicalities of the law, and then bragging about being clean afterwards." Hugh Sidey wrote in 1978: "Jimmy Carter is the closest thing to a scientist we have had in the White House since Thomas Jefferson. It may yet prove to be both a strength and a handicap. . . . Much of his trouble in the mystical arena of political leadership arises when he tries to apply these bloodless principles to human power and pride."[30]

As an ex-president in need of a research assistant, Carter hired Steven Hochman, a young historian who had recently collaborated with the aged Dumas Malone to help complete the sixth and final volume of Malone's prize-winning, cradle-to-grave Jefferson biography. Thus, Hochman, a graduate student at the University of Virginia, wafted from one retired southern agrarian president to another, effectively helping each to remake his image. The book he worked on, *Keeping Faith,* Carter's first post-presidential effort, contained but one Jefferson reference, and only in passing: "I had pledged during my campaign to emphasize fiscal responsibility and strive for a balanced budget," Carter wrote, reflecting on Inauguration Day, 1977. "This had not been a popular stand with some members of my party, but it was compatible with the beliefs of Southern Democrats and of Democratic Presidents I admired, like Jefferson, Madison, Jackson, and Wilson."

The Georgian's bold campaign for human rights could certainly be seen as an outgrowth of Jeffersonian democracy. In crediting Lyndon Johnson and Harry Truman for their actions in this regard, he traced back the impulse to "idealists" Woodrow Wilson and Thomas Jefferson. Carter's fiscal conservatism was an example of Jefferson's creed, as was his casual dress and rejection of the artificial trappings of the presidency: "The pomp and ceremony of office does not appeal to me," he said during an interview in the White House. "The people that I admire the most who have lived in this house have taken the same attitude. Jefferson, Jackson, Lincoln, Truman have minimized the pomp and ceremony."

It was Carter's "southernness" that most marked him, just as it had LBJ. Like Jefferson, he was a gentleman farmer. It was as a southerner that he allowed himself, on taking office, to see his role as that of a healer: "The possibility that the nation would actually choose as a leader someone from the Deep South meant that the bitterness of the past could be overcome." While he admired Jefferson, he was not a Jefferson worshipper by any measure. So there is no evidence that Jefferson's harmony-seeking first inaugural address came to President Carter's mind, though Carter's sensibility, like Jefferson's, was reflected in a central message about the moral conscience and essential compassion of Americans.[31]

In reading Hochman's doctoral dissertation, post-presidency, Jimmy Carter read in depth about Jeffersonian finance, and said he felt that he and Jefferson had something in common: once out of politics, they were still filled with energy and, as constant doers, "worked to relax." But it was Carter's successor, the buoyant older man who soundly defeated him, who most eagerly took Jefferson to heart. "Jefferson said that the people will not make a mistake—*if* they have *all* the facts," Ronald Reagan wrote cheerfully to a young admirer sometime before his presidency began. That affinity, expressed in private letters as often as in public speeches, fused with a commitment to the proudest incarnation of patriotism Americans had seen for a long time. He gave a dramatically different cast to the political world's understanding of Jeffersonian democracy. Moreover, as a savvy politico, Reagan succeeded in converting the Jeffersonian script into a political coalition with lasting impact.[32]

THE CONTROVERSIAL Fawn Brodie died at the age of sixty-five, just days before Ronald Reagan took the oath of office in January 1981. Her interpretation lived on in querying minds, and especially among African Americans who never doubted the oral history of Sally Hemings's son Madison and who firmly believed that Thomas Jefferson was as much an ancestor to black men and women as to his carefully documented white progeny. Brodie's Jefferson would not truly have his "day in court" for some years yet. As that Jefferson incubated, Reagan's Jefferson came onstage—the founder who stood for personal freedom above all else.

In his first inaugural address, from the steps of the Capitol, the new president invoked the great triumvirate whose memorials were around him: "Directly in front of me, the monument to a monumental man: George Washington, Father of our country. A man of humility who came to greatness reluctantly. He led America out of Revolutionary victory into infant nationhood. Off to one side, the stately memorial to Thomas Jefferson. The Declaration of Independence flames with his eloquence. And then beyond the Reflecting Pool the dignified columns of the Lincoln Memorial. Whoever would understand in his heart the meaning of America will find it in the life of Abraham Lincoln."

In his second inaugural address, four years later, Reagan ramped up the rhetoric: "We are creating a nation once again vibrant, robust, and alive. But there are many mountains yet to climb. We will not rest until every American enjoys the fullness of freedom, dignity, and opportunity as our birthright. It is our birthright as citizens of this great Republic, and we'll meet this challenge."

He consciously forecast how his own presidency might be remembered: a time "when Americans courageously supported the struggle for liberty, self-government, and free enterprise throughout the world, and turned the tide of history away from totalitarian darkness and into the warm sunlight of human freedom. . . . Let history say of us, 'These were golden years—when the American Revolution was reborn, when freedom gained new life, when America reached for her best.'"[33]

The Revolutionary inheritance loomed large in Reagan's formulation, and he devoted an unprecedented amount of room in the 1985 address for elaboration on the sublimity of meaning in Jefferson's language:

> Our two-party system has served us well over the years, but never better than in those times of great challenge when we came together not as Democrats or Republicans, but as Americans united in a common cause. Two of our Founding Fathers, a Boston lawyer named Adams and a Virginia planter named Jefferson, members of that remarkable group who met in Independence Hall and dared to

think they could start the world over again, left us an important lesson. They had become political rivals in the presidential election of 1800. Then years later, when both were retired, and age had softened their anger, they began to speak to each other again through letters. A bond was reestablished between those two who had helped create this government of ours.

In 1826, the 50th anniversary of the Declaration of Independence, they both died. They died on the same day, within a few hours of each other, and that day was the Fourth of July. In one of those letters exchanged in the sunset of their lives, Jefferson wrote: "It carries me back to the times when, beset with difficulties and dangers, we were fellow laborers in the same cause, struggling for what is most valuable to man, his right to self-government. Laboring always at the same oar, with some wave ever ahead threatening to overwhelm us, and yet passing harmless . . . we rode through the storm with heart and hand."[34]

Arriving at the White House on day one of the Reagan Revolution, the speechwriter Peggy Noonan noticed: "Everyone wore Adam Smith ties." She was referring to the philosopher whose *Wealth of Nations* (1776) was praised by modern conservatives for its market focus. Noonan elaborated: "The ties of the Reagan era bore symbols—eagles, flags, busts of Jefferson—and the symbols had meaning."[35]

Reagan had been writing down useful and incisive quotations on 4" × 6" notecards for years—perhaps since he traveled around the country as a paid spokesman for General Electric in the 1950s. Some of these citations, as, for example, an extended quote by John Adams in signing the Declaration of Independence, are apocryphal. But among the most numerous and forceful are his Jefferson quotes, encompassing matters of married life, religious faith, as well as politically charged axioms on the dangers of consolidated government. It's not just his Jefferson citations that are obviously selective. An FDR passage from 1935 decries government giveaways: "To dole out relief . . . is to administer a narcotic, a subtle destroyer of the human spirit." The longtime Reagan speechwriter Peter Robinson explained recently that the president "used to love quoting Tom Paine's remark, 'We have it in our power to remake the world,'" and felt he was "operating in a context something like that of the founders themselves. He wanted a *conservative* revolution. Even as the government of Lord North had begun to encroach on the colonists' traditional liberties, the Great Society and the bloated federal government had in Reagan's time violated the deep

American traditions of self-reliance, federalism, and so on. Reagan wanted to reassert something that had *already existed*."[36]

Some of Reagan's handwritten Jefferson quotes were popular among Democrats, such as the "no nation can be both ignorant and free" passage that Lyndon Johnson and Claiborne Pell, among others, had drawn upon. Other quotes in the collection were plainly self-sustaining: "If we can prevent the govt. from wasting the labor of the people *under the pretense of caring for them,* they will be happy." The italics are Reagan's, but the quote is actually a compound of two Jefferson letters written fourteen years apart.[37]

Every April, it seemed, some columnist for a major national journal would remind readers that Jefferson's birthday, once widely celebrated, ought to be again. In 1982, that role belonged to a senior advisor in the Reagan White House, who wrote in the pages of the *New York Times:* "It is unfortunate that Thomas Jefferson's birthday, today, is so rarely commemorated, for Americans need to be reminded of the enduring philosophy of that great, many-sided man." Converting Jefferson's tenets into Reagan-era policy, the Vermonter John McClaughry noted:

> Jefferson saw that America's experiment in liberty and democracy could not succeed unless most of its citizens were economically independent. . . . His prescription of a widespread distribution of ownership of private property, opportunity for the energetic and talented to succeed in competitive free enterprise, and curbs on all forms of monopolistic conduct continue to command the allegiance of most Americans. Today, his policy would call for strong encouragement not only of family-owned farms but also of independent owner-operated businesses and increased employee ownership of larger corporations.

This was the Jefferson who abhorred public debt, who rewarded "labor, industry, and thrift, and thus the economic health of the republic." He would not have thought much of the Federal Reserve Board, which printed however much paper currency it wanted, potentially leading to the "destruction of honest value, and a swindling of the ordinary citizen." The Reagan Republican believed in "keeping the functions of government limited and close to home, while relying upon the people themselves for works of charity and civic improvement." This was "another Jeffersonian passion" that Reagan's America meant to recover.

McClaughry invoked Jefferson quintessentially: "'A wise and frugal government,' he announced in a first Inaugural Address similar to President Reagan's, 'shall restrain men from injuring another, shall leave them otherwise free to regulate their own pursuits of industry and improvement, and shall not take from the mouth of labor the bread it has earned.'" A small-government Jefferson appreciated local initiatives as much as he detested concentrations of power.

"The curious question," McClaughry prodded, "is why no political leader has arisen—in either party—to explicitly make the Jeffersonian creed his own. Liberal Democrats, wedded to ever-increasing government spending, taxes, and printing of money, are obviously uncomfortable with the Jeffersonian tradition that dominated their party's history until 1844. Republicans, for the most part, do not question Democratic claims to Thomas Jefferson as one of their own." Yet, McClaughry slyly reminded, lest the twists and turns of party histories be entirely forgotten, the Republican Party's national platform, when it came into being in 1856, held that "election of the Republican ticket would 'restore the action of the Federal government to the principles of Washington and Jefferson.'"

Now for his ultimate message: "In Ronald Reagan, this country has probably the most Jeffersonian president since Martin Van Buren. Four years ago, he paid tribute to Jefferson in these words: 'Yes, Thomas Jefferson has gone on to that corner of heaven reserved for those who fought for Liberty and the Rights of Man. But we Americans, his spiritual descendants, would do well to pluck a flower from Thomas Jefferson's life, and wear it in our soul forever.'"

Though McClaughry did not explain how it was that corporate culture (which Jefferson would not have championed) adored Reagan Republicanism so much, he had otherwise laid out a strong case: "A more conscious affirmation of Jeffersonian principles, and a creative effort to give them practical application in today's circumstances, would do much to win new support for the Administration, and to recapture for America the wisdom and vision of its third President."[38]

But what would that creative effort be, and what practical application might be seen? The family farm did not prosper in the 1980s, and giant agribusiness was rapacious. Amid large federal deficits, anathema to true Jeffersonians, the gap between rich and poor continued to widen. Surely Jefferson would not have liked those trends. But perhaps he would have ascribed them to something other than Reaganomics. After all, Jefferson had a strong capacity for rationalization—he rarely if ever changed his mind once he had made it up. And if Reagan froze the minimum wage and demonstrated indifference to the antipoverty programs of his Democratic predecessors, it could just as easily be said that Jefferson expected philanthropy to engage citizens individually, without requiring federal programs. Inflation was cured under Reagan, which would have suited Jefferson just fine. Who's to say? Indeed, why do we imagine that Jefferson had anything to say to Reagan's America or to America today?

"Jefferson" made regular, if questionable, appearances in Congress. The early spring of 1983 in and of itself provides three instructive examples. Senator Jesse Helms of North Carolina employed Jefferson's argument concerning religious establishment to criticize the partisan use of compulsory union dues: "Thomas Jefferson said, 'To compel a man to furnish contributions for the propagation of opinions which he disbelieves is sinful and tyrannical.' Yet a loophole in the federal election laws grants to organized labor a special privilege enjoyed by no other organization—the right to take money from American workers . . . and to contribute that money to political causes and candidates the workers themselves do not necessarily support."

In debating a tax law, Senator Edward M. Kennedy of Massachusetts told a story to illustrate the Senate's "fundamental responsibility to serve the public interest, not the private interest of a powerful lobby." It was "according to a well-known tradition," said Kennedy, that "Thomas Jefferson once asked George Washington why the Senate was needed at all as a separate chamber in the Congress. Their discussion took place over coffee after breakfast, and Washington said to Jefferson, 'Why did you pour that coffee into the saucer?' 'To cool it,' Jefferson replied 'And that,' said Washington, "is why we pour legislation into the Senatorial saucer—to cool it.'" Kennedy felt it was time to "cool the public passions. . . . In fact, the present circumstance is precisely the situation for which the Senate was created."

In yet another odd appropriation of Jefferson that congressional season, Representative Ron Paul of Texas, a member of the House Banking Committee, drew upon the founder to criticize monetary policy. Speaking in favor of the gold standard, he stated: "In the 1784 debate concerning the handling of our country's currency, Thomas Jefferson said, 'If we determine that a dollar shall be our unit, we must then say with precision what a dollar is.' But . . . we don't know from day to day what a dollar will be worth. It's very clear—at least to those of us who advocate hard money—that if you have something *real*, such as an ounce of gold, it remains the same from day to day."

The inexact construction of Jefferson by Senator Helms sounds at least plausible. The problem with the "well-known tradition" in Kennedy's fable—and it was repeated, almost word for word, by Senate

Democrat Robert Byrd of West Virginia in 2006—was that it dated only as far back as the early 1870s, when it was reported in Moncure Daniel Conway's *Republican Superstitions.* Not only was Conway's mention of the historical anecdote used as a means to show that the Senate had failed when it most mattered—to cool the hotheads who called for the expansion of slavery and thereby provoked the Civil War—there is no credible evidence that Jefferson and Washington ever had the conversation in question.[39]

In the instance of Congressman Paul, his application of Jefferson's economic theory transports the founder beyond his actual relevance, from his harsh agrarian existence to our giant economy, from a slow-moving market to a system driven by global banking concerns and instantaneous communications. In 1784, western Pennsylvania was America's frontier, the states pretty much ruled themselves, and the central government was toothless. Did Jefferson theorize a relationship between gold-based economies and price stability? Hardly. Why, then, bring his eminence to bear?

Politicians, by habit, exaggerate. They love their colorful charts and statistics. Wielding Jefferson is just another way to sell dreams and magical solutions to their constituents who have to have a reason to reelect them. Jefferson was, of course, quite good at converting beautiful thoughts into political capital. At the crossroads of morality and politics, whether or not he lived up to his fine ideals, we relish the humanity he so well captured. But on matters of economy, we are well beyond his imaginings.

ONE WEEKEND toward the end of his first term as president, Reagan received an injection of Jeffersonian springtime when he visited Monticello and called it "a place of surpassing beauty." He made a different sort of pilgrimage on the morning of July 3, 1987, when he went to the Jefferson Memorial to announce "America's Economic Bill of Rights." This was probably the most Jefferson-centered address he ever gave. He touched upon the evidence he had stored up over the years that convinced him he was guiding America in the precise direction Jefferson would have chosen, had he been alive at that moment.

The president began his warm-up lightheartedly, as was his wont, but soon got to his core message: American exceptionalism. It was, he said, a "love of liberty . . . at the heart of our national identity" that distinguished America's experience from that of most other nations. "Down through history, there have been many revolutions, but virtually all of them only exchanged one set of rulers for another set of rulers. Ours was the only truly philosophical revolution. It declared that government would have only those powers granted to it by the people."

Repeating in full Jefferson's language of liberty in the Declaration of Independence, Reagan emphasized the preeminent phrase, "life, liberty, and the pursuit of happiness," calling attention to the "inspired ideals" etched into the wall behind where he stood.

> It was this revolutionary concept of representative government and individual rights, as well as the cause of national independence, to which the Declaration's signers pledged their lives, fortunes, and sacred honor. Each generation has done the same, and tomorrow [Fourth of July] we'll make that pledge again. Let no one charge, however, that ours is blind nationalism. We do not hide our short-comings. Yes, we have our imperfections, but there are no people on this planet who have more reason to hold their heads high than do the citizens of the United States of America.

He went on to use such phrases as "courage of conviction," "commitment to truth and justice," and "decent and humane values" to describe the essence of Americanism. Reagan affected a belief, as Jefferson had before him, that the power of ideals ultimately meant more than any other form of outward expression of national power. "We're still Jefferson's children," he attested, "still believers that freedom is the unalienable right of all of God's children." And then he approached the definition of freedom that his combined anticommunism and domestic conservatism led him to advocate, which was predicated on limited government:

> Freedom is not created by government, nor is it a gift from those in political power. . . . It is absence of the government censor in our newspapers and broadcast stations and universities. It is the lack of fear by those who gather in religious services. It is the absence of official abuse of those who speak up against the policies of their government. . . .

> Jefferson so fervently believed that limited government was vital to the preservation of liberty that he used his influence to see to it that the Constitution included a Bill of Rights, ten amendments that spelled out specific governmental limitations. "Congress shall make no law," the first amendment begins. And thus, the basic law of our land was meticulously constructed to limit government. . . .

Jefferson understood that our political freedoms needed protection by and from government[;] our economic freedoms need similar recognition and protection.

And so he spelled out the economic summons, instantly codifying his populist view of Jefferson's democracy:

> The working people need to know their jobs, take-home pay, homes, and pensions are not vulnerable to the threat of a grandiose, inefficient, and overbearing government—something Jefferson warned us about 200 years ago. It's time to finish the job Jefferson began and to protect our people and their livelihoods with restrictions on government that will ensure the fundamental economic freedom of the people—the equivalent of an Economic Bill of Rights. I'm certain if Thomas Jefferson were here, he'd be one of the most articulate and aggressive champions of this cause. The reason I'm certain is that in 1798 he wrote: "I wish it were possible to obtain a single amendment to our Constitution. I would be willing to depend on that alone for the reduction of the administration of our government to the genuine principles of its Constitution; I mean an additional article taking from the federal government the power of borrowing."

Thereby, Reagan proposed Jefferson's amendment: a balanced budget amendment to the Constitution. One effect would be to make it much harder for Congress to raise taxes—in Reagan's terms, "the harnessing of a free people." He saw America's founding principles as having been debased by big government:

> Our forefathers fought for personal and national independence, yet 200 years later, our own overly centralized government poses a threat to our liberty far beyond anything imagined by the patriots of old.

> Jefferson, in his first inaugural, spoke for his countrymen when he said: "A wise and frugal government, which shall restrain men from injuring one another, which shall leave them otherwise free to regulate their own pursuits of industry and improvement, shall not take from the mouth of labor the bread it has earned. This," he said, "is the sum of good government." Well, that vision of America still guides our thinking, still represents our ideals.[40]

Not since Roosevelt had a president so clearly, so extensively, identified Jefferson as his touchstone. Yet the vision of Jeffersonian democracy that conformed to the so-called Reagan Revolution was not based on the same Jefferson whose liberal spirit Roosevelt had found a way to modernize in accordance with the needs of a more diverse population of 125 million. Roosevelt's Jefferson wanted government intervention when it was the best way to support individual initiative—recall that, in this regard, candidate Roosevelt had said in 1932: "Government to him was a means to an end, not an end in itself." Reagan might have said the very same thing, but the statement would have had an entirely different meaning. For he had returned Jefferson to the inflexible Old Republican that the Virginian was in his own time, the guardian of unobtrusive government.

In responding to anxieties born of the Great Depression, Roosevelt found government solutions, from the protection of bank deposits to Social Security, as the way to allay fears. Reagan, as president, believed that times had changed sufficiently that the uncontrolled expansion of government programs had seriously undermined the Jeffersonian concept of limited government as a means to secure individual freedom.

To some, it appeared that Reagan's retrenchment showed insensitivity to the underprivileged—especially when he ran up large deficits. The late historian John Patrick Diggins had a unique take on that: "My personal reservation about Ronald Reagan is not that he was a conservative; on the contrary, he was a liberal romantic who opened up the American mind to the full blaze of Emersonian optimism." As much as one might see in Reagan an eager Emerson—the dream enthusiast who treasured the mind's capacity to produce good—the original American optimist was, in fact, Jefferson, who embraced an individualized spirit of independence and wanted his republic to function as an extended community modeled on the neighborhood "ward republic" and yeoman decency. It was "morning in America" when Jefferson reflected on his election, too.[41]

Each president employed subtle language in claiming Jefferson for his own ideological persuasion. If FDR's adaptation of Jeffersonianism can be called a "loose construction" of Jefferson, we can label Reagan a "strict constructionist." He railed against government bureaucracy the way Jefferson railed against aristocracy. To call the fortieth president a hard-headed utopian makes him a blend of the two oppositional founders. To his detractors, he was Hamiltonian, because despite his celebration of individual enterprise, he was first and foremost the president of the wealthy; otherwise, by letting the South be itself, he was a states'-rights Jeffersonian.[42]

IN 1793, as the first man to serve as secretary of state, Jefferson received a diplomatic note charging the United States with carrying out an aggressive policy directed at Florida, then a Spanish colony, by "exciting" the Chickasaw tribe to acts of war against the Spanish-allied Creeks. Writing to the U.S. envoys in Spain, Jefferson took a hard line, point by point denying American complicity, and asking his representatives to convey the administration's indignation to the authorities in Madrid. "We love and value peace," said Jefferson, self-righteously. "We know its blessings from experience." Protesting his nation's good intentions toward the government of Spain, he pressed for a complete acknowledgment that the United States had done nothing inappropriate. If Spain challenged the U.S. position, he warned, it should know that "we confide in our own strength, without boasting of it; we respect that of others, without fearing it. . . . If Spain continues to consider our defence against savage butchery as a cause of war to her, we must meet her also in war, with regret, but without fear."[43]

Confronting the Soviet Union, which he famously dubbed the "evil empire," the bullish Reagan could not have stood up for America any better. It was not simply his drawing of ideological distinctions—comparing an abundance of freedom in one against the absence of freedom in the other—that returned him to the Jeffersonian script on foreign policy. A Jefferson passage that Reagan commonplaced supplies all the justification he needed to acquiesce to, if not directly authorize, the Iran-Contra affair, a scandal that came to light on November 6, 1986. Jefferson had written in 1810: "A strict observance of the written laws is doubtless one of the high duties of a good citizen, but it is not the *highest*. The laws of necessity, of self-preservation, of saving our country when in danger, are of higher obligation. To lose our country by a scrupulous adherence to written law, would be to lose the law itself." We have already seen where Richard Nixon seized on this malleable axiom.

To make a case for the ethical principle at hand, Jefferson supplied historical evidence dating to the Revolution, invoking the late, lamented General Washington. He based a second, purely hypothetical example, on the real political circumstances of Jefferson's second term as president: supposing news of Spain's willingness to sell Florida to the United States had come to his desk a few weeks before Congress convened, he offered. The president ought, then, to supplant Congress's role in authorizing funds, and unilaterally agree to the sale if he could reasonably anticipate that one recalcitrant member of Congress might tie up that body in debate long enough to cause so popular a land opportunity to expire before the necessary legislation was drafted. It sounded almost exactly like what actually happened with the Louisiana Purchase.

The Reagan administration had quietly approved the sale of arms to Iran's radical government, which was officially under an arms embargo. The funds from this covert transaction were diverted to the anticommunist rebels of Nicaragua, or Contras, whom Reagan referred to publicly, in 1985, as that nation's moral equivalent of America's founding fathers. The problem was that Congress had barred further funding of the Contras.

Jefferson saw his actions in making his deal with Napoleon for Louisiana (and doubling U.S. territory) as an essential move—a slow-moving Congress might not accomplish the same before the French emperor changed his mind. Reagan would have seen the nasty business with Iran—which, at the time the plan was conceived, had been holding American hostages—as the greater good, despite its overturning the will of the people's representatives. He might have written down the Jefferson quote that LBJ had weakly used to defend his Vietnam policy, when he submitted to "the melancholy law of human societies," and was "compelled sometimes to choose a great evil in order to ward off a greater." But he did not. Or he might have helped his cause with a simpler axiom that Jefferson had penned in 1802: "What is practicable must control what is pure theory." Indeed, that one does sound Reaganesque.[44]

BIDDING farewell to the country at the end of 1988, President Reagan chose the University of Virginia as his venue. Addressing the students in the audience, he alluded to the general familiarity with "Mr. Jefferson" among all who traversed the sloping lawn he had laid out as an active ex-president in the 1820s. "Well, you're not alone in feeling his presence," said Reagan. "Presidents know about this, too." And he dressed up President Kennedy's statement at the Nobel laureates dinner for his hearers, many of whom were not alive at the time it was delivered. (For extended excerpts of the speech, see the appendix.)

President Reagan's speech captured that Jefferson we have anointed "democracy's muse," the memory of whom could still excite, whose singularity aroused eloquent testimonials. If he did not say precisely what it was about Jefferson's enlightened mind that made the founder so irresistible, Reagan knew how to sustain the mood and beseech the indulgence of his hearers: "Directly down the lawn and across the Ellipse from the White House are those ordered, classic lines of the Jefferson Memorial and the eyes of the nineteen-foot statue that gaze directly into the White House. A reminder to any of us who might occupy that mansion of the quality of mind and generosity of heart that once abided there and has been so rarely seen there again." Generosity of heart. It sounded like lines from a film of the 1930s or 1940s, which was the outgoing president's point of reference. His career had been fashioned by playing roles in which nostalgic dramatization brought a historical character back to life.

Seeing politics as unruly and sometimes vitriolic, Reagan used Jefferson to explain the world: "So he knew that governing meant balance, harmony. And he knew from personal experience the danger posed to such harmony by the voices of unreason, special privilege, partisanship, or intolerance." A certain amount of disorder had necessarily accompanied the American Revolution, and yet Jefferson, the architect of democracy, "also believed that man had received from God a precious gift, an enlightenment, the gift of reason, a gift that could extract from the chaos of life: meaning, truth, order."

This philosophic interlude in a speech devoted to foreign policy aimed to underscore that Jefferson was the proponent of a restrained federal government. The Jeffersonian Reagan believed in managing democracy by knowing how to achieve equilibrium in an untidy republic, "balancing, for example, on the one hand, the legitimate duties of government—the maintenance of domestic order and protection from foreign menace—with government's tendency to preempt its citizens' rights, take the fruits of their labors and reduce them ultimately to servitude." These words of President Reagan were particularly strong, the "servitude" of "excessive regulation and taxes" reminiscent of the Revolutionaries' questionable use of enslavement as a metaphor for Parliament's taxation of the American colonies.

As to the foreign menace, Reagan was pleased to report that at the end of his two terms, the Soviet Union, left in the hands of the reformer Mikhail Gorbachev, no longer constituted an "evil empire." The American president had strolled through Red Square, chatting easily with passersby. Democratic institutions did not yet exist in the East, but a liberalization of daily life was now evident in both Moscow and Beijing. More nations were embracing democratic elections, and free market economies had changed Asia for the better. Reagan said he thought the mood around the world was probably something like it had been when Jefferson was president and had made America the example for freedom-seeking everywhere.

The retiring president showed that he could just as easily preach the practical as the fabulous. It troubled him that the Russians, though reformed, still kept company with tyrannical regimes: "Let us remember that the Soviet preponderance in military power in Europe remains; an asymmetry that offends our Jeffersonian senses and endangers our future. So, we must keep our heads. And that means keeping our skepticism." Gorbachev deserved some credit for taming the beast, but "the democracies—with their strength and resolve and candor—have also made a difference."

We had "Jeffersonian senses" that were easily offended, by which Reagan presumably meant a predisposition to associate political justice with an open and tolerant society. There was an imaginable consistency to be found, whether it was historically verifiable or not: Jefferson's stand against "all forms of tyranny" was ostensibly Lincoln's, too, and emotionally accessible to any age.

As he summed up the experience of the 1980s, Ronald Reagan reprised his second inaugural address, finding solace in recurring to the Adams-Jefferson letters and to the lesson contained in the two men's shared nostalgia for days of yore, when as young Revolutionaries, "struggling for what is most valuable to man, his right to self-government," they were, metaphorically, in the same boat. Reagan extended the quote from Jefferson: "Laboring always at the same oar, with some wave ever ahead threatening to overwhelm us and yet passing harmless we rowed through the storm with heart and hand." And then, of course, they both died on the day America turned fifty, July 4, 1826.[45]

The goodwill that subsisted between the two long-estranged political warhorses was instructive for Reagan. It said to him that love of country superseded all else for the pair, which provided "insight into America's strength as a nation." As patriarchs, Jefferson and Adams understood implicitly what the future held. It was in this vein that President Reagan concluded his address, and effectively his presidency, with classic, if hackneyed words: "A great future is ours and the world's if we but remember the power of those words Mr. Jefferson penned not just for Americans but all humanity."

And then, exiting political life, the professional actor recited the Declaration's preamble, from "We hold these truths" to "life, liberty, and the pursuit of happiness." Mere platitude? Perhaps for anyone else, yes. But Reagan had long been convinced that the nation was ultimately a collection of free spirits, good men and women who got ahead when they did things right. As he put it some years earlier in a private communication: "Government exists to protect rights which are ours from birth; the right to life, liberty, and the pursuit of happiness. A man may choose to sit and fish instead of working. That's his pursuit of happiness. He does not have the right to force his neighbors to support him (welfare) in his pursuit, because that interferes with their pursuit of happiness." Justice stopped being fair and appropriate when it valued those who took from the system more than those who put into the system—because a nation's strength derived from its people's hard work and innovation.[46]

Reagan bought into supply-side economics, because it coincided with his conservative brand of optimism. The earnest Senator Warren B. Rudman, a moderate Republican from New Hampshire, signed on to the Reagan program, but subsequently saw folly in economic theory that quickly resulted in a doubling of the national debt. "I agreed with Thomas Jefferson," Rudman wrote in his political autobiography, "that for one generation to incur public debt and pass it on to the next generation is a violation of natural and moral law. I felt betrayed by Reagan and his advisers."

Nothing, it seemed, could redirect Ronald Reagan from his central faith in another of his favorite Jefferson quotes: "That government is best which governs least." He preferred, like Jefferson, to give the states more options, while identifying with the small businessman's hopes (the modern equivalent of Jefferson's mythic yeoman farmer). Yet a certain Hamiltonian bent also informed his view: let capitalists be capitalists. Reagan found no lessons in the grubbier side of history; his sustenance came from an idealized view of tradition.[47]

All nations require symbolic vocabulary, rooted in a storied past. That was Reagan, too, in striving to articulate a unifying sense of national belonging. Beyond his obvious attachment to 1776, he revived Puritan John Winthrop's imagery of a City on a Hill, which he intended as a vehicle of uplift. Reagan was not conventionally religious, but he did embrace civil religion, exploiting patriotic ritual and presenting in clear moral language what he regarded as the founders' gift to their posterity. In ministering to his flock, the twice-elected president was ecstatic about the role of a leader and the positive uses of nationalism. By all appearances, he venerated the nation's benefactors more than any of his predecessors in the modern era did—Jefferson above all.[48]

Reagan could charm. In his case, delivering quaint stories about a nation conceived in liberty was not a pitchman's vulgar means of persuasion. His millions of parishioners welled up when they heard him talk about freedom. They did so because it was what they had been waiting for, not because he had slyly disarmed them. To millions of others, however, patriotic platitudes appeared thin rather than expansive. A cruel caricature rendered Reagan an intellectual lightweight who lived on his pipe dreams, the man whom Clark Clifford, the otherwise mannerly advisor to Democratic presidents, called an "amiable dunce." But that wasn't the totality of Reagan, either.

To a certain extent all presidents invent personae and pander to the crowd. When he came to the University of Virginia to bid the nation farewell, Reagan was doing more than performing the rituals of civil religion. Conscious of his own symbolism, he was resurrecting the values of a time when democratic impulses were restrained—and not meant to promote turbulence among the have-nots or promise material ease and comfort to the masses. Perhaps these were the values of the Hollywood he knew, but it could be argued, too, that the values he promoted were legitimately connected to late-eighteenth-century currents of political thought, when individuals were encouraged to develop an unprejudiced sense of both dignity and responsibility, unencumbered by gluttonous government or an interventionist religious order.

4

"THE BOISTEROUS OCEAN OF POLITICAL PASSIONS"

Jefferson since William Jefferson Clinton

IN HIS post-presidential memoir, Bill Clinton reflected on the so-called character issue that dogged him during the 1992 campaign, and resurfaced six years later when he faced impeachment. "Presidents going back to George Washington and Thomas Jefferson have guarded their reputations jealously," he wrote, citing Jefferson's alleged "weakness for women." He admired the way Jefferson had handled all such attacks, and quoted the third president's humble words directly:

> When the accident of situation is to give us a place in history, for which nature had not prepared us by corresponding endowments, it is the duty of those about us carefully to veil from the public eye our weaknesses, and still more, the vices of our character.

From here, Clinton went on to explain: "The veil had been ripped from my weaknesses and vices, both real and imagined. The public knew more about them than about my record, message, or whatever virtues I might have." Among politicians, his was a unique way to recover the Jefferson image.[1]

On January 18, 1993, President-elect William Jefferson Clinton was at Monticello, beginning the final countdown to Inauguration Day festivities. Along with Vice President–elect Albert A. Gore Jr. and their wives, he toured the house and grounds, afterward entertaining questions from young people. If Thomas Jefferson were alive today, a boy asked, what position would you appoint him to?

"I would suggest to Senator Gore that the two of us resign so he could become president," joked the man with the middle name of Jefferson. As the laughter subsided, and he meditated on the question some more, the president-elect came up with an alternative plan for his namesake: "Secretary of Education." Another student asked what Jefferson's reaction would be to modern America, and Clinton stuck to the same theme: "He would be upset that we have not done more to provide a good education for all our people so that freedom can be more generally held. . . . Today many more people need an education just to function in the modern world."

Clinton was tapping essential Jefferson, for whom education was both a humane and a utilitarian concern for a modern republic. In working toward the establishment of the University of Virginia, in 1818, he emphasized the critical importance of citizenship training, so that the superior student might gain both the ethical composure and practical judgment needed to govern others; or, if not so predisposed, "to choose with discretion the fiduciary of those he delegates; and to notice their conduct, with diligence, with candor, and judgment." In other words, Jefferson sought to keep government in the hands of the best people. Believing that the capacity for improvement through exposure to ideas was meant to be extended across the social spectrum, Jefferson rejected "the discouraging persuasion that man is fixed, by the law of his nature, at a given point, that his improvement is a chimera, and the hope delusive of rendering ourselves wiser, happier, or better than our forefathers were." Clinton's credible association of education with individual autonomy matched up well with Jefferson's uncompromising principle.

His offhand replies to questions about social issues from schoolchildren were actually quite instructive. He thought Jefferson would be startled and disappointed by America's crime rate. "What was the greatest thing Thomas Jefferson did?" another child asked. Clinton: "His absolute unshakable conviction that if you could secure political freedom and . . . pursue freedom of thought, any problem could be solved." Appropriate optimism for one who had not yet taken occupancy of the Oval Office.[2]

From Charlottesville, the Clinton party rode on to the national capital, where a different welcome was in store. As reported on NPR's *Morning Edition:* "Bill Clinton's arrival in Washington was accomplished with his trademark mixture of glitz and populism. He used his favorite blue-collar form of transportation, boarding a bus to trace the route that Thomas Jefferson took from Monticello 192 years ago." In his day, the informal, outwardly modest Jefferson tied his own horse to the hitching post at the Capitol; in contrast, Clinton arrived at the Lincoln Memorial to preside over a celebrity-studded musical event. "Pure Hollywood," the radio news reporter Mara Liasson explained.

William Jefferson Clinton pre-inauguration button, 1993. Approaching the 250th anniversary of Jefferson's birth, the forty-second president was willing to share the limelight with a predecessor whose ideals were as much a part of him as the middle name he embraced.

"At Monticello, Clinton said he'd chosen Thomas Jefferson's home to begin his bus trip because Jefferson was a populist president and the bus trips were the populist symbol of his campaign."[3]

During his first months in office, President Clinton kept Jefferson's modern relevance very much in focus. In April, as several of his predecessors had done, he delivered an address at the Jefferson Memorial. This time, the occasion was the 250th anniversary of the prestigious founder's birth. Clinton reminded those assembled that it was also fifty years to the day since Franklin Roosevelt had dedicated the national monument, and he called FDR "a worthy heir to the spirit of Jefferson." Then, in a burst of progressive enthusiasm, he said: "Were Jefferson here today, I think he would not want very much to talk about the America of his time. Instead he would be talking about the America of our time."

If Reagan's Jefferson was a symbol of an admired past and a simpler, more manageable government system, Clinton's Jefferson was sensitive, experimental, and future-directed. "The genius of Thomas Jefferson was his ability to get the most out of today while never taking his eye off tomorrow," he said during his speech at the Jefferson Memorial, as he proceeded to quote from one of the panels inside the domed shrine to democracy: "Laws and institutions must go hand in hand with the progress of the human mind. . . . Manners and opinions change. With the change of circumstances, institutions must advance also to keep pace with the times."

The president continued to speculate on how Jefferson would react to the late twentieth century. True, he would delight in the worldwide expansion of knowledge; but even as the Soviet Union was disintegrating before the human passion to claim freedom, he would be troubled by the persistence of ethnic conflict and race hatred. And as a lover of the natural world, he would be deeply depressed by the state of the environment. "He believed in government constantly being reformed by reason and popular will," Clinton assured his audience.

There was much to be done to turn back the destructive man-made trends Clinton found on taking office. The nation's debt had increased fourfold in the twelve years past. We must try "to put our people first again," he said, in a rephrasing of the Jeffersonian code. As for the memory of Jefferson: "We can honor him best by remembering our own role in governing ourselves and our nation: to speak, to move, to change—for it is only in change that we preserve the timeless values for which Thomas Jefferson gave his life over two centuries ago."[4]

"Timeless values" were meaningless if society did not keep pace with changing conditions. The new Democrats were ready to put their active-government Jefferson back in the spotlight. Meanwhile, the *Economist* offered an addendum to the celebratory pronouncements that accompanied Jefferson's 250th: "He is the intellectual's president; the president of the uncalloused hands." Though aimed at the unmartial Bill Clinton, and meant to encompass the patrician Democrats Roosevelt and Kennedy, the statement could as easily have included Ronald Wilson Reagan—that unabashed Jefferson lover with far more film credits than greasy overalls in his closet.

At least Jefferson would have been pleased that the commission created to honor his special birthday drew minimal funds from federal coffers.[5]

IT WAS not clear, after twelve years of a Republican in the White House, how Bill Clinton would govern. His predecessor, whom he had ousted from office, did not incorporate Jefferson into his worldview in any measurable way. But the language of liberty was ubiquitous during George H. W. Bush's single term, when the Soviet Union collapsed and a decade-long liberalizing trend in China came to an abrupt end when the tanks rolled and bullets flew across Tiananmen Square on June 4, 1989.

Writing in *U.S. News and World Report* as a new decade opened, the outspoken Fouad Ajami, an American-educated scholar with personal ties to Iran and the Middle East, took the pulse of the times: "Each present arranges and adopts its own past," he wrote. "We choose the ancestors we want. Thomas Jefferson . . . is clearly the right ancestor for a moment such as this, when liberty is ascendant." The first President Bush had restored something of America's pride as the protector of liberty abroad with the short, relatively bloodless defeat of the Iraqi tyrant Saddam Hussein in the first Gulf War.

Like many others who observed the United States from abroad before they knew it from within, Ajami held a modern immigrant's perspective as to why Americans paired their magical ideas of liberty and exceptionalism: "Americans love the myth of their own innocence," he said. "In the myth, the innocent Republic ventures abroad only to be sullied by the ways of the world; she then retreats home. But even in isolation, she remains an exemplar. . . . That myth has in Jefferson its most compelling embodiment and expositor." Few Americans were introspective enough to have picked up on the fact that an ecstatic innocence attached to their belief in their exceptional qualities as a people. "Is there not a bit of Jefferson in all of us today?" the Lebanese American asked.[6]

There was more than a bit of Jefferson in General Secretary of the Communist Party Mikhail Gorbachev, who in recognizing his nation's political flaws hastened the end of the Cold War. During his April 1993 visit to Monticello, Gorbachev informed Daniel P. Jordan, the longtime executive director at Jefferson's landmark estate, that he had returned often, and at critical times, to a college text he had mastered that laid out Jefferson's political principles. Other foreign leaders who made fond pilgrimages to Monticello in the mid-1990s included the former British prime minister Margaret Thatcher, Japan's Emperor Akihito, and the Dalai Lama. When the president of the Republic of Bulgaria took a special detour from a state visit to Washington in order to see Monticello, he told Jordan that Jefferson's philosophy had inspired many in eastern Europe, and that the Revolutionary thinker was "widely quoted" in Bulgaria.

It could almost be described as intoxication. Jefferson's rhetorical construction of America presupposed a culture that had broken with the cruelties of earlier-constituted nation-states: it could be great without forfeiting its virtue. While his words inspired resistance to political tyranny elsewhere in the world, Jefferson, as in Fouad Ajami's view, would stare in horror at the capitalist empire, the government bureaucracy, and the size and scope of U.S. military involvement abroad. But, institutions aside, an embrace of Jefferson somehow immunized one against corruption and fed a devotional spirit. Ajami again: "America's insistence that it stands for something entirely new under the sun, that this Republic's ways abroad represent a break with the ancient ways states conduct themselves, demonstrates the tenacity of the Jeffersonian legacy." No matter how big it got, America pretended it could stay forever young.[7]

Boyish Bill Clinton suited that image in the 1990s. But if Clinton was titularly in charge of the national narrative for a time, Republicans in Congress were by no means ready to cede Jefferson back to the Democrats. The GOP was in an awkward stage of redefinition as it contended with the uncertain ideology of the Bush presidency. The Reagan legacy did not yet shine for die-hard conservatives as brightly as it would in the early twenty-first century. Bush, a more institutional Republican than his predecessor, had dismissed key Reagan officials in order to rule in his own name, a "kinder and gentler" version of Reaganism. But his patrician temper was unexciting; as a result, "the vision thing" (as Bush framed the Reagan magic he knew he lacked) would remain elusive for Republicans for some time to come.

Setting aside Clinton's dramatic summoning of his namesake, Jefferson belonged most to Republicans in the 1990s, if one measures his value to political discourse by tallying up the number of quotes aired on Capitol Hill. The prize for the most intensive application of the Revolution's master wordsmith in a single speech has to go to Senator Alan Simpson of Wyoming, a colorful speaker who never minced words. As he shopped around for Jefferson quotes in 1996, Simpson settled upon a previously untried axiom from the 1816 Kercheval letter: "We must make our election between economy and liberty, or profusion and servitude." And from another Jefferson letter of the same year: "I place economy among the first and most important of republican virtues, and public debt as the greatest of the dangers to be feared." It was all about debt. Jefferson again: "If we can prevent the government from wasting the labors of the people, under the pretense of taking care of them, they must become happy."

"I certainly agree with that," Simpson enfolded his Jefferson. It was "dangerous," "cruelly deceptive," productive only of "misery," "poverty," and "hunger" to go on spending as Congress had. "One simply cannot read many of the statements of our third president," he prodded, "without coming upon repeated, potent references to the necessity of eliminating public debt." The senator knew his Jefferson and knew history better than most: "Mr. Jefferson was fully acquainted with the dangers of mounting public debt," he concluded. "Indeed, one might say that the principal challenge of the young republic was how to discharge the massive debts compiled by the individual States in the course of the American Revolution."[8]

This was his party's issue, now more than ever before. During one of the many rounds of debate on a balanced budget amendment, in the spring of 1994, fiscal conservatives tried to seize the initiative. Representative Gerald B. Solomon of New York: "Thomas Jefferson was right when he expressed regret that the Constitution did not include a restriction on borrowing. And Mr. Speaker, if Thomas Jefferson could only see us now, like a bunch of drunken sailors on a never-ending spending spree." Charlie Stenholm, a conservative Texas Democrat, chimed in: "The threat of economic and political harm from continued deficit spending is the type of governmental abuse appropriately proscribed by the Constitution. The point was made by Thomas Jefferson, who said: 'The question whether one generation has the right to bind another by the deficit it imposes is a question of such consequence as to place it among the fundamental principles of government.'"

While Republicans did all they could to own this issue, liberals saw the merits of Jeffersonian frugality, too. Professor Laurence Tribe of Harvard, a leading opponent of the amendment, admitted to the Senate Budget Committee in 1992: "The Jeffersonian notion that today's populace should not be able to burden future generations with excessive debt, does seem to be the kind of fundamental value that is worthy of enshrinement in the Constitution. In a sense, it represents a structural protection for the rights of our children and grandchildren." The spirit of the Constitution would be upheld by a balanced budget amendment. As Tribe underscored: "It would protect the fundamental rights of the people by restraining the federal government from abusing its powers." Liberal Illinois senator Paul Simon concurred—again quoting Jefferson on the inadvisability of binding a future generation to debts incurred before. Less spending, urged the Right; smart spending, urged the Left.

For a brief while, then, debate in the 1990s lacked the clear-cut partisan contours Americans have come to expect in the current century. It was about the means, not the principle, of deficit reduction. President Clinton and his economic team were working to find a bipartisan solution. Representative Steny Hoyer of Maryland rose in support of the balanced budget amendment, sternly reminding Republicans how the problem began: "There is no question that we have taken significant action under the leadership of President Clinton to reverse the dramatic increasing deficits the country suffered under Presidents

Reagan and Bush." And then he quoted Jefferson's thesis: "I place economy among the first and most important of republican virtues, and public debt as the greatest of dangers to be feared."

Putting a modern Democratic twist on Jefferson's intent to protect minority interests under majority rule, Hoyer explained: "Why Jefferson saw public debt as the greatest danger to be feared was because he realized that future generations were even more vulnerable to abuse than the minorities of the present—because they were disenfranchised. As silent sufferers, unable to join the debate of today, they would be uniquely vulnerable to the ability of the majorities of the present to commit and spend their resources of the future. We've done that, we need to stop it." Who would best protect the future, then—flexible Democrats who would not abandon New Deal and Great Society projects, or purebred Republicans who feared the long-term implications of government ascendancy? Both parties claimed the Jeffersonian principle.

Perhaps the most unrestrained participant in the balanced budget debate of 1994 was Colorado Republican Joel Hefley. "Two hundred years ago," he noted, "Thomas Jefferson wrote that if he could add just one amendment [it would be] prohibition against Congress borrowing money. Such an amendment, he reasoned, would defend the American people from the tyranny of government." And then the congressman added a witticism all his own: "If Jefferson thought taxation without representation was bad, he should see it *with* representation." Lamenting that such an amendment had never passed, Hefley said that modern government had come to embody "the culmination of [Jefferson's] fears—a bloated and ineffective mass that stretches its constitutional authority to the limit."[9]

After the Republicans' strong showing in the midterm elections that year, the debate resumed in February 1995. Senator Bob Smith, Republican of New Hampshire, warned of the evils of spending, as members of his party would continue to do for as long as big-borrowing Democrats survived as a political species. He sounded the alarm: "There will not be anything in the Social Security trust fund. There will not be anything for Medicare. There will not be anything for Medicaid. There will not be anything for national defense because there will not be anything left. It will be gone." For backing, he turned to Jefferson directly:

No less an authority than the distinguished author of the Declaration of Independence himself, Thomas Jefferson, spoke about this.

He spoke, he even thought ahead about this type of debate that we are having right here. He said this: "The question whether one generation has the right to bind another by the deficit it imposes is a question of such consequence as to place it among the fundamental principles of government. We should consider ourselves unauthorized to saddle our posterity with our debt, and morally bound to pay those debts ourselves."

Jefferson had made the foregoing statement to his son-in-law, Virginia congressman John Wayles Eppes, in 1813, as an ex-president. President Madison had just broken ranks with his friend and predecessor, pursuing a different business model when faced with an active war. If he was to fight on the scale required to contest the British in the War of 1812, the federal government had to tax and spend. Or so Madison recognized.

Jefferson was married to a different idea. Each generation was, in effect, a nation unto itself, and not subject to invasion from without in the form of debt. To burden the rising generation was, he said, a "slavish imitation" of Britain. Jefferson advocated short-term notes only, to restrain the federal government from accruing long-term debt. But Jack Eppes failed to convince enough in Congress, and the ex-president's plan was rejected as insufficient to the moment at hand. Madison turned to bankers, much to Jefferson's dismay, in prosecuting an aggressive naval war.

History tends to be less readily transferrable than politicians are aware when they invoke the hallowed past to score political points. As we see here, a problem arises when the founders are removed from context, or when the circumstances of one decade are conflated with those of another. The well-intentioned Senator Smith had plucked a paragraph from a compendium of Jefferson's best quotes, unaware of the complexity of history. He did not realize, in this case, that he was saying James Madison had to be wrong for Jefferson to be right. He did not grapple with the unique problem that occasioned their debate either: the War of 1812.

With respect to the dangers inherent in federal involvement with private bankers, Jefferson had been saying the same things for twenty years. In the 1790s, under a Federalist regime, he and Madison saw eye to eye on issues of finance. In its first decade under the federal Constitution, the nation was wholly inexperienced. Power was distributed in untested ways, and the two-party system was yet to be formalized (and seen as a threat to republicanism). By 1813, the stakes were entirely different, with once-dominant Federalists a disappearing force in politics. So in 1813, whether he liked it or not, it was Madison whom Jefferson was writing *against*.

If Mr. Smith went to Washington to enact Jefferson's vision, he, like most lawmakers, saw little daylight between the consolidated genius of the founders and perceived implications for the political present. "Lest there be any doubt where Thomas Jefferson would have stood on the balanced budget amendment," Smith said blithely, "that doubt ought to be laid to rest by the following statement he made in 1798: 'I wish it were possible to obtain a single amendment to our Constitution. I would be willing to depend on that alone for the reduction of the administration of our government to the genuine principles of its Constitution. I mean an additional article taking from the federal government the power of borrowing.'"

This line from the Jefferson of 1798 would become a staple for modern-day Republicans in their war on federal spending. But what had prompted Jefferson to confide in Virginia senator John Taylor, a close ally, the secret wish that Smith was using as his trump card? *It was to make it hard for the United States to go to war at all.* That's what government borrowing was usually for in Jefferson's lifetime. In 1798, Federalist John Adams was president, and Jefferson was dead certain that his political opposition nurtured the desire to enact arbitrary government. Jeffersonian Republicans were at their weakest during that year, as Federalists clamored for war with Revolutionary France and passed the Alien and Sedition Acts in order to shut down protest—under penalty of jail time or deportation.

Jefferson's statement to Taylor was part of a litany of complaints about government abuse. To his mind, state governments at that moment were more republican than the national authority, which was then operating out of Philadelphia. Fearmongering Federalists had deluded a good many people into accepting rule by a group of men who didn't really care about the general welfare. But, Jefferson assured Taylor, "this disease of the imagination will pass over, because the patients are essentially republican." He always believed in the ultimate wisdom of ordinary folks, who were not to be deceived for any length of time. Ronald Reagan, altogether Jeffersonian in his sunny optimism about Americans, had inserted the "power of borrowing" quote in his July 3, 1987, "Economic Bill of Rights" speech at the Jefferson Memorial.

Seized by the same sound bite, Smith crooned: "Taking from the federal government the power of borrowing. How right Jefferson was. If you want to modify it a little bit, if you want to borrow, pay it back. . . . Do not pay it back, and go to jail or lose your home or whatever it is that you put up for credit. But we are asking our children to pay the cost—selfish, immoral, unconstitutional, in my opinion." And so the rhetorical argument of fiscal conservatives has ever after remained, spurred on by Jefferson's resistance to forces by which he felt threatened under an economic system that bears no resemblance to ours.[10]

That is not to say the liberal media simply rolled over and permitted Republicans' statements about fiscal discipline to overwhelm the national conversation. The *Newsweek* columnist Robert J. Samuelson adopted a different view from that of Senator Smith: "The Constitution is not a sledgehammer. . . . You should not confuse balancing the budget, which is generally a good idea, with the undesirability of using the Constitution to do it." Writing in the *New York Times,* the sociologist Paul J. Starr made the same point with unusual cleverness: "If the Constitution had required a balanced budget, many members of Congress would not sit there today: for one thing, Thomas Jefferson could not have completed the Louisiana Purchase."[11]

IN THE summer of 1996, as President Clinton campaigned for re-election, Republicans controlled both Houses, and Majority Whip Tom Delay of Texas spoke on behalf of an ambiguous bill establishing "Cost of Government Day." The GOP wished to highlight the statistic that "the American family has to give up more than 50% of what it earns to the government."

The Democrats, according to Delay, were hoping to "cover up" a problem: "Thomas Jefferson once said, a wise and frugal government shall restrain men from injuring one another, shall leave them free to regulate their own pursuits of industry and improvement and shall not take from the mouth the labor of bread it has earned. This is the sum of good government." It was one of the Jefferson quotes that Virginia senator Harry Byrd Jr. had favored in the 1970s, and the Reagan speechwriter John McClaughry had emphasized in the early 1980s. It has been in John Bartlett's *Familiar Quotations* for many decades. For Delay, the issue was that the Clinton administration stood by as the federal government continued to grow and, through taxes, take "the bread the American people have earned." This was the Texan's hobbyhorse.

Years earlier, Delay had been the owner of a pest-control business and had suffered, he said, "the very real sting of federal regulations and its costs on my business." He did not reveal, in his speech to the House, the fact that the Internal Revenue Service had in repeated instances found "The Exterminator," as Delay was known, seriously delinquent in meeting the obligations of payroll and income taxes. However, the congressman did complain, volubly, that "more people need to realize that government is a cost of doing business." He was part of the Republican cohort, led by House Speaker Newt Gingrich, that was responsible for provoking a government shutdown in late 1995 over the administration's spending on Medicare, education, and other social programs. Republicans were saying that benefits had to be cut in order to preserve the integrity of all that FDR and LBJ had unleashed—a case of Democrats' good intentions run amok. The course they proposed was understood as a Jeffersonian response to big government.[12]

Speeches poured forth. When the next Congress was seated in March 1997, the same arguments were reprised. The issue boiled down to one question: Who gets hurt by what spending reductions? Vermont Senator Patrick Leahy, a Democrat, elaborated on Paul Starr's year-old analogy: "Thomas Jefferson borrowed an amount that was equal to twice the budget of the United States for the Louisiana Purchase. I mean, this would be like borrowing trillions of dollars today. Had President Jefferson had a balanced budget amendment, . . . North Dakota would have had the chance to speak Spanish, not English. . . . Certainly the United States would not be a country described as 'from sea to shining sea.' These are some of the historical, as opposed to hysterical, facts in this debate."

Later the same day, long serving Senator Richard Shelby of Alabama, a conservative Democrat who had recently become a Republican, countered Leahy's logic by repeating, almost word for word, what Smith of New Hampshire had earlier argued. "As we debate the balanced budget amendment," Shelby said, "we would be wise to listen to the words of one of our Founding Fathers, Thomas Jefferson." And he launched into the theory of generations and obligations, circa 1798, repeating Jefferson's axiom: "We should consider ourselves unauthorized to saddle posterity with our debts, and morally bound to pay them ourselves." But Shelby also tried to be even-handed, noting that the federal budget had not been balanced since 1969, which made it a bipartisan problem. He offered up the statistic that a child born in 1996 was beginning life with twenty thousand dollars owed to Washington, "debt he had nothing to do with creating."[13]

President Clinton and congressional Democrats promised deficit reduction, but would not chain themselves to a constantly balanced budget. Republicans, aiming to drastically diminish the federal government's role in charting social policy, would not say precisely how they would effect balance. The result was stalemate. To the outsider looking in, one could either take pride in the Louisiana Purchase, with its once-exorbitant price tag of $15 million, or have a balanced budget suited to the existing size of the national economy. Jefferson, as usual, served both sides of the issue.

Libertarians especially loved Jefferson. The Southern California newspaper editor Alan W. Bock demonstrated his impatience with modern scholars whose critical appraisals of the Virginian seemed to be dominated by his record on slavery. No human being can be entirely consistent or without blemishes, he adjudged, and the scholars were missing the forest for the trees. Jefferson was "from an early age and throughout his life a proud and effective champion of human liberty." It was enough to keep the focus there, and on the evils of consolidated government.

Bock adopted the Jeffersonian maxim that when government advances, liberty retreats. "Most modern intellectuals and journalists, however consciously, are apologists for the powerful modern nation-state," Bock wrote, "and even more so for the idea that a powerful nation-state is the best or only path to peaceful progress and a better society, believing or hoping that its vast power can be and usually is used beneficently." Bock existed on the opposite side of the spectrum from Elbert Thomas's sentimental "World Citizen," presuming instead that Jefferson's libertarianism would have led him to scoff at the United Nations: "What would Jefferson have made of the Tower of Babble on the East River, and the imperial ambitions of the overstuffed, overpaid plutocrats who populate it and pretend to believe they are the last, best hope of earth?" (Note: In his first inaugural address, Jefferson had termed America "the world's best hope"; it was Lincoln who dubbed it "the last, best hope of earth.") Bock's distaste for the UN was rich. He explained why Jefferson was right in all the essentials, in having seen the dangers of bureaucracy and centralization when the United States was yet a modest nation. Jefferson maintained an "unflinching libertarian view of the world, tempered by experience and realism, and expressed so gracefully and persuasively."[14]

Jefferson's libertarian persona was examined by others besides outright ideologues. For a time in 1988, Senator Gary Hart, Democrat of Colorado, was a leading presidential contender. He returned to the practice of law after leaving government, and drifted in and out of public life before becoming a national security consultant and elder statesman. In a 1996 interview, the Democrat responded to questions about his intellectual preferences and literary tastes. Asked "which political figure, living or dead, do you most admire?" he answered: "Jefferson, the greatest American who ever lived."

By 2002, Hart had reshaped his résumé. With an advanced degree in politics from Oxford University, he had a new book out that promoted a political theory predicated on the Jeffersonian ideal of the "ward republic"—enhanced citizen participation in government at the local level. *Restoration of the Republic* celebrates mammoth federal initiatives such as Medicare, while projecting a larger role for "local republics" in displacing cumbersome federal bureaucracies and directing the administration of welfare and related poverty programs. Attempting to update Jefferson's language of republican liberty, the ex-senator held out an olive branch of sorts to small-government types, reviving the "ward republic" to function as a "therapeutic corrective to unwise or unjust national policies" (though Hart was mainly thinking about grassroots resistance to regressive environmental policies or unfair wages). "At their best," he wrote, as a neo-Jeffersonian, "local republics can become fountains of political energy and creative experimentation."[15]

DURING THE final years of the twentieth century, what was old was new again. Congress debated the balanced budget amendment, and Jefferson quotes were read into the record. The pivotal founder came up several times in a back-and-forth over term limits, again in the context of campaign finance reform, and subsequently in relation to the patent system, labor union activities, and a variety of other issues before Congress.

Amid a discussion of voting rights legislation in 1997, Democrat Major Owens of Brooklyn, New York, stepped up the pace of debate in Congress on the applicability of Jefferson to modern America's problems. He segued from the question at hand into a long meditation on Ken Burns's just-released PBS documentary special on Jefferson. Observed Owens: "Thomas Jefferson was a very complex man, also a very great man, a giant; so ordinary people are not expected to be able to really understand the psyche of Thomas Jefferson fully. He was the kind of individual who comes only once or twice or a few times in a century. He was the equivalent in politics to Einstein in science, as far as I'm concerned."[16]

Congressman Owens soon made it clear that he was contemplating democracy and race at the same time, and entertaining the possibility that the Virginia planter who became president had loved his slave

Sally Hemings. A big-budget cinematic treatment, drawing heavily on Fawn Brodie's 1974 portrayal of the Jefferson-Hemings affair, came out in 1995. *Jefferson in Paris* starred a ponderous Nick Nolte in the title role, as an ambiguous aficionado of salon culture who breathed in the dangerous air of the French Enlightenment. In this way, Jefferson was reintroduced to popular audiences as a man who exhibited cool charm in the midst of political upheaval; a quietly passionate man whose sex life in a racially charged environment was as intense and unsettling as it was historically meaningful. (The subject of race and sexuality will be discussed at length in the next chapter.)

In the years that immediately followed the release of *Jefferson in Paris,* the historical Jefferson found himself in for a stormy ride. Adding to the aura of inscrutability that came with this latest incarnation, the fickle cosmopolite had to contend with the Irish diplomat and politician Conor Cruise O'Brien, who made waves with *The Long Affair* (1996), a book that tore apart the liberty-loving founder. In advance of the book's publication, the *Atlantic Monthly* printed an article by its author, with an inflammatory tease following the title: "In the multiracial American future Jefferson will not be thought of as the Sage of Monticello. His flaws are beyond redemption. The sound you hear is the crashing of a reputation."

Jefferson, the Irishman argued, was no herald of modern values. His was "a wild liberty, absolute, untrammeled, universal, the liberty of a revolutionary manifesto." Bearing a poison pen more deadly than anything Jefferson's irritable contemporaries kept in their inkwells, O'Brien found Jefferson's conception of liberty ugly and debased. A Jefferson who would keep the spirit of rebellion alive could be directly associated with incendiary acts around the world.

O'Brien was convinced that in spite of the pragmatism he exhibited throughout his presidency, the radical core of Jefferson had survived intact. This was the Jefferson whose rhetorical quip, "The tree of liberty must be refreshed from time to time with the blood of patriots and tyrants," had inspired the Oklahoma City bomber Timothy McVeigh to carry out mass murder in 1995 (he was convicted in 1997). In O'Brien's extremist reading of the lying icon, Jefferson's extreme judgments separated him from the other founders.

Extreme judgments extended from a contentious Irish politico to the president of the National Rifle Association, who admired Jefferson for an imagined posture. In his largely ceremonial role at the NRA, the charismatic Charlton Heston, star of motion pictures—and most notably historical epics—quoted John Adams, saying: "Arms in the hands of citizens [may] be used at individual discretion"; which he fortified with: "Thomas Jefferson wrote, 'No man shall ever be debarred the use of arms.'" An entirely new sport had been invented.[17]

Jefferson's fans undertook damage control, but these were difficult days for any who held on to the Rooseveltian-Kennedy image of the man. Misconstrual of Jefferson's "tree of liberty" quote became increasingly common. One academic squashed O'Brien's interpretation in a single sentence: "Only a one-eyed prosecutor would ever turn this statement into a justification of a contemporary act of political mass murder." As the century's final decade wound down, revisionists both popular and scholarly converted the admittedly paradoxical Jefferson—slaveholding freedom-lover, freethinker who found sublimity in the morals of Jesus—into a psychically damaged, cold-blooded, and occasionally predatory renegade.[18]

For Bill Clinton, who owned a rare copy of Jefferson's *Notes on Virginia,* and recurred to it from time to time in private moments, Thomas Jefferson never really lost his luster. A political scientist who analyzed the number and character of the references Clinton made to past presidents during his two terms has found that Jefferson was, during most of that period, his favorite—especially on ceremonial occasions, and especially while abroad or in the company of foreign leaders. During his first term, he emphasized Jefferson on education and as a political exemplar; in 1993 alone, he invoked Jefferson on 25 separate occasions, followed by FDR (19), Truman (17), JFK (12), and Lincoln (11). Nearer the end of his presidency, he reached out more to Theodore Roosevelt—who had preferred Hamilton to Jefferson—and to Hamilton himself. This was the period when President Clinton was celebrating entrepreneurship and recalled, to quote from one speech, that "Hamilton identified new ways to harness the changes then going on so that our nation could advance." Jefferson was not the best source for appeals to an enlarged economy, when the president's message was as bold as: "We have the honor of designing the architecture for a global economic marketplace."[19]

At the end of the Clinton era, Jefferson was placed in calloused hands. In 1998, his political persona suddenly took backseat to his private life, when his DNA made national headlines. The latest science had found that the genetic material passed down through the male Jefferson line was present in the known descendants of Sally Hemings. In 2000, CBS aired a miniseries titled *Sally Hemings: An American Scandal.* If a formal poll had been taken that year, it is not inconceivable that more Americans would have known of Jefferson's sexual history than of his authorship of the Declaration of Independence.

THE OUTGOING century had been dubbed the "American Century," and the year 2000 naturally invited as many retrospectives as prognostications. The syndicated columnist and television news analyst George Will took a long view. "Jefferson was, I think, the man of this millennium," he intoned. "The story of this millennium is the gradual expansion of freedom and the expanding inclusion of variously excluded groups. He exemplified in his life what a free person ought to look like, that is, someone restless and questing through a long life under the rigorous discipline of freedom. Freedom's not the absence of rigor; it's the absence of restraints imposed by others."

Here was JFK's Jefferson of the capacious mind melded with a conservative's grudging acknowledgment of government as a "necessary evil." America's political schizophrenia could still be expressed in the same terms Claude Bower Democrats had identified in the 1920s: *Jefferson's ideals ruled the day, while Hamilton's moneyed elite really ran the show.* Something had been lost in the translation of Jefferson to modernity. Why? Because Jefferson's optimism about individual rights emanated from a minimalist government in a simpler world. Somehow, though, that cold, hard fact did nothing to limit his relevance. His gift to posterity was a clearly articulated political morality: he created a standard meant to endure. According to the conservative columnist Will, Jefferson had done nothing less than "define the American mind," and render the nation's founding ideals as universal ideals.[20]

The election of 2000 between Vice President Al Gore of Tennessee and Governor George W. Bush of Texas, as close and as controversial as it was, did not seem to require dignified appeals to Jefferson and his generation. In its focus on financial security for middle-class Americans, the two moderate-appearing candidates traded observations about honor and fairness at home and keeping peace abroad. The closest their three televised debates came to bringing up the hallowed annals of America's creation was Gore's comforting allusion: "We can renew and rekindle the American spirit and make our future what our founders dreamed it could be." Neither candidate sounded particularly lofty at any point.[21]

Yet again, with a change of administrations, change came to the walls of the White House Cabinet Room, although this time it was minor. His father had hung portraits of Presidents Jefferson, Lincoln, the first Roosevelt, and Eisenhower; Clinton had substituted Washington for Eisenhower. George W. Bush returned Eisenhower (removing Lincoln). At least in terms of portraiture, the one man the forty-first, forty-second, and forty-third presidents had in common was Thomas Jefferson.[22]

Tea Party Republicans were still years from designating themselves as such, but the first inkling of what was brewing could be felt in calls to return money to taxpayers and drastically limit the reach of government. In June 2001, freshman congressman John Culberson of Texas addressed his colleagues on the $1.3 trillion in tax cuts enacted by President Bush. As a fiscal conservative who wished the cuts had been even greater, Culberson presented himself as a Jeffersonian in spirit, symbolized in part by the slogan he came to adopt: "Let Texans run Texas." He would join the Tea Party caucus, and in 2011, publicly favor a most un-Jeffersonian idea: requiring Christian prayers to be read at all military funerals.

During Culberson's first season in Congress, the Houston-area representative spoke about the "core philosophy" of Republicans: "limiting the size, power, and cost of the federal government." He devoted the last quarter of this lengthy speech to thoughts on Jefferson and his legacy; he read from a short political biography of the founder, highlighted his legislative accomplishments in Revolutionary Virginia, and marveled at the unpretentious words on his tombstone at Monticello. From here, however, recounting Jefferson's pride in resisting John Adams's "federal principles and proceedings," the congressman lost his way:

> In modern parlance, in the language of the year 2001, Mr. Jefferson is telling us that his greatest achievement in his entire life was being a partisan Republican. It mattered to him more than anything else he had done, because they created, James Madison and Thomas Jefferson, created political parties to ensure the election of Republicans, of people that were Republicans, as they called themselves. Mr. Jefferson never called himself a Democrat. He called himself a Republican, their political party was the Republican Party, because they were committed to the preservation of the American republic, the core principles that made the country great: reducing the size, power, and cost of the federal government, preserving the power of the state governments to control the things that affected their lives. . . . Mr. Jefferson set forth as his highest priority the elimination of the national debt, reducing taxes, abolishing the income tax.

It would be absurd to think that Thomas Jefferson understood the terms *democrat* and *republican* (or *Democrat* and *Republican*) in the same way as twenty-first-century Americans. Language and meaning are never constant. Aside from the outrageous implication that the Federalist Adams administration was a "tax and spend" regime because its party nomenclature involved the term *federal*, Congressman Culberson thoroughly disfigured American history when he suggested that the party designation "Republican" (also known as Democratic-Republican in Jefferson's day) had somehow morphed into the party of Abraham Lincoln; or that the Republican Party of 1856–60 subscribed to the values of the party of Harding and Coolidge and Hoover and Reagan.

At the risk of belaboring the point, the Texas congressman's misguided argument in favor of tax cuts neglected to take into account that a federal income tax did not exist in Jefferson's lifetime, and that it was enacted for the purpose of raising revenue to conduct America's wars. Income taxes were made a permanent feature of a worker's civic obligation only in the twentieth century. Oblivious to history, Culberson proudly concluded: "I hope the American people will remember this tax cut as one of the most vivid examples of why it is important to preserve a Republican majority in the House and in the Senate."[23]

While the foregoing is an outrageous instance of "Jefferson abuse," it demonstrates how Jefferson's malleability was a critical part of his legacy. Rebellious Confederates and adherents of Union alike adopted him; Calvin Coolidge celebrated Jefferson's attachment to the Bill of Rights, and Franklin Roosevelt honored him with a stately memorial. John and Robert Kennedy, William Jefferson Clinton and Ronald Wilson Reagan, all sought political justification by consulting Jefferson's dynamic lexicon.

On September 11, 2001, after three hijacked commercial jets took aim at American complacency, the Jefferson symbol came easily to Washington's representatives. The country was looking for ways to express a common sense of national belonging, beyond the widely shared shock and horror. Democratic congresswoman Shelley Berkley of Nevada: "Yesterday's attack was an attack on everything that we believe in as Americans, everything we hold sacred as a nation. . . . As Thomas Jefferson once said: 'I have sworn upon the altar of God eternal hostility against every form of tyranny over the mind of man.' We will persevere over the tyranny of terror, and we will persevere over tyrants everywhere." Another Democrat, Lloyd Doggett of Austin, Texas, praised President Bush's strong remarks in the wake of the attacks, adding a personal reflection: "As I passed the Tidal Basin yesterday and witnessed the smoke rising from behind the Jefferson Memorial coming from the still-burning Pentagon, I will concede to being moved by the juxtaposition, the gray smoke from the Pentagon against this classic white marble structure where the words of Jefferson are inscribed: 'I have sworn upon the altar of God eternal hostility against every form of tyranny over the mind of man.'" Tyranny—the Satan of America's civil religion—had reentered the vocabulary with urgent cause.

In the U.S. Senate that same day, Republican John Ensign of Nevada conveyed a profoundly different sensibility: "As our nation prepares to confront the threat of terrorism, we must be careful not to destroy the freedom which makes this country great. We must not abandon civil liberties within our borders or our ability to act unilaterally outside our borders if we want to be safe. As Thomas Jefferson warned us, 'Those who desire to give up Freedom in order to gain Security, will not have, nor do they deserve either one.'" Ensign's information was flawed; Jefferson never recorded those words (and one wonders where he or his staff found them). However, Jefferson did, with similar purpose, write to John Jay in 1785: "The justest dispositions possible in ourselves, will not secure us against war. It would be necessary that all other nations were just also. . . . Weakness provokes insult and injury, while a condition to punish often prevents them." To use the vernacular, "Them's fightin' words."[24]

Jefferson's presidency soon became a comparative model, a window through which to assess how the nation ought to regard its relations with the Muslim world. The Barbary Wars were vaguely familiar to Americans from a single phrase in the Marine Corps hymn: "to the shores of Tripoli"—where Jefferson had dispatched armed vessels. Even before the American Revolution, though, Mediterranean pirates had regularly harassed commercial vessels, demanding ransom payments for captured crewmen. So, from its very inception, the United States was engaged in difficult negotiations with representatives from North Africa—Algiers, Tunis, Tripoli, and Morocco—over the tributary arrangement to which other seagoing nations had agreed.

Prior to 1776, Jefferson had acquired a copy of the Qur'ān. He examined Islamic law and remained cognizant of the history of violent conquest undertaken by Islamic nations. From the 1780s through his presidency, he took a harder line than most of his peers, preferring war with the "piratical States" to any agreement of annual payments for protection of commerce. During his first term, he sent an American fleet to the Mediterranean; by 1806, a less obnoxious working relationship was in place.

Nevertheless, the absence of a visible U.S. military presence in ensuing years allowed for a reinfestation of piracy in the Mediterranean. It was not until 1815 that the American naval fighters William Bainbridge and Stephen Decatur demonstrated their total resolve and brought a complete end to tribute. This left the United States in a superior position, compared to the European powers, vis-à-vis the Barbary States. Interestingly, too, during a frustratingly long period of contention, both Jefferson and his successor, James Madison, separated the threats posed by Muslim piracy from the practice of Islam. As Jefferson's secretary of state, Madison explained to U.S. consul Tobias Lear that "universal toleration in matters of religion" was official policy.[25]

After 2001, the lesson taken from Jefferson's experience was that, in a case of state-sponsored terrorism, religious toleration without military decisiveness achieves nothing of lasting value to American security. And while Jefferson, as a debt-removal strategy, trimmed the budget of the army and navy, he was obliged to issue government bonds in support of the Barbary action. The old tension revived between republicanism and consolidated government. A republic remained free only as long as it remained stable, a condition requiring a degree of security that necessitated central coordination and placed limits on freedom.

In the twenty-first century's opening decade, as national security issues became a preoccupation and the Bush-Cheney foreign policy team led the United States into a questionable war in Iraq, free speech concerns formed a critical part of political discourse. With leadership responsibilities front and center in the election year of 2004, *Time* devoted its Independence Day cover story to Thomas Jefferson, promising "A Look at the Most Controversial Founding Father." Describing the peace-loving Revolutionary as an accomplished statesman with his share of quixotic ideas, the editors took a predictable tack: "Trying to picture Jefferson now and apply his ideas and policies to 21st century American issues, one first has to imagine a sort of figure who hasn't existed for a long, long time and seems unlikely to appear again soon: a philosopher-President." Would Jefferson have invaded Iraq? the editors asked uselessly.[26]

George W. Bush, war president, was no Jeffersonian. He did not value his elite education or have big ideas. He resorted to politics because he understood politics, while gamely exploiting the money-making opportunities that came his way as the privileged scion of a prominent political family. He governed without subtlety, resorting to the "big stick" without walking softly. Al Gore, the Democrat he overcame in 2000, was also a political son with dollar signs in his eyes. But in defeat, Gore became a champion of humane causes and a student of science—a progressive. His 2007 book, *The Assault on Reason,* was an outright critique of the improvident, closed, and heavy-handed Bush-Cheney practices. Gore aimed to show how the public sphere had become a place where policy was dictated instead of argued, and the enemies of reason prevailed. In this exercise, his apostle of reason was Jefferson, the forward-looking humanist whom Franklin Roosevelt and his Democratic successors had embraced.

Speaking of the founding era in general, Gore wrote nostalgically in praise of an imagined "public forum . . . where the people held the government accountable." Here, "the fate of ideas contributed by individuals depended, for the most part, on an emergent meritocracy of ideas . . . regardless of the wealth or class of the individual responsible for them." This, to him, was what democracy was supposed to be about. The former vice president had a rosy picture in mind when it came to the conduct of politics in Jefferson's America, but like so many others, he was able to draw upon Jefferson's enlightened sensibility to lament the absence of a republican ideal: mindful civil discourse.

The problem that Gore and many other progressive Democrats had encountered of late was the rise of unreasoning political passion in a spiteful environment where honest debate no longer thrived. Reflecting on the misinformation disseminated about Iraqi strongman Saddam Hussein's alleged attempt to acquire nuclear materials from the African nation of Niger, and the Bush administration's questionable pretext for war more generally, Gore averred: "A free press is supposed to function as our democracy's immune system against such gross errors of fact and understanding." Which led him to a higher authority: "As Thomas Jefferson once said, 'Error of opinion may be tolerated where reason is left free to combat it.'" The phrase came from Jefferson's first inaugural address.

For Al Gore, a political language borne of fear had supplanted the founding script, coupled with what he called "vicarious traumatization" from excessive television viewing. There is an ironic touch in this observation; for when Jefferson looked upon his political opposition, he, like Gore, applied the operative neuropolitical terms of his times. For Jefferson, hardened conservatives (Federalists) literally suffered from damaged brains, from diseased minds, which rendered them constitutionally incapable of supporting healthy social growth.

The political crowd that could not but identify with money power was composed, he wrote, of "nervous persons, whose languid [nerve] fibres have more analogy with a passive than active state of things." Fearing openness, "timid" and "deluded," they tended to accept arbitrary power easily.

When former vice president Gore surveyed the political scene of the early twenty-first century, he cited the latest neuroscience to back him up: "Our mental life is governed mainly by a cauldron of emotions, motives and desires we are barely conscious of . . . and conscious life is usually an elaborate post hoc rationalization of things we really do for other reasons." The Enlightenment philosophy that moved Jefferson to an exquisite idealism about the outcome of the American Revolution was not the force that swayed modern American minds: "Television-created memories have the same control over the emotional system as do real memories," Gore explained.[27]

In the last year of his presidency, George W. Bush went to Monticello on the Fourth of July to deliver the keynote address at the naturalization ceremony that each year welcomed one hundred or so new American citizens. It had long seemed a fitting place to honor the patriotic instincts of immigrants who cherished freedom. Three of Bush's predecessors as president had spoken at the annual naturalization event: Roosevelt in 1936, Truman in 1947, and Ford in 1976. The year before President Bush took his turn, the actor Sam Waterston had done the honors. Waterston's earnest tones had won him the coveted role of Manhattan district attorney Jack McCoy in the long-running TV series *Law and Order;* he was also the voice of Jefferson in the Ken Burns documentary biography. The actor delivered an uplifting message about the quest for national self-understanding through citizen participation, noting: "History shows that America is the all-time greatest self-correcting nation."

In 2008, the forty-sixth year that Monticello held its naturalization ritual, the documentary filmmaker Ken Burns was scheduled to give the Fourth of July keynote speech; he generously yielded when, on short notice, Monticello received a request from the White House. On Jefferson's birthday three months earlier, President Bush had gathered a smaller group at the White House, where he spoke of Jefferson's having changed the world with a single sentence. "After countless centuries when the powerful and the privileged governed as they pleased," Bush said, "Jefferson proclaimed as a self-evident truth that liberty was a right given to all people by an Almighty." In an effort to expand the Jeffersonian principle to the Bush Doctrine in international affairs, the president had also said at that time, with reference to the Tidal Basin memorial: "The power of Jefferson's words do not stop at water's edge. They beckon the friends of liberty on even the most distant shores. They're a source of inspiration for people in young democracies like Afghanistan and Lebanon and Iraq."

For the unpopular war president, though, the Fourth of July speech did not go nearly as smoothly as the invitation-only White House event of April. As he thanked the various dignitaries present on the summery mountaintop, some boos were heard. When he spoke of the revolutionary character of Jefferson's immortal Declaration, dissenting voices again rang out. When he got to honoring "newcomers" to the United States, members of the audience reacted even more sharply. A northern Virginia schoolteacher held up a pink banner that read "Dissent Is Patriotic." The cry "War criminal!" was audible, and the president responded calmly: "We believe in free speech in the United States of America." The protest did not immediately die down: "He has brought fascism to our shore!" yelled one man. The single word "Impeach!" was shouted. The president was interrupted by protesters at least four separate times. It could have happened anywhere, but the impulses nurtured in the university community Jefferson made possible gave this event a special cast. There were no arrests.

Monticello had known to expect some interruption of the proceedings, which were open to the public. Concerned citizens wrote letters and sent e-mails to Monticello: "I regard Thomas Jefferson as the ultimate antithesis to G. W. Bush," went a representative complaint. In all, Monticello received some 350 telephone calls in advance of the president's visit, most registering dismay at the decision to host him; more than one hundred protesters lined the route to the mountain. One bore a sign that read, "I Am Rolling Over in My Grave—Thomas Jefferson." County police had an established protocol, and of course, Secret Service staff remained wary, knowing when and when not to intervene. As a result, the vocal protesters were painlessly escorted off the property—private property.[28]

In the wake of the protest, the eighty-year-old Iranian-born scholar Ruhi Ramazani, a distinguished professor emeritus of government and foreign affairs at the University of Virginia, signed his name to an op-ed in the *Richmond Times-Dispatch*. He contrasted Presidents Bush and Jefferson both on the impetus to go to war and on the value of cultivating the self, which Ramazani saw in this instance to be related: "Jefferson understood that tyranny can be imposed, democracy cannot. Democracy comes from within; it must be chosen." And, whereas the Declaration of Independence required "a decent respect to the opinions of mankind," the Bush administration had ignored the same in favor of imposing an outside order. "Enlighten the public generally," Jefferson had written in 1816, "and tyranny and oppression of mind and body will vanish like evil spirits at the dawn of day." At a time when talk of tyranny was reviving, with implications for U.S. policy both abroad and at home, Jefferson's language remained current.[29]

ALL THE talk of tyranny unleashed a political force on the American Right that came to be called the Tea Party. It regarded itself as Jeffersonian in publicly protesting budget deficits, high taxes, and government stimulus of the economy. It believed in the Protestant founders' notion that hard work reaped rewards. Its target, therefore, was an overreaching central government, though with the 2008 election it quickly found its personification of the enemy in the untested recipient of the Nobel Peace Prize: Barack Hussein Obama.

As the Obama era took shape, the appearance of a spirited, young African American president with Ivy League credentials and street smarts energized the rising generation and produced outright euphoria on Election Day. But in the emerging Tea Party, the new president appeared both elitist and secretly anti-American. Reaction from the Right to the "Hope and Change" slogan that catapulted Obama to the presidency was sharp and bitter. The Tea Party came to power within the Republican Party as a pressure group, with a loud, petulant, absolutist call to shut down the top-down processes of government. As correct patriots, they would no longer be talked down to by the overeducated. They were, in short, a theatrical caricature of Jeffersonian populism as the Federalists of 1800 might have styled it. But Jefferson's message was filled with sympathy and tolerance (whether or not real), and the Tea Party lacked empathy to the same degree that it lacked reserve. Many assumed that the Tea Party would disappear when the economy improved, or when libertarians got sick of the Christian Right.[30]

Barack Obama began his historic quest for the presidency in February 2007, with an official announcement from the Old State Capitol in Abraham Lincoln's Springfield, Illinois. When he noted, on that frigid day, that he stood "in the shadow of the Old State Capitol, where Lincoln once called on a divided house to stand together," he made it clear that the sixteenth president, not the third, was the chief executive whose life experience resonated with him most. It was really not until February 2014, when French president François Hollande came to Washington on a state visit, that President Obama contemplated using Jefferson's symbolism for political advancement. For the first time ever, a sitting president accompanied a foreign head of state to Monticello. It was Obama himself, in fact, who came up with the idea of smoothing the way for talks by traveling together to Jefferson's home. Jefferson, for five critical years in the 1780s America's minister to France, was, in Obama's words, "a Francophile through and through"; for his part, Hollande recalled the close camaraderie of Jefferson and the Marquis de Lafayette, whose efforts were instrumental in securing American independence. "Allies we were at the time of Jefferson and Lafayette," he crooned. "Allies we are today."[31]

Even without Obama's instigation, the Jefferson image attained prominence in the political environment that his historic election created. Internet traffic in Jefferson quotes was disseminated so vigorously and in such varied ways that Monticello's research department compiled a long list of spurious Jefferson quotes floating in cyberspace, and posted explanations designed to set the record straight.

The high point in counterfeit quotes was reached in 2008, the year of Obama's ascendancy. A widely distributed e-mail blast that year featured ten quotes, some legitimate, none properly contextualized, all of which found their way onto multiple websites. These included the easily exaggerated "tree of liberty" quote (another old favorite from Bartlett's Familiar Quotations) and the wholly invented, "The democracy will cease to exist when you take away from those who are willing to work and give to those who would not." Among other well trafficked quotes Monticello investigated, "Bad government results from too much government" is not something Jefferson ever wrote. "Dissent is the highest form of patriotism," is another axiom frequently attributed to Jefferson that was bandied about during the 2004 campaign and actually appears to have emerged from sentiment voiced during the Vietnam War era. "When injustice becomes law, resistance becomes duty." Never said. And so on.[32]

In the first decade of the twenty-first century, more books were published on Jefferson than on any of the other celebrated founders, including Washington and Adams. In fact, there were more books about Jefferson than about the American Revolution itself. With peacetime partisan rancor at a level of toxicity comparable to 1800, when Jefferson contested Adams, the red-headed Virginian continued his active afterlife in the highly democratic format provided by the World Wide Web. Online, vengeful writers peppered their rants with warring Jefferson quotes.[33]

The ongoing "war on terror" was never far from the headlines. Days after his January 2009 swearing in, President Obama was asked in a television interview about prospects in Afghanistan. "We are not going to be able to rebuild Afghanistan into a Jeffersonian democracy," he replied. A Jeffersonian democracy was one that could only spring from a republican foundation, which Central Asia historically lacked.

At the end of his first year in office, the foreign affairs expert Walter Russell Mead assessed the forty-fourth president: "Neither a cold-blooded realist nor a bleeding-heart idealist, Barack Obama has a split personality when it comes to foreign policy," he wrote, constructing a useful historical typology: "In general, U.S. presidents see the world through the eyes of four giants: Alexander Hamilton, Woodrow Wilson, Thomas Jefferson, and Andrew Jackson." Hamiltonians promoted a strong military, while believing in a federal government with strong business ties. Wilsonians stood with Hamiltonian internationalism, but privileged democracy and human rights over big business. Jeffersonians aimed for a federal government without complicated commitments and with a limited military footprint. Jacksonians, Mead wrote, were "today's Fox News watchers . . . , populists suspicious of Hamiltonian business links, Wilsonian do-gooding, and Jeffersonian weakness."

Thus, John F. Kennedy was a Wilsonian, and Theodore Roosevelt and George H. W. Bush were practical-minded Hamiltonians. Democratic doves, as well as Dwight D. Eisenhower, were confirmed Jeffersonians; and Ronald Reagan and the Far Right of the twenty-first century were chauvinistic Jacksonians. One could argue that the Barack Obama who extricated the United States from Iraq before the end of his first term, stayed for a bloody spell in Afghanistan, authorized an uptick in drone attacks and the Seal Team Six assault that killed Osama bin Laden, altogether proved a Wilsonian, Hamiltonian, and Jeffersonian at different times. He was less Jeffersonian than libertarian isolationists would prefer, less Wilsonian than those who had prematurely awarded him the Nobel Peace Prize hoped to see, and more Hamiltonian than many others expected of him. That said, Jefferson, in office, was not always Jeffersonian either. He understood the practical limits of restraint in a dangerous world.[34]

Presumably, nothing would have pleased Jefferson more than First Lady Michelle Obama's initiative in growing vegetables on the South Lawn of the White House. As president, Jefferson routinely monitored the appearance of spring peas, beans, and other produce at the Washington, D.C., farmers' market, and he routinely supplied his friends with seeds obtained from abroad. With his "fixation on gardening," and in having inaugurated the White House dinner party, Jefferson was hailed as a "Founding Foodie." At the same time, one wonders how excited he would be about the Thomas Jefferson Award given out since 1992 (generally to Republican legislators) by the Foodservice Distribution Industry: its announced purpose was to honor those who cast votes in Washington "to protect America's businesses, stimulate economic growth." Jefferson's "business ideals," in this odd construction, were those that limited the role of government in regulating businesses.[35]

LIMITED government. Personal liberties. Gun rights. Fear and loathing of all who would coddle illegal Mexicans. Obama as outsider, secret Muslim, convicted socialist. Meet the extreme wing of the Tea Party.

"It is time to water the tree of liberty" read the aggressive taunt of an undisguised protest sign, with its seizure of the Jefferson line. The Oklahoma City bomber Timothy McVeigh had worn a "blood of tyrants" T-shirt on the day he blew up the Murrah Federal Building. In the first years of the Obama administration, the same blood-soaked totem of homegrown radical sentiment that Conor Cruise O'Brien had held out as a symbol of Jefferson's anarchic tendency revived. In the summer of 2009, an aggrieved Second Amendment activist showed up at an Obama town hall meeting in New Hampshire, locked and loaded.

Tea Partiers were not interested in constructive dialogue. The executive director of the Coalition to Stop Gun Violence appealed for a renewal of American community by reminding his readers that in the same 1787 letter containing those radical words about the "tree of liberty," Jefferson made clear to his London-based diplomat-friend William Stephens Smith, that he was not "all in" when it came to rebelliousness: "The people cannot be all, and always, well informed," he said. "The part which is wrong will be discontented in proportion to the importance of the facts they misconceive." Angry impulse was no part of the Jeffersonian creed. But that did not give pause to those in the Tea Party who lived by aphorism only.[36]

Liberal-leaning television programs and progressive-minded websites found a perverse pleasure in their regular mockery of Republican failures to convey the American historical experience accurately. This proved especially true in representations of the founders, whose intellectual attainments were celebrated by both political parties equally, but who were hailed as demigods more often by conservatives.

The Tea Party darling Glenn Beck was a primary target of the Left.

He owned a pulpit on Fox TV News and sounded off nightly against the Obama administration. Early in 2010, Beck was pumped up about the ongoing "war on terror," when he launched into a militaristic history lecture: "I mean, if you're going to mess with us, we're going to pound you," he blared. "Thomas Jefferson created the Marines for the Islamic pirates that were happening, right?" His guest of the moment nodded, which elicited the following: "And so they didn't take any guff. But they weren't spreading democracy. Progressives spread democracy and gooey goodness."

Beck was especially fond of Thomas Paine, a fighter for social justice whom he somehow imagined a patron saint for modern criticism of government social programs. At the same time, he was nauseated over the "gooey-goodness" spread by the income-taxing Woodrow Wilson. Beck adopted the freedom-fighter Thomas Jefferson as a model for vigilance whose rhetorical power Obama aimed to match— aiming wide.

One problem with Beck's invective-laden political analyses was a highly selective reading of the founders' texts. He erred in essential facts, and conflated them easily. To take, as examples, the statements quoted above: (1) the U.S. Marines were created at the start of the Revolution, long before Jefferson took office; and (2) they were called up in the late 1790s by John Adams, when the presumptive enemy was France, not the Barbary powers. Beck's "Islamic pirates" of Jefferson's time were interested in enriching themselves, not in spreading any kind of pan-Islamic agenda that could be seen as the precursor to twenty-first-century terrorism.[37]

Tea Party chauvinism proclaimed its "love of freedom" and "love of country," but also a deep resentment toward comprehensive federal programs and the very idea of federal authority. One elected official who captured Glenn Beck's interest was former Alaska governor Sarah Palin, a onetime beauty pageant contestant who spoke of "fresh ideas for the future" without enumerating them, and whose public speeches featured unabashed boasts of "America's greatness." When she was chosen by Arizona senator John McCain to join the Republican ticket in 2008, the erstwhile governor provided an extended moment of excitement for a political party in need of reinvigoration; but she soon proved a liability, in no small measure owing to her slippery engagement with the lessons of history.

In her ghostwritten post-campaign biography, *Going Rogue,* the shrill-sounding headliner accused CBS interviewer Katie Couric of being rude when the University of Virginia–trained reporter asked:

"What newspapers and magazines did you regularly read?" And when she visited Boston's Old North Church, Palin stuttered her way through a recapitulation of Paul Revere's ride: "He warned the British that they weren't gonna be taking away our arms, by ringin' those bells and making sure, as he's riding his horse through town that we were going to be secure and we were going to be free." Among her hordes of fans, some tried to provide cover by reworking the Wikipedia entry for Paul Revere in order to reflect her version of a galloping Revere "sounding his warning shots."

Millions saw her as a godsend. When Glenn Beck scored a prime-time interview with Palin, advertised with a Jefferson-accented visual labeled "Refounding America," he spoke softly and fawningly, as the two of them each wondered aloud who "the next George Washington" might be. It was as though the Tea Party was waiting for the return of a political messiah. Beck: "Who is your favorite founding father?" Palin: "Well, all of them, because they came together . . . collectively, they came together to form this Union, and they were led by, of course, George Washington." Vagueness was okay, as long as it sounded patriotic and the messenger could deliver it spiritedly.

In 2010, at a star-studded gala in New York, put on by Time, Inc., the "100 most influential people" of the year were feted. Palin and Beck were high on the list. That evening, as she faced the gaffe-attuned reporters, she delivered an ironic toast "to all at this press event who agree with Thomas Jefferson, who said that our liberty depends on the freedom of the press." She hit the high notes of Tea Party hero worship with: "I want to lift a glass to those who defend that freedom. Our finest, the men and women in uniform who defend that freedom, our Constitution, and our exceptional way of life in America."[38]

No ideology so captured the minds of Beck, Palin, and enthusiastic patriots across the political spectrum as a belief in American exceptionalism—the idea, rooted in principles Jefferson set forth in the Declaration of Independence, that the United States of America has held the moral high ground throughout its history as the ultimate repository of liberty and storehouse of exportable values. "President Obama and the Left hate American Exceptionalism," declared former Speaker of the House Newt Gingrich of Georgia in promoting his 2011 book *A Nation Like No Other: Why American Exceptionalism Matters.* Gingrich (with his writing partner) wrote thickly and with condescension, saying that Obama "simply does not understand this concept." The Left was defeatist, declared Gingrich, and all too ready to abandon the principles bequeathed by Jefferson's generation. It was, after all, Jefferson who declared America "the world's best hope" in his first inaugural address. Gingrich's corollary was: we don't have to treat other nations as equals, and whoever shows respect to un-American countries is un-American himself.[39]

Gingrich's treatment of President Obama was rich in irony, and his celebration of Jefferson a bit odd. The foundation created by Gingrich and his third wife named the Thomas Jefferson Foundation (Monticello) its "Charity of the Month" in July 2011. The nonprofit institution the Gingriches so appreciated was reimagining the slave quarters on Mulberry Row—the wooden cabins, long since dismantled, just below Jefferson's stately mansion. The same Thomas Jefferson Foundation officially acknowledged the biracial Hemingses as a part of the Monticello family, and had rewritten the official tour to give the house servants their due. And yet, running for the Republican presidential nomination in 2011–12, Gingrich was the candidate of angry white people who decried race-mixing, and insisted that nonwhites were overindulged and just needed to work harder.[40]

The disconnect was obvious. Gingrich railed at Obama and the Left for failing to appreciate American exceptionalism. But did *he*? Wasn't the election of a biracial president—raised by a single mother and her middle-class parents from the American heartland—yet another signal achievement of American exceptionalism? Wasn't the unprecedented success of this hardworking, public service–oriented citizen a decisive exhibition of the American Dream and the principles of liberty and equality that Thomas Jefferson espoused? How could Gingrich have failed to celebrate such an event, instead of seeing in the undeserving Obama a "hatred" of American values?

The *St. Louis Post-Dispatch* columnist Kevin Horrigan pointed out the absurdity of the various poses adopted by Gingrich and fellow conservative Rick Santorum of Pennsylvania, as the two vied for the GOP nomination in 2012. These well-educated Washington insiders felt obliged to deny their own pedigree while castigating the "elitist" president and his "phony" overeducated abettors, who would "rob" Americans of their vaunted freedoms. "Was there ever an American more elitist than Thomas Jefferson," Horrigan taunted, "the smartest man in every room, a sociophobe intellectual who imported books and wine by the case from France? Jefferson revered the common man, but only from a distance." What made competence objectionable? the columnist asked. How would we be better off electing a president whose intellectualism was on a par with our most ordinary next-door neighbor, or that scene-stealing "hockey mom" Sarah Palin?[41]

The hostile nature of Gingrich's language betrayed his Tea Party constituency's confused logic. As their numbers grew, their grasp of history foundered. The confrontational Gingrich campaigned in New Hampshire after the appearance of his book, and a voter asked him how the founders who grew hemp would have regarded the possession of illegal drugs. "I think Jefferson and George Washington would strongly discourage you from growing marijuana," the candidate bombastically replied, "and their tactics to stop you would be more violent than they would be today." More violent?[42]

Upholding a resilient political system was never the Right's plan. Rather, it aimed to resist, to subvert, to demonize a duly elected president, by imagining him a radical, radically dangerous to America. Tea Party activists organized to overthrow the system that had produced a president with a Kenyan surname; as they did so, they professed an intuitive understanding of the founders' intent. At the end of Obama's first year in office, the Tea Party appealed, in the vaguest of terms, for "commonsense principles" and "commonsense solutions" to complex problems.

Resentment plus noise equaled the Tea Party in 2010. A newly emergent "outsider interest" was buoyed by calls for those untainted by Washington-style politics to step up and lead. Speaking at the National Tea Party Convention in Nashville, in February of that year, Sarah Palin embraced a "ground-up call to action," decrying the administration for being "out of touch and out of date," and routinely in violation of the Constitution. With a logic that only the faithful truly understood, the movement that Beck, Palin, and a loose-lipped gang of would-be congressmen spearheaded saw in the historic Jefferson a man of the people whose "love of country" mirrored theirs. He belonged to the age of giants. A Revolutionary vocabulary—self-evident truths—made him an eternal watchdog on behalf of the disquieted freedom-lovers who stood united to resist tyranny; this was a tyranny that emanated from professional politicians who ignored "the people" at their own electoral peril.[43]

It wasn't enough just to have a Jefferson who fought government spending in the manner of Ronald Reagan. Now, Jefferson had to embrace every value that the long excluded (as they dubbed themselves) were looking to bring back. With the Tea Party's political takeover of Republican talking points in advance of the 2010 midterm elections, traditional supporters of the GOP bent over backward to express sincere interest in the populist insurgency. The Weekly Standard posed the question this way: "Does the Tea Party draw on long-standing American constitutional, political, and economic traditions, eddies of thought that one can trace back to James Madison, Thomas Jefferson, and Andrew Jackson? Or is it of more recent vintage? Are the Tea Partiers simply the same folks who once were called Reagan Democrats?" According to this excited rumination, their "strength" derived from their identification with the founding era; they stood for the Tenth Amendment and against "out-of-control spending" in Washington; they were known to "devour" books on Thomas Jefferson and Samuel Adams. They regarded the Constitution as a direct offspring of the Declaration of Independence, and the Bill of Rights as the culmination of it all.

In this instance, the *Weekly Standard* was not providing the complete picture. Lest it be thought that orthodox Hamiltonians welcomed the Tea Party movement with open arms, we need to remind ourselves that populism in any political era is a hard sell for conservative intellectuals. The Tea Party challenge was a challenge not just to liberals but also to Republicans who were more comfortable with the Wall Street crowd that came to the party in BMWs than they were with country-music enthusiasts who drove up in pickup trucks. Republican intellectuals had to mask their urbanity in courting the Tea Partiers. To defeat congressional Democrats, they did so.[44]

It was in the summer of 2010 that the Tea Party caucus was launched in the House by outspoken Minnesota congresswoman Michele Bachmann, another whose allusions to historical events were constantly challenged. (She famously claimed that the founders succeeded in putting an end to slavery.) As the 112th Congress convened in January 2011, the Tea Party caucus gathered steam—mainly in the House, but with a modicum of support in the Senate. Its importance was recognized by the Republican leadership with a ritualized reading of the Constitution on the floor of the House for the first time in history.

Predominantly white, united in their anger toward Obama, and banking on the shock value of their message, Tea Party caucus members made antipathy toward big government the centerpiece of founding-era thinking. Among their number, none invoked the name of Thomas Jefferson so often in speeches as Texas Republican Ted Poe. On that day in January, he expressed his conviction that President Obama's signature piece of legislation, the Affordable Care Act, or Obamacare (passed in 2010), was an unconstitutional government takeover. The stated purpose behind the president's initiative was to insure millions who could not afford insurance, and to reduce the growth in health-care costs generally. But Representative Poe saw things differently: "Congress must repeal this totalitarian act," he charged.[45]

Ted Poe thanked Jefferson for stating in the preamble to his Declaration that human dignity was the gift of God, not government. He opened another speech by reciting Jefferson's "tyranny over the mind of man" quote; and when Somali pirates were on the prowl in the Indian Ocean, he lionized the third president as a man of his word: "Jefferson sent a clear message to the Barbary states and their pirates: don't mess with the United States. And they didn't for 200 years. The Somalian pirates should study a little American history. . . . Thomas Jefferson destroyed them. We will see what happens now." In 2012, the *Washington Post* reported that Congressman Poe had finally gone too far, and that in his urgency to locate Jeffersonian support for his stand against the welfare state, Poe had cited Jefferson saying something Jefferson never said: "The democracy will cease to exist when you take away from those that are willing to work and give to those who are not." The quote had actually come from an encyclopedic text of 1986, authored by one "John Galt," a name lifted from Ayn Rand's fictional libertarian hero.[46]

House Democrats did not let the co-optation of Jefferson proceed entirely without comment. In the spring of 2011, in response to the Republicans' attempt to "own" the federal Constitution, Congressman Mike Quigley, a Chicago Democrat, rose to criticize what he labeled the Right's "misguided . . . fundamentalism." "The Constitution is our national charter," he began his speech. "It protects our basic freedoms, it grants power to the government, and puts limits on those powers." But it was "a first draft of liberty," he stressed, and not a perfect document composed by perfect men; it included, for instance, a provision that fugitive slaves were to be captured and returned to their owners. "We should talk a lot about the Constitution," Quigley proceeded, "but we should talk about it the right way. . . . The Framers deliberately used broad, open-ended language because they wanted their words to be read flexibly as times changed. Freedom of speech, due process of law—these terms don't define themselves."

In offering a progressive interpretation, and pointing out the problem of "collective amnesia about our past mistakes," Quigley drew on the expansive letter Jefferson wrote to Samuel Kercheval in 1816, and closed his remarks with a pertinent quote from the letter: "Some men look at constitutions with sanctimonious reverence and deem them like the ark of the covenant, too sacred to be touched. Let us follow no such examples, nor weakly believe that one generation is not as capable of taking care of itself, and ordering its own affairs."[47]

While the Republican Party of 2012 continued to invoke Jefferson's limited government mantra, its eventual standard-bearer in that year's presidential contest made his hundreds of millions in the manner Jefferson most abhorred. Mitt Romney was a risk-prone financial speculator who bought, stripped, and sold businesses to which he felt no enduring attachment, with only one goal in mind: rewarding investors like himself. All perfectly legal. His running mate, Wisconsin congressman Paul Ryan, had come to the public's attention as a budget specialist, championing limited government by reducing federal expenditures on health care and education, and gradually privatizing Social Security.

Ryan reserved most of his Jefferson comments for campaign stops in the swing state of Virginia. Speaking at a rally in Roanoke in August 2012, he scored points with vintage lines that exemplified America's national self-image: "We want to be an independent, free people" and "We want to live in our communities where we're free to take care of one another, to help each other in our communities." Which led directly to: "Thomas Jefferson, he said it so beautifully. There's— you can't top these words—the idea of America is so precious. We're the only country founded on an idea. And that idea is basically this: our rights as individuals, they come from nature and God, not from government. [APPLAUSE] That's the American idea. That's who we are." Jefferson's name was enough, automatically associated with the watchwords "liberty" and "freedom," and the sanctifying idea that "independence" pertained to individuals as well as the collective national consciousness. Just not to "government programs."[48]

IN DIVIDED America, "life, liberty, and the pursuit of happiness" resonates differently across the political spectrum. In 2013, a group of antigovernment purists announced their plan to construct a spacious utopian community in northern Idaho called the Citadel. Its website projected a population of thousands, and promised "an affordable, safe, well-prepared, patriotic community," without property taxes, abundantly armed, and founded on "Thomas Jefferson's ideal of Rightful Liberty." To the promoters of the Citadel, Jefferson could be boiled down to suspicion of government tyranny, along with the same requirement to which Boston-area Minutemen were held in 1775: proficiency with firearms. Evidently reflecting a similar conception of the founder's intent, the rural region along the California-Oregon border (centered in Siskiyou County) also amped up its anti-Washington gun-rights talk in 2013, as part of a local secessionist movement that dated to 1941, when the would-be breakaway state was first given the name of "Jefferson." In some quarters, then, small-government Jefferson was *never* at peace with FDR's big-government Jefferson.[49]

Thomas Jefferson has been a part of every dramatic moment in American history. With unintended irony quite typical of Jefferson's pose, he wrote to a Virginia planter and state legislator: "I wish to avoid all collisions of opinions with all mankind." Leaving office at the conclusion of two conflict-filled terms, he protested that his studious nature had intended him "for the tranquill pursuits of science," and only "the enormities of the times" had compelled him "to commit myself on the boisterous ocean of political passions." Overspreading American history from his day to ours is one incontrovertible truth: our national politics is almost always boisterous and impassioned.[50]

The Obama era is, of course, no exception. Dramatic speech and extreme solutions have flowed from the Jefferson-loving Right. The Left's earlier complacency when it came to "ownership" of Thomas Jefferson may be one reason why he has receded somewhat from his once commanding place in Democratic discourse; second, with his commitment to human rights deemed defective, the gap between golden rhetoric and historical reality widened to the point at which the entire concept of "greatness" had to be challenged. Seen through the liberal lens, Jefferson, once clearly envisioned, has gone out of focus.

Meanwhile, traditional Republicans have remained consistent, regarding Jefferson as he was on his best day—July 4, 1776—when he metaphorically stood up, speaking to the world in a strong voice, and announced a new nation conceived in liberty. For old-style conservatives, he remains in the pantheon of spiritual fathers who "grounded" the United States in the values it has consistently tried to uphold: a safe and secure, reasonable, family-oriented, and fairly homogeneous moral community.

Tea Party enthusiasts are an entirely separate breed. As reluctant Republicans, they embraced Jefferson's radical individualism in ways that went beyond the dictates of conventional patriotism. Their Jefferson encompasses the pure populism of the grassroots, the identity Americans once drew from the rustic, homely, boastful, defiantly confrontational Andrew Jackson image. For Tea Partiers, Jefferson belongs to the vernacular, and to a new-fashioned political moralism that combines a belief in exceptionalism with belief in the power of self-expression—even if that self-expression is disconnected from either social responsibility or actual historical experience.

PART TWO

Culture Wars

5

"MISERY ENOUGH, BUT NO POETRY"
Race and the Remaking of a Symbol

ON OCTOBER 18, 1945, six months after the death of Franklin Roosevelt, Congresswoman Helen Gahagan Douglas of California challenged her colleagues on a question of national self-definition: what, in moral terms, did the United States stand for? The subject on her mind was racial justice, and she made her case by reciting the most famous section of the Declaration of Independence.

The former Broadway star and Hollywood actress, wife of the popular actor and enlisted man Melvyn Douglas, was an Eleanor Roosevelt liberal and an intimate of the young Texas Democrat Lyndon Johnson. Ronald Reagan had endorsed her for office. She did not know what to make of Harry Truman, and as yet had very mixed feelings about the unintended president's decision to drop the atomic bomb on Japan. "This new age demands of us an entirely new concept of our responsibilities toward one another," she prodded House members. "These responsibilities must be based fundamentally on a fully Christian, moral attitude."

The congresswoman had decided it was time to revive the issue of the African American vocalist Marian Anderson. Before Pearl Harbor, the contralto had been barred from performing at Constitution Hall, which the Daughters of the American Revolution (DAR) operated, tax-free, under a federal exemption. First Lady Eleanor Roosevelt withdrew her membership in the organization over the incident, and arranged for Anderson to give an outdoor concert at the Lincoln Memorial. It was an act of moral conviction that Douglas did not want forgotten.

With the war over, a new era in civil rights advocacy was about to begin. Although it was her first year as a member of Congress, Douglas was not one to sheepishly follow the lead of others in the male-dominated body. That autumn day, she proposed that the national legislature withdraw the tax-exempt status of the DAR if it continued to bar commercial use of its premises on the basis of "race, creed, color, or national origin." Detailing for the record how her grandmother Hannah, a longtime DAR member, regaled her with the story of Crispus Attucks, a man of color who died in the Boston Massacre of 1770 at the hands of the British, the congresswoman broadened the definition of patriotism to encompass every individual associated with the historic fight for liberty. And she did not stop there. "Freedom is not won on the battlefields," Douglas insisted. "The *chance* for freedom is won there. The final battle is won or lost in our hearts and minds."

As outraged as she was by racist rule, Douglas was not impossibly idealistic. "We cannot legislate equality," she acknowledged. Yet she did think it possible to legislate equal opportunity. If the most powerful nation in the world was "indivisible, with liberty and justice for all," she said, then Thomas Jefferson's words in the Declaration of Independence had to be taken literally. "We hold these truths," she recited, and did not stop until she was done with the preamble. There was no doubt in her mind what the modern meaning of "all men are created equal" should be.[1]

The civil rights era would usher in critical new understandings, but the 1950s and 1960s did not constitute the first period in U.S. history when rights discourse forced a reexamination of Jefferson and his fellow founders. Revolutionary values always sounded less universal and the transcendent geniuses of 1776 and 1787 less pure or prophetic whenever a substantial part of the population was shown to be artificially held back and implicitly deemed unequal.

A century earlier, it was a tireless generation of women's-rights activists who exposed the founders' limitations. They called conventions, and replicated in such widely divergent towns as Worcester, Massachusetts, and Salem, Ohio, the famed Convention of 1787 in Philadelphia. Delegates to these latter-day conventions argued for gender coequality on the basis of Jefferson's foundational example. The supposition of male chivalry and the assumption of female political incompetence had, they said, divested female citizens of essential rights and legal protections. The 1848 Declaration of Rights, promulgated in Seneca Falls, New York, rephrased Jefferson's preamble to read, "all men *and women* are created equal."

At the same time as the women in Seneca Falls were challenging tradition, abolitionists, male and female, white and black, held that the slave's right to an independent life constituted nothing less than a struggle for the soul of America. Jefferson himself had used the combination "human rights" when he announced an end to the slave trade in his last year as president. But on July 4, 1852, Frederick Douglass, the best-remembered of the abolitionists today, delivered an oration titled "What to the Slave Is the Fourth of July?" His answer was stinging: "a sham." He shamed his audience: "Your boasted liberty, an unholy license; your national greatness, swelling vanity; your sounds of rejoicing are empty and heartless; your denunciations of tyrants, brass fronted impudence; your shouts of liberty and equality, hollow mockery."[2]

FREDERICK Augustus Bailey took the name Douglass from the hero of an adventure story. The actress Helen Gahagan took the name Douglas when she married. But they have something else in common: they lit fires when they spoke out.

If symbols mean something, then we should linger a moment or two longer in the year 1945, as Congresswoman Douglas began her term. The nation was still reeling over the death of its fatherly leader, who had been elected and reelected four times, and had now joined Jefferson and Lincoln among hard-nosed politician-presidents who, in death, became something more: advocates of unrestricted human advancement. On the eve of World War II, FDR had established by executive order the Fair Employment Practices Committee, which effectively ended racially discriminatory hiring in the federal government. It was a start, but merely that. The armed forces remained segregated.

Another symbol of historic dimensions takes us beyond the institutional and deeper into the soul of a separated citizenry. It is the moment of somber transition from Roosevelt to Truman, preserved in an iconic photograph most have seen, which captured a sobbing black accordionist mourning a president's death. The image of Graham Washington Jackson that graced the cover of the ever-popular *Life* magazine was not that of a generic African American, but rather a Virginia-born Georgian who had more than once played for Franklin and Eleanor Roosevelt. In the pain-filled photo, the musician performed a dirge as the president's funeral train left Warm Springs, Georgia.

In April 1945, President Roosevelt was composing the Jefferson's birthday speech he would never deliver, when the Associated Negro Press ran the headline: "Remember Thomas Jefferson Prophet of Democracy and a Great Foe of Slavery." It stated, erroneously, that "Thomas Jefferson was a lifelong anti-slavery man," and pinpointed his statement in *Notes on Virginia:* "Nothing is more certainly written in the book of fate than that these people are to be free." One of the panels inside the Jefferson Memorial contained this line—and what could be more authoritative?

The author of the retrospective piece, a minister, hoped that history would uphold the progressive narrative: "One clearly sees in Jefferson's writings a background for Abraham Lincoln's philosophy." His perspective was in line with the historiography of this era: In *Thomas Jefferson, World Citizen,* Elbert Thomas included a chapter on the scourge of slavery, highlighting Jefferson's "high moral sense" as a courageous slavery opponent, and writing that "the force of his logic became the driving force of a nation which finally freed its slaves." For his argument, Senator Thomas drew heavily on the opinion of a distinguished soldier, Brigadier General Jefferson Randolph Kean, a Jefferson descendant who took pains to emphasize Lincoln's appreciation for the "Jeffersonian policy of attack on slavery." As rosy about Lincoln as they were about Jefferson, a host of writers, black and white, overlooked Lincoln's long-held preference for the solution Jefferson always had in mind: recolonization of America's freed slaves beyond the country's borders.[3]

It may seem perverse that substantial numbers of African Americans were given to praising slave-owning founders at the end of the Roosevelt era. Professional historians today would pounce on their misreading of Jefferson, who, simply stated, did not at any time in his career resist or reject the slave economy. He certainly never envisioned black liberation in any modern sense of the term. What he wrote of, he wrote of fearfully: enduring black-white antagonisms, the prospect of race war. To his credit, he did recognize the violence of thought that transgenerational enslavement had produced.

Of course, there were many cruder, less sensitive white supremacists than the master of Monticello, so it is not easy to pass final judgment on the eighteenth-century man who tempered his "scientific" musings about African inferiority with the common rationalization that one who inherited his human property could yet be a good master by providing well. There were those, like Jefferson, who considered their thought liberal and enlightened when they contemplated, over the long haul, an exchange of unfree African laborers for European peasants. This dream presumed that the process of recolonization (i.e., whitening the population) would carry forward.

Jefferson philosophized about rights in a measured way, that is, measured by the norms of his age. We learn the most about his thought process by regarding how he wrote about blacks' diminished capacity for cultural improvement. He demeaned free blacks in ways that were entirely gratuitous: "Among the blacks is misery enough, God knows, but no poetry. Love is the peculiar oestrum of the poet. Their love is ardent, but it kindles the senses only, not the imagination."

Here we are introduced to the remarkable lexicon of an eighteenth-century bookworm. The "oestrum," or period of sexual arousal in an animal, is a curious choice of words. Without reading too much into it, Jefferson does not intellectualize as much as corporealize his cultural criticism of blacks, whose natural coloration is "eternal monotony," whose secretions are odorous, and whose bravery only arises from "want of forethought."

The well-published New England slave Phillis Wheatley struck him as too religiously inspired to be any good as an original poet. Ignatius Sancho, freed in England, wrote with too much affectation and too little "head," absent of "reason and taste." And Jefferson could not help but suspect that the Maryland mathematician and almanac author Benjamin Banneker had help from a white person. When Virginians Madison and Jefferson traveled in upstate New York, Madison complimented a skilled black farmer. Jefferson never committed any such thought to paper. He did not like his established beliefs to be challenged, and resisted evidence of free blacks' attainments.[4]

Jefferson subscribed, then, to a flawed taxonomy of humankind that he did not invent but that he bought into easily. He left us with an unambiguous defense of natural inequality and racial separation. But it is too simple, and simply wrong, to mark Jefferson as a monster. If we acknowledge the obvious—that perfect social equality has never existed in America—it follows that each generation is equally subject to future historians' judgment. He was not greatly different from the majority of southern slaveholders, true. And to the north, Alexander Hamilton and Supreme Court Chief Justice John Jay, leading members of the New York Manumission Society, were not above owning household slaves, either. Indeed, as the historian Shane White has explained, fully one-half of the society's members were slave owners, "genteel and paternalistic," conservative rather than abolitionist. The African Free School they established was designed to keep free blacks "from running into practices of immorality."[5]

It is not hard to understand why it is that Jefferson bears the brunt of modern criticism for the general failure of elected leaders to find a humane way to end slavery. He committed to paper more explicit meditations on race than others of his celebrated time cared to do.

That the author of the Declaration of Independence was a slave owner makes his hypocrisy all the more conspicuous. He sacrificed little on behalf of the oppressed.

Jefferson has always been a lightning rod. The range of his correspondents was great and global. He was, then, as he is now, eminently quotable; and the moral element in his writing struck his contemporaries as it strikes us. That is why Douglass and Douglas invoked the Declaration.

THOMAS JEFFERSON is the irresistible starting point for discussions of American content and discontent alike, for all the reasons given above. The problem this book chronicles, the politics of memory, finds expression in the subjectivity of those in public life who extract quotes from historic texts and apply them loosely to modern, or momentary, concerns. It is a problem that goes well beyond Jefferson's blemished stand on slavery and racial difference.

In any generation, self-defense can become self-delusion. Americans have harmed themselves, if unthinkingly, over the years, by holding up the nation's founders as a league of inspired nation builders unsurpassed in wisdom, instead of encountering them as the interest-conscious politicians they actually were. Roosevelt-era Jeffersonians employed the stirring language of liberty to conciliate an anxious and aggrieved people amid crisis. The era's Jeffersonian message offered blanket assurance that Revolutionary ideals were being revived, and that government was attuned to the just needs of all. Clearly, the African American press at the end of World War II was not alone in succumbing to Jefferson's brightest notions. It was not yet time to see Jefferson in any less refulgent light.

"All men are created equal." The grandest of all political metaphors was reworked for the umpteenth time at the 1948 Democratic National Convention in Philadelphia, when Harry Truman's vice-president-to-be, Senator Alben Barkley of Kentucky, channeled the best Jefferson imaginable in his keynote address:

> He did not proclaim that all white, or black, or red, or yellow men are equal; that all Christian or Jewish men are equal; that all Protestant and Catholic men are equal; that all rich or poor men are equal; that all good or bad men are equal. What he declared was that all men are equal.

Barkley, popularly known as "Veep," borrowed the ethic of Helen Douglas when he pronounced that the "free world" was increasingly "being challenged by the world of slavery. For us to play our part effectively, we must be in a morally sound position." Warning against a moral double standard, he identified the religious sentiment underlying his vision of broad social betterment: "We are God-fearing men and women. We place our faith in the brotherhood of man under the fatherhood of God." And then, this ultra-liberal senator got to the political reality of the moment: "There are those who say this issue of civil rights is an infringement on states' rights. The time has arrived for the Democratic Party to get out of the shadow of states' rights and walk forthrightly into the bright sunshine of human rights." Yes, he really was talking about the germinating seeds of the civil rights movement.

President Truman had okayed Barkley's language. It was Truman, in fact, who in late 1946 had appointed the Civil Rights Commission, and he welcomed its 1947 report, *We Hold These Truths*, which came out in favor of domestic legislation to right the wrongs of the past. Early in 1948, the president called for the creation of a Civil Rights Division within the Department of Justice, as he spoke to the nation of the promise contained in Jefferson's Declaration: "We believe that all men are created equal and that they have the right to equal justice under law. . . . We believe that all men are entitled to equal opportunities for jobs, for homes, for good health and for education." It was a bold beginning.[6]

At the stately Waldorf Astoria in Manhattan on April 11, 1948, the Council Against Intolerance in America presented the "Thomas Jefferson Award for the Advancement of Democracy" to Jackie Robinson, the Brooklyn Dodgers infielder and 1947 Rookie of the Year who had integrated Major League Baseball. Next came desegregation of the Armed Forces. Yet when the Minnesota senatorial candidate Hubert Humphrey attempted to include the integration issue in the 1948 Democratic Party platform, he shocked party regulars who were seeking to avert a convention walkout by southern Democrats.[7]

It was the year of the Dixiecrats. South Carolina senator Strom Thurmond splintered the Democratic Party and ran as a third-party candidate on a platform of white supremacy. Southerners had already boycotted the Jefferson-Jackson Day dinner that year, with one Alabama delegate threatening to make a stink at the convention. He repeated Jefferson's "tree of liberty" quote menacingly, as he vowed that "no southern jury would convict an employer for refusing to take a Negro into his white office force." Then, after Truman's victory, two hundred concerned citizens from across the South gathered at Monticello to discuss a course of action on behalf of civil rights. Monticello was chosen because of the words in Jefferson's Declaration, and Jefferson's ready association with "the idea of brotherhood" across cultures.

In 1950, the University of Virginia School of Law admitted its first African American student, Gregory Swanson. His suit to obtain admission was assisted by none other than Thurgood Marshall, the successful civil rights attorney who would become the first African American to sit on the Supreme Court. Yet, most tellingly, Swanson left UVA after only one year as a result of the hostile racial climate he faced. He was not even permitted to live on university grounds.[8]

Also at midcentury, five years after her dramatic statement on the House floor, Helen Gahagan Douglas ran for the U.S. Senate against Richard M. Nixon. In a sign of nasty politics to come, she was torn apart by the up-and-coming Republican for her softness—for qualities that made her susceptible to communist come-ons. It was during this campaign that the future vice president and president earned his nickname "Tricky Dick," as his female opponent was branded "pink right down to her underwear."

If a promising political career was brought to an end that year, it was equally clear that Helen Douglas's Christian approach to racial justice had found adherents. Harry Truman, once ambivalent, was now onboard. And just a few years later, the Reverend Dr. Martin Luther King would come to prominence, and momentously recast the Revolutionaries' message concerning human equality.[9]

Jefferson's solid reputation among black-owned newspapers persisted into the tumultuous 1960s. He was frequently praised for having attempted to incorporate antislavery language into the Declaration. In the uncommonly contentious election year of 1968, amid mourning for the slain Dr. King, the *Milwaukee Star* spread the word that the "key to black power" was to register to vote. Beneath a drawing of an old-fashioned ballot box was a Jefferson quote: "I know no safe depository of the ultimate powers of society but the people themselves; and if we think them not enlightened enough to exercise their control with a wholesome discretion, the remedy is not to take it from them but to inform their discretion by education."

These lines are especially curious because, unlike most Jefferson quotes of the period, they were drawn from an obscure letter to one William Charles Jarvis in September 1820. The letter was part and parcel of Jefferson's critique of the partisanship of unelected judges. He was writing at the same time that he felt passionately about the rights of states to determine how they dealt with the future of slavery. That's the Jefferson who irritates researchers, the one who won't be pinned down.

Also in 1968, the same Milwaukee paper reviewed a new book about the founders, in the course of which the reviewer elevated Jefferson above Lincoln, owing to his "ardent" abolitionism. But 1968 was a most volatile year, as witnessed by Eldridge Cleaver's thunderous *Soul on Ice,* which raged against the oppressive white regime as its author sat behind bars and fantasized having sex with white women. An edited collection called *The Black Power Revolt* was published that year, too. It opened with the eloquent appeal from the free black Benjamin Banneker to then secretary of state Thomas Jefferson, an urgent call to make the phrase "all men are created equal" credible. Jefferson's reply to Banneker was a poor, placating whisper by comparison—which was the apparent subtext in 1968 as the editor proceeded to lay out a modern concept of black empowerment.[10]

Despite the headlines and the marches and the stated resolve expressed by a host of outspoken leaders, America was playing a long game of catch-up. While the Thomas Jefferson Foundation, skilled caretakers of Monticello, had always been sensitive to Jefferson's complicity in a hated institution, Monticello did not address the lives of the plantation's slaves in significant detail until the mid-1980s. At that point, staff undertook archaeological work on Mulberry Row, the section of the mountaintop where a number of Jefferson's slave cabins stood; the word *slave* replaced the softer-sounding *servant* in guides' descriptions of Jefferson's unfree workforce; and the Visitors Center exhibit displayed information about (and later photos of) slave descendants. By the 1990s, Monticello's interactive "slave-life tour" was generating positive conversation. In the words of Daniel P. Jordan, executive director of the Thomas Jefferson Foundation from 1985 to 2008: "The premise was straightforward: to understand Jefferson, one had to understand slavery. . . . To understand Monticello, one had to understand the Monticello slave community."[11]

ROBERT H. COOLEY III, the son of a civil rights attorney, was the first African American to be appointed a magistrate judge within Virginia's federal district court system. In 1993, he was an invited guest at a special Monticello-sponsored banquet that was attended by the former Soviet leader Mikhail Gorbachev, who gave the keynote address on the lawn at the University of Virginia on the occasion of Jefferson's 250th birthday, and praised Jefferson as an influence on his own reform agenda.

The reason Bob Cooley was part of the celebration actually had little to do with his attainments in the law. It had more to do with a claim he had made that the Thomas Jefferson Foundation chose to take seriously. Cooley had good reason to believe that he was a descendant of Jefferson and his slave Sally Hemings, and that the two had maintained a wholesome, loving relationship for more than three decades. In 1954, a short piece in the popular black magazine *Ebony* had highlighted the founder's "Negro grandchildren," establishing the fact that among black and white Americans there existed markedly different views of Thomas Jefferson's historical personality. In 1961, an article in the *Journal of Negro History* contended similarly. So Bob Cooley was by no means alone in his conviction.[12]

There was at least one white chronicler of all things Jefferson who took an unusual interest in the 1954 *Ebony* feature. With an open mind, John Dos Passos initiated a correspondence with, among others, the premier Jefferson expert, Princeton's Julian Boyd, querying whether anything new had come to light in the matter. Placing the word *descendants* within quotes when referring to African Americans' claims, Boyd informed Dos Passos that Jefferson was "simply too fastidious" to turn to his slaves for "the gratification of an appetite." Black oral history was mistaken. While he would go on to deploy Boyd's argument aggressively in his 1966 book, *The Shackles of Power*, Dos Passos, lecturing at Princeton in 1957, made a particular point of telling his audience: "There were no prudes among the Founding Fathers."[13]

In 1995, two years after the Jefferson 250th anniversary celebration, Bob Cooley recorded an audio interview as part of Monticello's "Getting Word" project. He recalled that at the age of ten, in 1950, he was told by his grandfather that he was a direct descendant of Jefferson and Hemings. He repeated his grandfather's exact words: "You are part of a special family." The connection came through Thomas Woodson (1790–1879), the child Hemings was purported to have conceived in Paris. This would have occurred not long before she and Jefferson and Jefferson's two young daughters sailed home to America, and Jefferson became the first secretary of state. He had, said Cooley, sold his unacknowledged child to a nearby planter named Woodson.

Instructed at a young age that no one in the wider world would believe him if he went around boasting of his blood connection to a founding father, Cooley had preserved the family secret for all these years. The Woodson family history had it that the historic relationship was built on love, "as if Sally were his wife." That morsel, the attorney knew, would not go down well in white America.[14]

Eventually, Bob Cooley broke his silence. From the lawn of Monticello, he went on NBC's *Today Show* on April 13, 1993, the bicentennial of Jefferson's birth. He was interviewed by the program's host, Katie Couric, herself a graduate of "Mr. Jefferson's University."

> Couric: According to oral history, the first offspring of [the Jefferson-Hemings] union was Thomas Woodson, a man who had an uncanny resemblance to Thomas Jefferson, so much so that he was sent away from Monticello. . . . Why do you say that?
>
> Cooley: Because it's true. And it is a result of our global history that's been in our history for over 200 years.

Lucia "Cinder" Stanton, research director at Monticello, was brought into the conversation next. She remained agnostic, because the evidence was as yet inconclusive.

> Couric: There is no written documentation of this liaison or of children being fathered by Thomas Jefferson. What's your take on this?
>
> Stanton: Well, we listen to the oral tradition, five generations of belief in Mr. Cooley's family is very significant. . . . There is very strong belief on the other side of the issue through Jefferson's Randolph descendants. [Jefferson's one long-lived child from his marriage, his daughter Martha, married Thomas Mann Randolph, and bore eleven children.][15]

And so things stood for a time.

Annette Gordon-Reed's 1997 book, *Thomas Jefferson and Sally Hemings: An American Controversy,* constituted a legal scholar's interrogation of historians' assumptions. Gordon-Reed called into question the textual record produced by the Jefferson-Randolph clan; she compared it to the competing African American oral tradition and to the extraordinary published interview of 1873 with Sally Hemings's son Madison.[16]

For most professional historians, absent a DNA solution, the "logical" judgment was to accept the explanations of Jefferson's white grandchildren that their deceased cousins Peter and Samuel Carr were sexually active with Monticello's enslaved, and that one or the other was Sally Hemings's lover. To Professor Gordon-Reed, scholars assumed too much when they disregarded the descendants of slaves and took the self-protective Jeffersons at their word.[17]

It was shortly after President Clinton was sworn in for a second term that Bob Cooley was at a White House gathering in February 1997, as one of the "talking heads" in the Ken Burns PBS documentary

Thomas Jefferson. An abbreviated version of the film was screened for President Clinton, Hillary Rodham Clinton, members of Congress, and dozens of invited guests. After the screening, the president engaged his guests in conversation, expressing interest in the personal life of his namesake. Cooley confidently made his case. Then the president wondered aloud whether Jefferson had remained celibate throughout the last forty-four years of his life, after the death of his wife. Family lore had it that he promised the dying Patty Jefferson in 1782 that he would never remarry.[18]

As the nation subsequently learned, President Clinton was engaged at the time of his reelection in an adulterous relationship with a female intern. When the 1998 DNA test results revealed that a Jefferson male had fathered Eston Hemings, the youngest of Sally's sons (that's as close as DNA could come to definitively establishing Thomas Jefferson's paternity), the press made much of the comparison, in effect asking whether Clinton was looking for "cover" from Jefferson. In his memoir, however, the president wrote that he was focused that fall on the outcome of congressional elections. "I went with Hillary to Cape Canaveral, Florida, to see John Glenn blast into space," he framed this interlude. "The Republican National Committee began a series of television ads attacking me [on moral grounds] . . . , and news reports indicated that, according to DNA tests, Thomas Jefferson had fathered several children with his slave Sally Hemings." The historical revelation was part of what stuck in his mind as he mulled over the midterm elections (the Democrats picked up five seats in the House), with impeachment charges for lying about sex hanging over his head.[19]

That season, the famously contentious Christopher Hitchens, no fan of the sitting president, wrote an invective-filled (if somewhat chaotic) piece for *Salon,* the online journal of politics and culture. It was titled, "What Do Jefferson and Clinton Have in Common (Except Randyness)?" Targeting the president's vocal defenders, Hitchens took offense at the suggestion that blame for both scandals lay with sensationalizers in the press rather than with the carnal power brokers themselves. At the same time, Nancy Isenberg drew a more sober comparison in the *Nation,* observing that the Clinton sex scandal "verges on the pathetic, in part because nothing is left to the imagination. Indeed, if we had all the details of sexual activity at Monticello, we might view Tom and Sally with less nostalgia."[20]

In the wake of Fawn Brodie's scintillating study, Barbara Chase-Riboud's tremendously popular 1979 novel *Sally Hemings,* and the 1995 film *Jefferson in Paris,* there was little nuance possible anymore. With both Clinton and Jefferson, the public had its choice between ogling the male lead and punishing him; between accepting and rejecting the exciting premise of transgressive sex. Even the age difference between the presidents and their paramours was similar: they both had daughters close in years to the forbidden women.

NARRATIVES about sex and the powerful have never fallen out of fashion, beginning with eighteenth-century novels of seduction, and encompassing the class-crossing romances of the nineteenth century. In terms of social taboos and heart-pounding sensation, one could easily argue that these were directly succeeded by the race-centered novels of the twentieth century. In 1961, it was John Howard Griffin's *Black Like Me*, describing a white journalist's experience in the South after a physician helped to temporarily alter his skin pigmentation. In 1976, Alex Haley's blockbuster *Roots* reminded white as well as black Americans that when personal histories are recovered, they can exert a tremendous influence on perceptions of the present.

So, what America had in 1998 was a unique conjunction between an active president's intimate affairs and the rewriting of a historic debate. Both invited satire. And both women, in spite of the newsprint they "earned," doubtless realized that there was nothing empowering for them in having sexual relations with a "great" man. Sally Hemings spent her adult life as Monticello's seamstress, not the mistress of the mansion, or anything close. It is only the lurid imagination of the modern Peeping Tom, snooping from the other side of the TV screen or from a temporal distance, that conjures a message of significance in what amounts to the compartmentalization of sex in men's lives, and continuing subordination for the women concerned. In the late 1990s, renewed attention was being paid to the first published novel by an African American: *Clotel; or, the President's Daughter* (1853) began to pop up in more college literature courses. Its author, William Wells Brown, was a runaway slave who tapped into familiar lore, and made his heroine the mixed-race daughter whom Thomas Jefferson had sold into slavery. No social climbing there, either.[21]

In the final quarter of the twentieth century, then, the mixed-race Sally Hemings became an imaginable alternative to the common portrait of an abused and too infrequently dignified black underclass whose life stories were underdeveloped. After Fawn Brodie, Chase-Riboud's *Sally Hemings* led the way with a heroine, wholly invented, who exhibited her inner strength. The novel's Sally was far more than a servant with benefits; she was a woman with complex thoughts who also had a spine, and who had won the heart of a well-above-average Virginian.

Though advertised as romance, *Sally Hemings* the novel was actually nuanced and psychologically rich, imagining well the unsatisfying reality of slave concubinage. As well, the casting of Thandie Newton, the actress who played Sally in the film *Jefferson in Paris,* was ingenious, even if the silly, ill-informed script converted her into an initially childish, but ultimately self-possessed, artful, and vivacious companion. Newton is British, the product of a white father and African mother—a Shona princess from Zimbabwe. Just twenty-two when she shot the film, she spoke of her experience in school in England, where she was regarded as "dark-skinned"; and of her visits to Africa, where she was thought white. She called herself "an anomaly."[22]

Sally Hemings is anomalous, too. She was an individual held back by her gender, her "one drop" of Negro blood, and her class status as a household servant, despite being the much younger daughter of the wealthy planter John Wayles, whose daughter (by a white wife) was married to Thomas Jefferson from 1772 until her death ten years later. As many have pointed out before, Sally Hemings and Martha (Patty) Jefferson were half sisters. Sally's siblings, nieces, nephews, and cousins were trained in skills necessary to the smooth functioning of a working plantation. Though enslaved, they were privileged and relatively autonomous, certainly in comparison to those who labored in the fields. But like virtually every historical actor who does not play a role in the political life of the nation, their history remained obscure before the 1990s, when the scholarship of Stanton and Gordon-Reed produced a fuller picture of day-to-day reality on Jefferson's estate. Monticello was a stylish dreamworld for its architect because of those who labored for his happiness. As biological relatives, the Hemingses were a parallel, subordinate family living meaningfully in the midst of the white Jefferson-Randolph clan.

Were Americans not obsessed with the need to possess intimate, scandalous details about those they turn into celebrities, we would never have become aware of the existence of the Hemingses. In the late eighteenth century, powerful men of the landed class, slave-owning southern planters, grew up seeing enslaved women of any hue as sexually available. In *Notes on Virginia,* Jefferson famously expressed a generic distaste for the physical qualities of Africanness. But Sally Hemings, three-quarters white, was someone he had always known. The racism in his writings may or may not have accurately reflected his private impulses; either way, it is hard to conceive that she would have been a register of Africanness, as Jefferson would have found nothing generically offensive in the physical person of his deceased wife's half-sister.

Race issues flood the popular media, generally trumping class and gender components of a given situation, thus generating an incomplete understanding. The lesson to take from the experience of Thandie Newton, the onscreen Sally Hemings, is that Western tradition cares most about the male line—almost to the point of distraction. Why else was Barack Obama hounded from the moment he decided to run for president? His merits, or "worthiness," were bound up in the fanciful association his enemies made between an African American president and the Kenyan father who played no actual part in raising him.

It is hard to imagine that Obama's detractors would have been any kinder to him if he had been married to a white woman. Visceral responses, conditioned by inherited social guidelines, come into play here. Yet Thandie Newton (and the historical Sally Hemings?) are not denied assimilable traits when they stand before the white gaze. Look, then, at what society has done: *The undesirable blackness of the male descends to the son, while women of color who have sex with white men are more or less allowed to assimilate.* It is an odd disjunction, and yet another uncomfortable fact about our culture when it comes to the valuation of skin color and reactions to sexual activity.

We should address (at least briefly) the obvious question: How is skin color perceived? As the body's background, the pigmented surface delivers the first impression one person has on sighting another. Before a white person makes the acquaintance of a nonwhite person for the first time, before a word is even uttered and with personalities unknown, awareness of color kicks in. Physiognomy. Hair form. At about the same instant, attractiveness or unattractiveness is considered. It's just how it is. And then we hear how that person talks, and we render a judgment that has racial—and often class—elements attached.

We make assumptions based on surface impressions no matter who it is we are meeting. In the United States of America, by conditioning, a white's encounter with a nonwhite person automatically carries a history of cultural perplexity with it. Long before (and ever since) Jefferson pondered in *Notes on Virginia* whether the "eternal monotony" of that "immovable veil of black" meant more to him than it should, a silent conversation has gone on in the minds of white people that has to do with feeling comfortable.

People with African American ancestors have been "passing" into white society since Jefferson's time, since the Hemingses' time. For many (if not most) who did, they did so without bettering the black condition. Their power was limited to "stealing" their way into whiteness, without fully owning a white identity. As one scholar puts it: "By treating blackness as a damaging secret, those who passed actually showed that their racial identity was an inescapably inferior status." It is meaningful that no one who is one-eighth or one-fourth white has ever been thought other than black, while someone one-fourth or even one-eighth black may be at pains to deny blackness.[23]

Even (or perhaps especially) in an age of "political correctness," when tolerance is positively preached and practiced, setbacks occur and the sordid history of racial preference periodically reemerges in press reports. The idea of a postracial America might be spoken of, as it was in the shockingly brief moment of transition between Barack Obama's election and the activation of the Tea Party, but it is abundantly clear now that the postracial society we desire lies somewhere in the future.

Though consensus lags, the future is coming into focus anyway. The monoracial type is increasingly less common in America's cities and suburbs, a Jeffersonian racial nightmare that has placed the aggressive promoters of white privilege on the political fringe. Outspoken right-wingers insist that the Left, having surrendered to multiculturalism, now engages in a form of blackmail by accusing all who refuse to accept the Jefferson Hemings liaison of being racists.

Owing to the long life of Notes on Virginia, Jefferson has symbolized the cause of depopulating the United States of dark-skinned Africans, and he continues to symbolize the remnant confusion over an outdated term: miscegenation. We are having a psychically charged conversation in the twenty-first century when some nod agreeably (or, at least, unperturbed) and others choose to resist the implications of a Jefferson-Hemings sexual connection.

Even if that resistance is not a passive form of racism, it is still denial. Today, as multiracial Americans achieve an unprecedented level of social prominence, the dynamic that pitted white supremacism against Afrocentric nationalism in the latter decades of the twentieth century collapses. And as standards of purity become irrelevant, those who were once thought of as pioneering cross-racial lovers can now focus more attention on emotional stability within their families instead of implicitly defending their love before a prurient public.[24]

We need to recognize, too, that gradations of color have mattered not only to whites who have historically policed the racial frontier, but also to African Americans. This has been so from at least as far back as the pre–Civil War years, when free black social clubs denied admission to the darker-skinned. In high schools in the 1990s, as the Jefferson-Hemings question received its most dramatic public hearing, black kids were getting into fights over insults traded about color. When one earned higher grades, another would say, "That's because of the white blood in you. You fit right in."

Light skin indicated privilege. In 1994, accused of a double homicide, the football great O. J. Simpson was pictured on the cover of *Time* in a touched-up photograph that artificially darkened his facial features; the public was in an immediate uproar, because he had been made to mirror a stereotypical criminal profile. It is an oft-repeated fact that in white-dominated Hollywood, lighter-skinned black females are more likely to get ahead, and to be seen on-screen, than their darker sisters, because they represent, in the words of a distinguished journalist, "an ethereal region of racial drift." It is all part of that anomaly to which Thandie Newton referred.[25]

History continues to matter. The biracial American (the "tragic mulatto" of nineteenth-century literature) lives on in the modern imagination, and continues to play an important role in American society's unending conversations about purity and degeneration, affinities and repulsions, power and privilege. A series of novels have appeared since the 1990s that feature sexual tension between black women and white men, and white grandparents' concern in having to embrace as family the biracial offspring of these unions. The themes momentously staged in the film *Guess Who's Coming to Dinner* (1967) do not disappear.

The "one-drop rule" that applied to Sally Hemings and her children resonates in various forms of modern media. Characters think they are white who are not quite; half siblings meet, separated by race and uncertain how to define what they are and how they should feel. If copper-colored biracial women of the modern era are "hit on" by white and black men both, and are not as easily welcomed into black women's circles as they'd like, might we not wonder whether Sally Hemings herself identified more with white culture or with slave culture? As a "mighty near white" quadroon with privileges, did she chiefly identify with her family's socioeconomic position as she was growing up, as seems quite possible; or was she constantly hampered by the impossibility of forgetting that as a woman born into slavery, she would bear slave children, by law? This scenario would seem equally possible. We don't know, and that is why her story is foundational, and can be reworked again and again.[26]

It matters, too, that the never-pictured Sally Hemings is (and in literature always was) imagined as physically alluring. As the pages of fashion magazines and the world of entertainment are today proving, biracial beauty is greatly elevated in elite circles. In 2002, the light-skinned Halle Berry (white mother, African American father) was the first woman of color to receive a Best Actress Oscar. Winning the 1997 Master's at the age of twenty-one, the multiracial Tiger Woods (Thai/African American/Chinese/Dutch/Native American) emerged as golf's ultimate superstar. Indeed, it can be argued that no one so clearly embodies the multiracial future of America from an early-twenty-first-century perspective as Woods. By 2050, it is said, at least one in five U.S. citizens will be racially mixed.

Americans are proving that as much as they need fictions to celebrate the imagined past, they need fictions that take them out of that past. It explains, again, why the "Tom and Sally" story, with its dramatic revitalization in the late 1990s, was useful in bringing out the primal struggle over acceptance of racial reality. *Tom and Sally: A Love Story* had a successful run off-Broadway. In 2012, a musical revival, *Sally and Tom: The American Way,* was staged for Manhattan audiences, with one song that rhymed "democracy" with "hypocrisy." Curiously, the actress who was cast as Sally was darker-skinned than previous Sallys, and the Jefferson character comes across as rather spineless. The strongest voice was that of their son Madison Hemings, who brought "believable complexity" to the stage, according to one reviewer.[27]

THE WOODSON family historian Bob Cooley passed away in the summer of 1998, just months before the results of DNA testing came in. He was right about his underlying premise, insofar as Jefferson's DNA lives on in the descendants of Sally Hemings. But the oral history about which he was so certain proved inaccurate: he and his grandfather did not match the male Jefferson Y-chromosome haplotype. There are a good many living descendants of the Jefferson-Hemings union, exhibiting widely varying skin pigmentation, but apparently none is related to the Thomas Woodson who claimed kinship.[28]

When the DNA results were published, the Monticello Association had to face the music. This was a group of some seven hundred white Jefferson descendants, formed in 1913 to maintain the family graveyard. Prominent among them was fifty-two-year-old Lucian K. Truscott IV, who embraced the DNA findings and, after appearing on the *Oprah Winfrey Show* with several Hemings descendants in January 1999, welcomed all Hemingses to attend the next annual meeting as his guest. At the traditionally all-white meeting, four months later, thirty-five of Sally Hemings's descendants sat in, only to find themselves caught in a family squabble of mammoth proportions. When the "guests" were given the cold shoulder, the maverick Truscott compared his relatives' resistance to rednecks of the 1950s refusing to seat blacks at a diner. (His statement was a reminder that cemeteries across the South were segregated.) Those who opposed inclusion of the Hemingses demanded further study before accepting the implications of the science. "We're not racists, we're snobs," said Theresa Shackelford, one of the old guard. Meanwhile, a spokesman for the Woodsons refused to let go of their truth, doubting the implications of DNA from the other side of the spectrum.[29]

A battle promptly arose over whether mixed-race descendants were to be given the right of burial in the Monticello graveyard. Being denied entry into the family association, they were automatically denied rights to be buried on the mountaintop—a decision made official in 2002. As the years went by, it turned out that few Hemingses were actually keen on placing their bones in proximity to Jefferson's. No suit was filed, no more demands were made, and life went on. Yet the episode further illustrates the historical magic attached to Thomas Jefferson. How many other "founding father" burial grounds have established family associations designed expressly to oversee who comes and (eventually) goes into the sacred soil? "It's complicated," as people nowadays are wont to say. The Jefferson-Randolphs were white, and the Jefferson-Hemingses predominantly African American by outward appearance, though descendants of Eston Hemings were indistinguishable from any "white" Jefferson.[30]

One of the latter was Julia Westerinen (née Jefferson), sixty-five years old in 1998. Her father had intentionally hidden the facts of her mixed heritage when she was growing up outside Chicago in the 1940s. She was not even permitted to play with black children. Fawn Brodie's 1974 book awakened her memory of an Eston Jefferson having been mentioned at home. Westerinen made contact with the author and learned the complete story of her ancestry. Upon meeting some of her darker-skinned Hemings relatives on *Oprah*, Westerinen sought to make sense of past, present, and future. She speculated that Sally Hemings "had to have been intelligent." She figured, too, that Eston Hemings's 1852 move to Madison, Wisconsin, where he changed his surname to Jefferson (and his children passed for white) could only have been a heart-wrenching decision. He could not have truly felt he belonged in the white community. Born into slavery, coming of age in segregated society, Eston had taken the necessary steps to secure a better education and greater opportunity for the generations to follow.

Westerinen, a mélange of Scots-Irish, English, French, and African American, saw her own sudden celebrity, and her introduction to an extended family of black and white Jeffersons, as a harbinger of something better in America. It made her feel good to imagine that Thomas Jefferson's name would come to be associated with a more inclusive society, and that her own legacy would consist of having contributed in some small way to that end.[31]

With promptness and a scholarly sense of purpose, the Thomas Jefferson Foundation, which runs Monticello, commissioned a multidisciplinary group of specialists—from historians to medical experts—to evaluate the new DNA findings. Their conclusions were released in January 2000, as validation of the inference many had already drawn: Thomas Jefferson was the "most likely" father of *all* of Sally Hemings's children.[32]

DNA did not convince everyone. Ever since 1998, a stalwart group of white Jefferson descendants, politically conservative scholars, and patriotic Jefferson admirers has been quite outspoken in insisting that a Jefferson other than Thomas—one who shared the third president's DNA profile—had to be the actual father of Sally Hemings's children. Not long after Monticello issued its report, the Thomas Jefferson Heritage Society (TJHS) was born. Like Monticello, it convened a body of scholars to assess the evidence. Their report, prepared in 2001, reached a very different conclusion. Of the thirteen members of the Scholars Commission, twelve agreed that there was insufficient evidence to claim Thomas Jefferson as the "likeliest" father of the Hemings children.

The Scholars Commission majority presented its countervailing evidence. Other Jeffersons with a DNA match to Thomas were present at Monticello on occasions when the president came home. Thomas's brother Randolph, twelve years his junior and that much closer in age to Sally Hemings, was invited to visit Monticello nine months prior to Eston Hemings's birth; the same Randolph was known to play his fiddle in the slave quarters. Although, among the Jefferson clan, only Thomas Jefferson could be proven to have been present at the time of each and every one of Sally's conceptions (and she never conceived during his frequent long absences), that did not in itself end the debate. The written record was far from complete.

So reminded the TJHS, which offered an alternative explanation: When Randolph was in the vicinity, his presence might not have been noted. And as a man in his mid-sixties with health issues when Eston was conceived, Jefferson might not have had an easy time fathering the child. "Candidly, we don't know who fathered Eston Hemings," the TJHS scholars' report concluded. The evidence pointing to Thomas Jefferson struck only one of the commission's thirteen members as "compelling." The other twelve contested Monticello's conclusions.[33]

Other pertinent facts ought to be mentioned: (1) Randolph Jefferson lived twenty miles due south of his brother, which was a reasonable, but not a simple, distance to travel in 1800, when Randolph's first wife (and first cousin) left him a widower; (2) no information exists that could tie him to Sally Hemings before 1800, when she was bearing children every couple of years; (3) based on correspondence and financial accounts, his relationship with Thomas Jefferson consisted principally in discussing crops, exchanging seeds, and monitoring the education of Randolph's eldest son, who matched the brothers' Y-chromosome but was thirteen when Sally is first recorded giving birth at Monticello; and (4) if Randolph visited only irregularly, we do know that he sold two slaves to his brother in the mid-1790s.

For brother Randolph to have been the father of one or more of Sally Hemings's children, he would have had to remain at Monticello on each visit long enough to impregnate her, and only while Thomas was at home. Or else, in contrast to the Hemingses' well-documented understanding, the Hemings children would have to have had multiple fathers.

The TJHS had another problem. Until 1998, no one had ever suggested that Randolph Jefferson had fathered any of Sally Hemings's children. White Jefferson descendants had settled on the rambunctious Carr nephews; the slaves' descendants made no credible mention of Randolph, the introduction of whom seems like a red herring. While a dearth of information keeps the "mystery" alive, it would seem quite a stretch for a reasonable person to consider Randolph the *more likely* sexual partner of Sally Hemings, which is what the TJHS has argued. It remains, however, that neither the Monticello report nor the TJHS report expressed absolute certainty as to the paternity of Sally Hemings's four sons and one daughter.[34]

It is not evidence but attitude that most concerns us here. Monticello had nothing to gain by accepting Sally Hemings's offspring as the master's kin. Obvious speculation was contained in the January 2000 report in the extended inference that all of the Hemings children, and not just Eston (the last, and the only one tested), were fathered by Thomas Jefferson. In reaching its conclusions, the Monticello report accepted the word of Eston's elder brother Madison, circa 1873, when he clearly stated that he and his siblings were all the children of one man, and that their father was Thomas Jefferson. Monticello's assumption is striking, yes, but is not attributable to anything that could be termed liberal bias.

The TJHS, uniformly composed of political conservatives, has remained active and undeterred. Its friends have been responsible for a number of books denying the post-1998 consensus, and bloggers have adopted the term "hoaxers" for those who seek to impose the new race-mixing narrative. As of 2014, the main Web page of the Society featured a banner quote from Jefferson: "For here we are not afraid to follow truth wherever it may lead, nor to tolerate any error so long as reason is left free to combat it." Among the group's stated purposes are: "To further the honor and integrity of Thomas Jefferson"; and "to stand always in opposition to those who would seek to undermine the integrity of Thomas Jefferson."[35]

One is naturally tempted to ask how Thomas Jefferson's integrity is undermined by acknowledging the strong possibility that he enjoyed intimacy as a widower. Is his integrity as a sentient being only preserved if he engaged in sex with a woman of his own class? And were all the men in his era who had sex outside of marriage demeaned by dint of having done so? Questions of motive compound: Must expectations of conventional private behavior be greater for founders, for geniuses, for national icons?

The preconceptions of the Heritage Society are of the sort that differentiate twenty-first-century Republicans and Democrats. The Society feels that society at large has something to lose if Thomas Jefferson's sexual virtue is subject to dissection. In this regard, it has engaged in a desperate power struggle with Monticello, and those collectively designated "the Jefferson establishment," laying claim to the essential identity of a man who has been dead for close to two centuries.

Many conservatives critique any brand of scholarship that undermines the "great man" historical narrative with which they are most comfortable. The clear implication of their protest is that lavishing attention on slaves removes the focus of historical scholarship from the famous names that deserve it more—as though modern scholarship can do without treating all layers of society.

It is not clear whether those who established the Thomas Jefferson

Heritage Society with the intent of highlighting the founder's political achievements and moral rectitude uniformly insist that Jefferson ceased having sexual relations at the age of thirty-nine. Their and Jefferson's motto, to "follow truth wherever it may lead," ought to mean that, by probing all aspects of his admittedly awkward engagement with the institution of slavery, we do no injury to the memory of the man who wrote the Declaration of Independence and served two terms as president. Indeed, whether or not the Monticello report of 2000 is wholly accurate, blind obedience to a static vision of how history ought always to be remembered seems rather more controlling than Jefferson's unambiguous exhortation demands.

But why then choose brother Randolph, whom no one—neither Hemingses nor white Jefferson descendants—previously mentioned in this connection? The answer is this: because no living being has any real attachment to him. He certainly did not have the same regularity of contact with Sally Hemings that the master of Monticello did. The Randolph diversion seems to imply that modern-day promoters of the sexless Jefferson image read shame into the thought that a heroic founder could lust for a union less noble than republican nationhood.

A conservative, almost by definition, idealizes the strong, competent leader, the man who sits at the head of the table and delivers rational ideas and stands for moral order. That is the Jefferson the TJHS has steadfastly embraced. The edited collection produced by the TJHS in 2001, expanded and reprinted a decade later, posed nearly as many questions as Annette Gordon-Reed had in her book (pre-DNA), but with no effort to mask the contributors' agenda: the principal editor unabashedly stated that those who abided the Monticello report were "assassins of Thomas Jefferson's reputation." Uncomfortable in admitting to the moral flaws to which the flesh is heir, supporters of patriarchy saw Jefferson much as his sophisticated granddaughter Ellen Coolidge consistently painted him: a sweet, generous elder, a benign moral authority. He could not have so debased himself as to act the libidinous older man, taking his biracial house servant into his arms, again and again and again.[36]

The obvious question is the one no one ever seems to ask: *Why does he even need moral protection?* Why do any of the founders? The persistent myth of founder infallibility is a fantasy of almost biblical proportions. At the end of the last century, Annette Gordon-Reed described Jefferson as "completely predictable and depressingly familiar, a fairly garden-variety version of a white man, struggling (not too hard) to come to grips with this ultimately weird relationship with black people." Hers was a salient, if plainly argumentative, social commentary, and one that should be engaged head-on.[37]

Here is what we do know: (1) In their generation, powerful men of the landed class, slave-owning southern planters, grew up seeing enslaved women of any hue as sexually available; and (2) in *Notes on Virginia,* Jefferson famously expressed a generic distaste for the physical qualities of Africans and supposed a brute-like sexuality among all blacks—this being a common notion since Roman times. The eighteenth-century "science of man," as extracted from the books Jefferson owned, was decidedly racist and sexist. For Jefferson to have loved Hemings in the way the modern imagination encounters love is not likely, but it is also of minor import in our larger consideration of the ways in which emotionally charged Americans have been affected by the debate over the Jefferson-Hemings relationship since DNA.[38]

WE FIND a few key differences among historical approaches to the charismatic founders. In his autobiography, Benjamin Franklin admitted to sexual dalliance, a self-description that has remained a part of his popular portrait for more than two hundred years. He has always been the witty, even cagey, founder, a sharp-tongued, public-spirited celebrity—a remarkable presence, indeed, but in no way a perfect being. Jefferson, on the other hand, descends to us as the moral philosopher of democracy. He opted to make no comment about the published charges that he had fathered his slave's children, thereby encouraging his friendly posterity to contend that the most intellectually resilient of the Revolutionaries did not deserve to have his intimate life, whatever it consisted in, fodder for satirists—and much later, the subject of scholarly inquiry.

One should not be surprised that southern conservatives are especially inclined to mask the sexual "debasement" of the patriarchs by keeping secret the earthier aspects of their lives. This is how it always was in their section of the country. When intimate truths were peddled by scandalmongers, gentlemen ignored them or quietly took exception to the revelations, and wished them away. Even the conventional word for such behavior—"indiscretion"—bears a euphemistic tone. In the early twentieth century, before he entered his half-century-long political life as a South Carolina senator, a young Strom Thurmond had sex with the family maid and fathered a mixed-race daughter. The truth did not emerge until his final days, in the early twenty-first century.

Thomas Jefferson's post-marital private life was meant to remain in the shadows, too, and within the family. In that protective retreat, whatever it was that his actions represented—a form of love, male sexual prerogative, or some socially unacceptable, transgressive behavior—could work itself out and dissolve into the broader home narrative, taking its place within the cabinet of curiosities that family members dealt with in their own ways, over time, over generations.[39]

As a patriarchal set, the American founders are commonly granted an ethereal quality in order that the national creation story wear tasteful and attractive garb. To modern nationalists, the delegates who took their seats in Independence Hall, Philadelphia, are best appreciated as a class of men heroically untouched by sexual diversion or unpalatable opinions about race mixing. We are instructed that as full-time patriots, their minds were principally devoted to the solemn business of government: molding the central themes, the core identity, of America's being.[40]

In the minds of founder fundamentalists, patriots have a duty to protect the reputations of those unimpeachable sources of authority who carried the eternal word of the founding. As in religion, it is the wisdom of elders, the unblemished evidence of the patriarchs' meritorious leadership, that exist to inculcate good family values. Founding greatness is therefore nonnegotiable. For the guardians of our Revolutionary tradition, Jefferson's corporeality interferes with his ethereality as a man of words whose moral philosophy speaks eloquently and prescribes.

Founder fundamentalism requires that George Washington exist for his posterity in polished marble, stalwart, unflappable, pointed forward. Aspects of the real Washington—a tough-minded land speculator and impatient landlord, an imperfect strategist quick to blame subordinate officers for battlefield reverses—are, if not dismissed, obscured, and quietly folded into his overall grandeur as a natural leader. He is preserved as the republic's Solomon, the superior judge and serenely focused decision maker, his essential portrait on national currency, his name associated with innumerable counties, cities, towns, and streets. In like manner, as the putative father of an immortal Declaration, Jefferson is associated with a kind of holy scripture that is primal and irreversible; without its comforting essence, America as an idea is compromised.

In fact, though, ideology constrains us. Reluctance to accept any change in Jefferson's legacy that belittles his reputation demeans the discipline of history. The wishful ennobling of the light-skinned slave

Sally Hemings, a mother and a domestic for most of her life, into a heroic black woman, takes license, too.

It is the historian's job to reshape the conversation. Male sexual repression was not expected in Jefferson's world, a fact of historical life that the fundamentalists are loath to address. But neither was sexual conquest glorified; and among the lower sorts, southern courts regularly dealt with bastardy and punished sexual predators. Obviously, then, the anxieties we moderns attach to sexual behaviors cannot be transplanted to an earlier era thoughtlessly.[41]

Historical context is everything. Matters of personhood that applied to Jefferson do not apply to us, and vice versa. This is why, in modern life, he functions as a metaphor as much as anything. The Jefferson image exists at the margins of cultural criticism and at the core of national identity. His image is conditioned by the politics of memory, representing the tension between constructive and subversive forces in American life. As we lose the capacity to retain an actual memory of what is past, we are left with the natural distrust that accompanies all efforts to reconstitute it.

Before he left political office and officially retired to Monticello, Jefferson suffered from migraines—he termed them "periodical headaches." They could last weeks, requiring him to burrow away in a darkened room. In a sense, the Jefferson-Hemings affair revived a "periodical headache" of frustrated yearning in the late twentieth century among a patriotic corps that treats Jefferson as a reflection of their better selves.

NINETEEN ninety-eight was a historically significant year. It opened with President Clinton's memorable assertion: "I did not have sexual relations with that woman." In February, Osama bin Laden declared war on the United States, though no one noticed until the deadly August bombings that killed hundreds at U.S. embassies in Africa. Steven Spielberg's *Saving Private Ryan* presented the chaos of war with unparalleled realism, replicating the D-Day invasion on the big screen. In September, the Internet search giant Google, headquartered at that time in a garage, was first incorporated. Old and new were colliding, as Thomas Jefferson's DNA made national headlines.

In fact, more history massed at this crossroads moment than most were able to comprehend at the time. As a raucous century neared its end, the prospective impeachment trial of the president reminded the Nobel Prize–winning African American author Toni Morrison of something that should have seemed peculiar but did not. It was in 1998 that she famously dubbed Bill Clinton "our first black president," owing to his impoverished, small-town Arkansas origins, his having been raised by a single mother, his saxophone days, his fondness for junk food. Black Americans responded positively to Bill Clinton.

It is the nature of charisma to defy easy definition. If there was something about President Clinton that brought him close and made him knowable to black America, it was Jefferson, among the presidents, who first came to be viewed as a man of the people. In 1800, non-elites expressed their personal hopes that his elevation to the presidency would change the circumstances of their lives for the better. The lofty Washington did not lodge with strangers in country inns, or converse comfortably with regular folks. It was Jefferson who famously wore undistinguished clothing and preferred to hitch his horse to the post at the Capitol rather than ride to his inauguration in a presidential coach. But he never shed his aristocratic self-regard. His friends knew him for the honorable gentleman that he was. Which made the allegations about a black mistress all the more outrageous—at least it seemed so on the surface.

Toni Morrison was actually saying something different from what most thought. For her, Bill Clinton was being eyed in office just as a black man was accustomed to being eyed by the resistant old order: he had to be guilty of something. "I was deploring the way in which President Clinton was being treated," she explained a decade later, the year of Barack Obama's historic run for the White House. "He was treated like a black on the street, already guilty, already a perp."[42]

It didn't take long after his inauguration for social conservatives to charge the mixed-race Obama with various shades of illegitimacy. In 1967, when this future president, the product of a Kansas woman and a Kenyan man, was just entering grammar school, the case of *Loving v. Virginia* was adjudicated by the U.S. Supreme Court. Chief Justice Earl Warren and the eight other justices unanimously ruled that anti-miscegenation laws were unconstitutional. This overturned the Racial Integrity Act of 1924, which had divided all Americans into two racial categories: white and colored.

At once a victory for racial equality and marital autonomy, the *Loving* decision evidently did not do away with the inherited fear (among a certain set of white Americans) that light-skinned blacks (men, especially) would somehow usurp the privileges of whites. Indeed, that seems to be a part of what drove the Obama illegitimacy narrative. In the age of Jefferson, it was the existence of a growing class of free blacks, many of them mixed-race and with access to the still enslaved, that fed group suspicion of collusion and heightened fears of slave insurrection. In ways such as these, we are reminded of the often intangible, but nearly unbanishable, historical force of bigotry or xenophobia. Laws help, but laws do not alter the "DNA" behind the sensations that dictate aversion.[43]

During the same decade that the Jefferson-Hemings question was joined to the science of genetics, myths about racial difference and race mixing received their hearing in the works of southern fiction writers. In 1992, Bebe Moore Campbell wrote *Your Blues Ain't Mine*, fictionalizing the 1955 murder of the black teenager Emmett Till and the politics of sex and race that it evoked. In 1993, the celebrated Louisiana novelist Ernest J. Gaines, born to sharecroppers, published the classic *A Lesson before Dying*, a poignant story about empathy in a time of racial injustice. The author was raised by his aunt, Augusteen Jefferson, and his main character, also named Jefferson, sits in jail, accused of a murder he did not commit. Jefferson's trial brings out "Jeffersonian" assumptions, dating to *Notes on Virginia*, about the fundamental distinctions, biological as well as sociological, between whites and blacks. In the course of the narrative, the reader is told about the age-old problem of black men, "broken" by the legacy of slavery, who somehow keep abandoning their women. The story is less about laying blame than about feeling one's way out of the past. One subtheme in the book is the slow emergence of a friendship across racial lines in the slow-to-change South.[44]

Yet a demographic shift was also noted in the 1990s. As African Americans returned south, they appeared to be looking ahead and struggling less with the past. Surveys taken regularly from the mid-1960s to the end of the century revealed that both southern and non-southern blacks expressed positive feelings about the South and southerners generally; the percentage of black people surveyed who felt this way rose steadily, decade by decade, to the point of nearly equaling the percentage of pro-South southern whites, whose responses remained constant over the same period.

Before the civil rights movement chipped away at the last vestiges of slavery and Jim Crow, before memory started to deal honestly with the legacy of atrocities, whites generally referred to southern whites as "southerners," and to southern blacks as "blacks." But that fact changed some after the 1960s. The South became "home" to most all of those surveyed, black as well as white. As the descendants of slaves acknowledged their affection for a region where they had been so long victimized, their sense of alienation was meaningfully reduced. Modern African Americans learned to see history as a reminder of strong communities, and of a revitalized sense of purpose.[45]

It was in this context that Toni Morrison was able to take some comfort in the Clinton presidency, even if his "blackness" lay in negative experiences. By sharing some of the pain of black folks with southern roots, the president showed, just as they were showing, that a strong, positive attitude enabled one to surmount the obstacles presented by those who considered you vulnerable simply because of who *they* imagined you were.

THROUGHOUT U.S. history, intersecting concerns over race and national identity have risen among white conservatives whenever a demographic threat was newly perceived in the visible addition of "different" or dark-skinned people. As a cohesive ruling group, whites have tended at certain moments to feel their social power slipping. Elements within white America will then fixate on the behavioral characteristics of the feared group, the un-American character of its message, or the essential imperfection of its claimants to power, who are painted as dangerous demagogues.

With President Obama's election in 2008, the disapproving minds of consciously and subconsciously racist voters resulted in a substantial percentage of registered Republicans believing—despite ample evidence to the contrary—that the forty-fourth president was a political radical whose ties to the nation were somehow tenuous. No healing took place in consequence of the election of 2008. Quite the contrary. Like the 1998 DNA test, the Obama phenomenon became a flashpoint, a reminder of a demographic challenge more real for white people than ever before. While liberals accepted the fact that America has always been mixed-race, even when it was not being talked about, conservatives redoubled their efforts to preserve the white American essence through public school texts, home schooling, and other means. Patriotism was subtly racialized through reminders that the leading founders of the country were Anglo-Americans.

The race-transcending Colin Powell, a career soldier and highly decorated major general, was a registered Republican who embodied the leadership values and principles that the strong conservative looked for in a presidential candidate. Not only did Barack Obama never wear the uniform, but as an Ivy Leaguer with an African name, he chose instead the path of urban community organizer, and attended a controversial black church. These were signifiers of his "otherness." When General Powell threw his support to the African American Democrat, a presumed allegiance to his race served to nullify his conservative credentials rather than cause a reconsideration of Barack Obama.

As president, Obama could be made to appear on the verge of "reverting to" the radical theology that hyped-up conspiracy theorists said marked him. Others might be duped by the generous smiles and smooth talking, but not they. In a surprisingly similar manner, Federalist "scribblers"—as the socially conservative press was styled—could not accept the harmony-seeking public vocabulary of President Jefferson as legitimate. Like President Obama, President Jefferson courted the political opposition, but did so with very limited success. He might have undertaken certain experiments that no Francophobic Federalist would have tried, but he was not the dangerous radical they had claimed to know him as: he did not set fire to New Englanders' Bibles or bring on public licentiousness and French Revolutionary–style terror; he did not appoint common people to cabinet posts. Instead, he grew the country, acre by acre. The congenial Obama did not introduce socialized medicine or substitute any radical agenda in place of competence in his high-level appointments. Instead, he worked on growing the economy.

The political Right sees itself resisting the Left's attempts to wrest American history from the "actual" founding fathers, and to replace these giants with slaves and free blacks and other ethnicities—to promote, in other words, a sensitive, "politically correct" narrative. Their method, according to the Right, is to inflict a sense of guilt and shame, and to use emotional blackmail to reverse history's verdict. This mindset extended to President Obama and his supposed "apology tour," whenever he went abroad and represented the United States as a historically flawed, but ultimately reasonable, nation, no longer interested in imposing its will overseas.[46]

To the Right, Democrats are seen, then, as "soft," and liberal historians are seen as blinded by empathy for the lowly. Newt Gingrich insisted that a confused President Obama wavered on applying the lessons of American exceptionalism once he was lifted to the presidency. One might also construe Gingrich's charge as a veiled means of feeding the prevailing belief among social conservatives that Obama was not a "real" American. According to Gingrich, "a determined group of radicals" had decried and demeaned exceptionalism, convinced that the United States is a "uniquely brutal, racist, and malevolent country." He found obnoxious the mocking language of those, like the Washington Post columnist Matt Miller, who wrote: "Does anyone else think there's something a little insecure about a country that requires its politicians to constantly declare how exceptional it is?" By denying historical greatness, by denying American exceptionalism, the Left would corrode American power, ceding the future to the United Nations, self-defeating multiculturalism, and one-world government. Gingrich tried to avoid suggesting a racial dimension to the danger he perceived, but something in his puzzling attack on "elitism" seems to indicate anger about the replacement of a traditional elite with a new elite whose elevation is both artificial and unconnected to the founders' vision.

You didn't have to say "color" for the word to be understood. The racial divide was being redrawn, and more visible executive positions were being occupied by Obama-endorsed people of color. Meanwhile, having an African American president did not ensure improvements everywhere else: we know when racial justice is unevenly applied in the courts. In February 2012, an unarmed African American teenager, Trayvon Martin, was shot and killed by a volunteer neighborhood watchman in Sanford, Florida, who thought the youth did not belong in his community. President Obama felt it personally: "If I had a son, he would look like Trayvon," he said. Gingrich reacted, calling the president's comment "disgraceful." He posed: "Is the president suggesting that if it had been a white who had been shot, that would be okay because it didn't look like him?" Upon which Gingrich applied the Jeffersonian ideal as he understood it: "Every young American is endowed by their creator with certain unalienable rights, including life, liberty, and the pursuit of happiness. And we have to, as a movement, the conservative movement . . . be concerned about the quality of life and the sanctity of life of every American of every background." The inference here was that black America should get over the past and accept his view that in the modern era every American is equal: no one should expect special favors or dispensations from government. In short, African Americans were not exceptional—only America was.

Throughout his campaign to unseat Obama in 2012, Gingrich called the Democrat "the food stamp president" who encouraged continued dependency on government programs by African Americans who "choose" not to work. This recurrence to racial stereotypes, and the condescending attitude the Georgian adopted when he spoke about the black community, belied his claim to be inclusive in his conception of American community. In blaming African Americans for their condition, he denied the power of history and intentionally excluded a wide swath of the descendants of slaves from his exceptional population.

As the candidate of the frustrated and resentful social conservative, Gingrich spoke to the activist base of the Republican Party, principally southern, that harbored resentment toward people of color for supposedly reaping the benefits of others' tax dollars in "handouts." These were whites who felt cheated, and who accepted the premise that whatever unfairness existed was the direct result of Democratic initiatives. To understand the motivation of Gingrich backers (and the several other presidential contenders who appealed to the Tea Party in 2012), one must account for their anger. What was the evidence they drew upon when they insisted that America was "slipping away," stolen from them by left-leaning "community organizers" or "outside agitators" who favored the redistribution of wealth?

The answer lies not so much in economics as in demographics. Those responsive to Gingrich or to the radio provocateur Rush Limbaugh and others of their ilk imagine it is Jefferson's better, purer America that needs to be reclaimed. Jefferson's was a time when it was only natural for white people to police the comings and goings of people of color—when liberty did not have to be defined as all-inclusive. His small-government philosophy never had the welfare of black Americans in mind. Thus, the Right's association of Jefferson with a racially managed American exceptionalism made him "one of them."[47]

How had Jefferson, of all people, come to be associated with intolerance? From the 1990s forward, his controversial statements about slavery, along with the titillating Jefferson-Hemings question, were part of a confused attempt to understand multiracial America in historical relief. Under the newfound dictates of "politically correct" multiculturalism, pride in ethnic uniqueness competed against the long-held value of a common culture.

Old liberals had left the door ajar, and neoconservatives forced their way through. Onetime Kennedy aide Arthur Schlesinger Jr. worried in 1991 that American society was being pulled apart as a result of the impulse, emanating from the civil rights era, to counteract the racism "so deeply and shamefully inbred in our history," and enact fairness. What began as a therapeutic exercise, "a gesture of protest against the Anglocentric culture," had turned history on its head. Paying excess attention to people's ethnic and racial identities, he said, "belittles *unum* and glorifies *pluribus*," exacerbating perceptions of difference. Restoring a proper balance between the "many" and the "one" was imperative. America had not been anything like a homogeneous society since the nineteenth century. It was a composite of the whole world. But it still needed to promote a common culture.[48]

THE JEFFERSON image had been useful in establishing common ground before. But not in these years. What if Jefferson wasn't always right, wasn't always truthful? As of 1998, it became harder to think of the sexually active Jefferson as a man above the fray in America's culture wars. It was all too easy to brand him a racist, along with the overused appellation, "a man of contradictions." Liberal humanists loved him less; his resistance to government expansion plainly encouraged conservatives.

Jefferson wrote at length about race without feeling the pain of black people very deeply or losing sleep over the South's inertia. His beloved Virginia was proud, convivial, and, in his mind, free—that way of life known as "the Old South" and later the "Lost Cause" of the Confederacy. Tied to an insufficiently diversified economy, it had obvious drawbacks. Disparities seen in Jefferson's day became increasingly apparent in the manufacturing and logistical advantages the North held during the Civil War. Jeffersonian agrarianism worked against rational growth and only served to isolate the South. We still see the results of a region plagued by the combination of nineteenth-century farmers' incompetence and widespread indebtedness.[49]

If we are honest with ourselves, the enlightened patriot-nationalist who stands so tall inside his exquisite Tidal Basin memorial must coexist in memory with the southern provincial. Despite his adoration of science and moral philosophy, Jefferson was not above considering the breeding qualities of female slaves. The manner in which he dealt with the Missouri crisis in 1819–20, ardent about states' rights when it came to the expansion of slavery, constitutes strong evidence that Jefferson would have *acquiesced*—as he might well have put it—to secession in 1861.

Twenty-first-century founder fundamentalists have dutifully separated him from the other slave owners who fathered their slaves' children and marched off to war, with rebel relish, in hopes of preserving the Old South. But ever since Jefferson's time, the South has remained the poor relation in a booming economy, the most violent region in America, the most intolerant of difference, the most hateful toward government, and the most needy and dependent on government's largesse. Now as then, the white southerner did not have to feel threatened by the emancipated black to be conscious of his own political inadequacy.

Blame Jefferson the Virginian, if you must. If not the father, he is a grandfather of the Lost Cause. In 1798, when the Adams administration cracked down on opposition newspapers and subverted the First Amendment, Jefferson turned to a southern legislature and considered the right to nullify federal law. As the first prominent figure to question the endurance of the states' commitment to Union, he could always be called on, posthumously, to weigh in on questions of sectional power and economic leverage. As historians of the South will tell you, Jefferson was a Virginian, a southerner, before he was an American.[50]

We live with the legacy of all that. A century and a half after the Civil War, one encounters histrionic whites in considerable number who revere the Confederate flag. Southern politicians continue to gain traction by appealing to disaffected white men's fears. During and after the 2012 election season, sinister attempts by Republicans to place impediments in the way of minority voters refocused on problems that everyone else imagined were settled.

Braggadocio does not stop at the Mason-Dixon Line. Northern superiority also exists as an ingrained ideology. Jefferson railed against it for years. Sectionalized forever, the white ruling class in the Deep South suffers in being seen as wrong by everyone who doesn't belong there. "We got a town full of reporters from New York City to Los Angeles to London, all intent on making Mississippi look bad," says the white politico in Bebe Moore Campbell's *Your Blues Ain't Mine*. Outside judgment has been a constant theme in southern literature.[51]

The terms of our engagement with race will no doubt look different when future generations, less stung by the intractable history of slavery and white supremacy, pass judgment on ours. At election time, we keep track of the "white vote," the "black and Latino vote," the "female vote," etc., so as to suggest that skin pigmentation and gender outpace class distinctions or other measures of identity. In stark print, in searing still images, in captured videos, we tackle "the race issue," to use its shorthand designation. We know where it comes from. We know it doesn't quit.

The psychological choice to categorize opinion in terms of race engages another facet of the Jefferson-Hemings debate. Depending on how one identifies, the founder's role in race mixing can be positive or negative. An overt preference for an altogether cerebral Jefferson does not automatically represent an endorsement of white supremacy. Merrill D. Peterson, the senior Jefferson scholar who spoke passionately before a University of Virginia audience on behalf of civil rights in the 1960s, openly scoffed at the idea that Jefferson and the domestic dependent Sally Hemings could have been intimate. So, we cannot presume that deniers of the Jefferson-Hemings connection are dyed-in-the-wool racists; nor should we presume that those who are comfortable with the implications of the DNA findings are themselves immune to hidden biases.

Without having lost the admirable qualities of the polymath (as President Kennedy found him), Jefferson became, post-DNA, what African Americans long assumed him to have been. We are left with a new set of questions: What if the "garden-variety" male was not a garden-variety racist but, on some level, as Fawn Brodie projected, an exemplar of love across the color line? What if any Jefferson-Hemings communion we choose to see in terms of race relations was, for the participants, principally felt as sex across class lines? Could the supremely well-educated Jefferson even have "loved" (in the conventional sense of the word) his uneducated, biracial house servant? Will future students of history even care? So that's what the posthumous president does to us now: he leaves our libidinous questions unanswered.

Just as President Kennedy's brightly shining "Camelot," as transmitted to posterity by his widow, later yielded to the lustier image of a president with multiple mistresses, Jefferson has taken a step down from his beautifully constructed dreamworld, his sunny Mount Olympus. The mild-mannered philosopher, seated by acclamation at the head of the table, suddenly finds himself transformed into a "garden-variety" white man with predictable urges: like FDR, like JFK, like Clinton. The only difference (a very significant one) is that Jefferson's post-corporeal sex life is tied to his anxious theorizing about racial purification.

ON JEFFERSON'S birthday in 2001, the following headline appeared in the conservative *Washington Times:* "Bush Recognizes Black Jefferson Kin." By conferring acceptance of the Hemings-Jefferson genealogy, President George W. Bush dealt a blow not just to the all-white Monticello Association, but also to the conservative scholars who refused to tolerate the hijacking of Jefferson by "liberal" Monticello.[52]

That year, and over the next several years, the Hemingses received considerable press attention. The white Jefferson descendant Lucian Truscott IV, who had warmly embraced his Hemings cousins immediately after the 1998 revelations, stood nearly alone. Angered by the stubbornness of the family, he eventually stopped attending meetings of the Monticello Association. "Things have gone from bad to worse," he wrote in a *New York Times* op-ed in 2003. While the Association continued to distance itself from its unwanted relatives, it sought to defuse the situation by recommending that Monticello find a separate (but equal?) plot of land on the property to open to the plantation's slave descendants, including Hemingses. Still, the president of the Association would not, as he wrote in a letter to the editor of the *Times,* "sacrifice Mr. Jefferson on the altar of political correctness."

Between 2001 and 2005, that newspaper's Brent Staples contributed thoughtful pieces on the subject of the Hemingses, using them as a springboard to talk about slave offspring across the South who "passed" into white society. "The black intelligentsia did not spring fully formed from the cotton fields," he wrote. "It had its roots in the families of mixed-race slaves like the Hemingses." Where is Sally Hemings buried? asked others. The answer: possibly below the Hampton Inn on West Main Street in Charlottesville. But no one is sure.[53]

In 2010, three Jefferson descendants received an award from an international organization called Search for Common Ground. David Works (of the Jefferson-Randolph line), Julia Jefferson Westerinen (a Hemings, white in appearance), and Shay Banks-Young (a Hemings, dark in appearance) were honored for their work to heal the rift within a patchwork family that was reliving America's history of race enslavement. Speaking on National Public Radio, Works confessed: "I had behaved rather poorly" at the 1999 Monticello Association meeting. He called it "a very sleepy organization," and explained how he had been caught up in the moment when "it just appeared that the Hemingses wanted to break down the gates and get buried in our precious graveyard." After a series of honest discussions with his "cousins," Works came to understand the depth of the insult. Banks Young provided the parentheses: "I know that there are a lot of white Americans who don't know that they go back to black." Westerinen added: "If you look for the negative, you're going to find it." Together, the three started a new group, "Monticello Community," which reached out to all whose family history connected them to Jefferson's private mountain.[54]

In the nation's capital, in 2012, a rich exhibition of slavery at Monticello went up at the Smithsonian's National Museum of American History. Beyond the mixed-race Hemings clan, the other extended families who labored for Thomas Jefferson received their due; a complex and fascinating genealogical chart hung along the wall at the center of the exhibition, showing in unprecedented detail what it took to sustain plantation life on a large scale, over decades. Slavery was realistically represented, Jefferson depicted as a well-meaning master who, every so often, looks mean-spirited: to wit, he did sell slaves for profit. His absences and occasional missteps as a manager made way for cruelties perpetrated by one or more of his uneducated white overseers.

The exhibition's balanced presentation opened the eyes of many thousands of visitors. Monticello was its noisy nailery, its blacksmith's forge, its woodworking area, its merino sheep, its wheat and tobacco fields. It was a busy community, a very human place with complex characters and multiple interests, no less than it was a stately home with European paintings and a wine cellar for the world-class aesthete, his family, and distinguished guests to enjoy.[55]

Jefferson finally comes into clearer focus. He was robust and refined, stubborn and generous. His brightly domed domicile touched the sky, but in terms of personal needs, he was of the earth. He was never a disembodied thinker, and always a corporeal striver. He lived in close proximity to those he owned. He was important to them, and they were important to him in ways we do not fully comprehend, even now.

The Revolutionary generation's list of priorities are somewhat less nebulous. Slavery was founded long before their time, in rudeness and out of weakness. Most acknowledged (and despaired) a compounding problem. But cruel facts did not offset a stronger compulsion: *This nation was founded by those for whom attachment to property was primary.* Some of their ideas were noble and good, but they were not all-encompassing. According to Jefferson's flamboyant formulation in the Declaration, any person—white, black, and admixture—could lay claim to every individual right, to a pursuit of happiness. Practically speaking, only some could expect to enjoy those rights in the United States. This has remained true for the longest time.

Pundits speculate as to what will happen to the beleaguered white voter, so long in the majority and now betting against time. Will assimilative properties make bi- and multiracial people "insiders" and thereby "safe" for white conservatives to support? What will it take to reduce to manageable levels all the pent-up historical anxiety?

Today, we are not as far from segregated drinking fountains as we imagine we are. With increased acceptance of race mixing, those now living may (or may not) be the first generation to repudiate the sensory causes of America's social ills, that long-cultivated belief in the organic inferiority of people thought dirty and distasteful; presumed lazy, unproductive, and undeserving of assistance; said, on some level, not to belong. This is a class problem, too, not simply a race problem. But its racial aspects are outstanding, and particularly burdensome in the light of history. Once we make it our duty to understand the forms that alienation takes, we will start to recognize that the truly decisive separation of African and European occurred when the seed of American exceptionalism was planted—when European settlers justified their quest for wealth in land by pronouncing a divine purpose in the "benevolent" exploitation of a wild, inviting, yielding continent. It was then that they restricted opportunity to people like themselves.

They said: We found it. We made it. It's ours. We're an exceptional people.

These are all warning signs.

TESS TAYLOR is a direct (white) descendent of Thomas Jefferson. Her poems interrogate her privileged Virginia ancestors. She goes through wills, inspects shards, and grasps at shadows in pursuit of all that her family carefully hid—or inadvertently hid—or that had simply wasted away.

Lost-and-found is the poet's theme. Taylor reaches through the "portal to the gone world," as she puts it in the short lament "Graveyard, Monticello," and makes sense for herself of scraps of writing and atmosphere. The imagined lives of the slaves intrigue her even more than the tactile reminders of Jefferson's extended family. And in another poem:

I can trace the names of his white children's descendants.
Where the enslaved went after auction
   is partial—

"A Letter to Jefferson from Monticello" is in turn playful and brutal, with this curious appeal:

Families are still stories: Now we look
for them with DNA. DNA would have
fascinated you: It is
symmetrical, almost rational. . . .[56]

One suspects she is right about how Jefferson would have greeted DNA. He was too committed to advancing knowledge not to follow trends in evolutionary science. We can recklessly imagine his reaction to the 2007 follow-up study of the Jefferson male cellular material, which concluded that he and a good number of Jeffersons alive today in Britain belong to a genetic type that is rare among Europeans and far more common in East Africa. Scientists speculate that Jefferson's ancestors migrated north from the Middle East.[57]

The racial theorist would no doubt have been surprised by his remote African connections. But we cannot say more. We cannot know what might have changed his mind about race or anything else. We suspect he was a man whose house servant, his late wife's half sister, was an outlet for his sexual urges; he could also have been a confused hypocrite, repelled by Africanness, able to convince himself that his pretty concubine had had the greater part of the dark "stain" removed from her person. Or perhaps, as some prefer, he was an exemplar of interracial harmony who just wouldn't come out of the closet.

Efforts to reclaim the past lead us to recognize the easy corruptibility of memory amid competing truths. Let us embark on an entirely new journey of the mind, then, honest with ourselves and unafraid in discovering "a more perfect union" of the public and private Jefferson. No excuses need be made. His occasionally questionable political judgments and flawed humanity pose no threat to anyone in the twenty-first century.

The example of his white and black families reuniting at Monticello accomplished some good. Yet the definition of national "belonging" is nowhere near resolved. Resentments persist that are only artificially muted when, say, a once-common slur is redesignated "the N-word." If Hemings had been a white servant, there would be no story here. We should admit, then, that up to this point, debate over the meaning of "Tom and Sally" has produced more misery than poetry.

6

"ABORTION TO THEIR HOPES"

Jefferson versus Religious Authority

SELF-RIGHTEOUSNESS is no part of religion. If Jefferson had a critique of religion, it began there. His deep disgust for the sanctimonious clergymen who attacked him at pivotal moments in his career reappears often in his intimate correspondence. They made his personal faith a dangerous distraction when he stood for election in 1800. Well into his retirement years, he complained about their "pious whining, hypocritical canting, lying & slandering," incensed by the unreasoning preachers who duped the ignorant and spread fear.[1]

As impossible as it is to know where, as an eighteenth-century man born into a slave economy, Jefferson would have stood on issues of race and civil rights in our times, it is entirely possible to project with confidence how he would have weighed in on religiously tinged issues of today. That is because his critique of institutional religion related less to professions of faith than to public demonstrations of power by religious leaders. His hatred was reserved for religious indoctrination, for militant antimodernist conservatism. If citizens surrendered their power to reason before any man who insisted he knew what God wanted, democracy would rot.

Jefferson's own belief in God rested not in revelation but in scientific organization. His deity was a "superintending power" compatible with Newtonian science. It was only through scientific study, he felt, that the greatest of mysteries would ever be resolved. Jefferson was not an atheist or pure rationalist. God existed for him as the ingenious design power evident in the organization of our universe. He was quite capable of marveling at the mysteries of Creation.

Answers that did not lie in science lay for him in history. And in that regard, Jefferson's appraisal of pretentious, pontifical clergymen is uncomplicated: They blocked the way to usable knowledge. They had not studied history—or if they had, it was not with honorable intent. To him, their thinking was shallow, and their view of the life of Jesus and the age of apostles mired in delusion and superstition. "Superstition" is Jefferson's word. He paired it with "absurdities," and used both terms to describe the "perversions" of modern Christianity. He scoffed at the mass of stories invented at an unhealthy distance from the actual life and teachings of Jesus—a historical actor who, Jefferson was quick to add, never once declared himself "a divine personage."

At the age of eighty, Jefferson shared with John Adams a lifetime's frustration with the ideas promoted by those Protestant ministers who labeled him an atheist. "The day will come," Jefferson wrote, "when the mystical generation of Jesus, by the supreme being as his father in the womb of a virgin will be classed with the fable of the generation of Minerva in the brain of Jupiter." The "primitive and genuine" moral teachings of Jesus were unmatched. Protestants whom he termed "priests" (for their undemocratic tendencies) should have known when to stop dressing up tired old stories.[2]

Jefferson believed that a republic could accommodate honest differences in religious belief and practice, but he asserted that no one could arrogate to himself a superior knowledge of the all-consuming mystery of life's origins and death's ostensible rewards. In the Revolutionary era, he lobbied for freedom of conscience. When at the end of his life he reflected back on his political prime, he claimed credit for few things, but he eagerly accepted paternity of the Virginia Statute for Religious Freedom, forerunner to the First Amendment. One of its pithier, personifying lines goes like this: "Truth is great, and will prevail if left to herself." In Jefferson's moral-philosophical framework, religion began with humility.

In 1800, New England clergy painted him as an "infidel" who would disturb public morality by imposing a faith-free regime. Outwardly, Jefferson did nothing to combat the characterization, exercising restraint in the manner expected of an eighteenth-century gentleman. Privately, though, as we know, he composed eloquent words on the eve of his election, directed to Dr. Benjamin Rush, a Philadelphia friend who enjoyed a rich spiritual life: "I have sworn upon the altar of god eternal hostility against every form of tyranny over the mind of man." The line that followed referred to the illiberal men who had mislabeled him: "This is all they have to fear from me."

That assurance was true except in one detail, one public position from which Jefferson would never retreat: The religious conservatives who could not see the writing on the wall, who did not accept the

Virginia Statute as a sound template for the eventual disestablishment of state-sponsored religious sects everywhere, were right to fear in Jefferson a symbol of resistance. In the same paragraph of the stimulating letter to Dr. Rush, he stated that there was nothing he could do to assuage the *"genus irritabile vatum,"* or sacred order of the priesthood, those true believers in a permanently established church. As Jefferson saw things, each denomination believed that it would become the chosen sect, in state after state, as the nation grew. But, he confidently challenged, when a Jefferson administration ended the decade-long reign of the effete, antidemocratic Federalists, such tired old ideas would be rejected. "The returning good sense of our country threatens abortion to their hopes," he told Rush. If they believed he was standing in the way of their expanded power, he added, "they believe truly."

Dr. Rush, no wallflower himself, summed up his emphatic agreement with Jefferson by issuing a clever appeal to Christian ethics: "Were it possible," he replied, "for St. Paul to rise from his grave at the present juncture, he would say to the Clergy who are now so active in settling the political Affairs of the World: 'Cease from your political labors—your kingdom is not of *this* World. Read my Epistles. In no part of them will you perceive me aiming to depose a pagan Emperor, or to place a Christian upon a throne." Next, the inventive professor of medicine matched Jefferson's allusion to the *"genus irritabile vatum"* by volunteering his own Latinized list of detestable tyrants—leading off with the *"Odium Juris-consultum,"* or repugnant lawyers.[3]

SO NOW we know the origin of Jefferson's "altar of god" remark, its larger context, and what made it so expressive. When he felt he could write uncensored, as he did with his friend Rush, or Adams in their later years, literary gems and quotable thoughts poured forth.

Yet, as this book consistently shows, Jefferson could do little to control the ways in which even a fawning posterity would remake him. It would doubtless have perturbed him to know that his religious profile continued to matter to Americans after his death in 1826. The charges of nonbelief once used as a tactic in Federalist editorials and New England sermons did not go away. None so industrially addressed the matter as Jefferson's fond biographer Henry Randall, a New York Democrat. Working in collaboration with the late president's grandchildren on the eve of the Civil War, and perhaps at their behest, Randall sought to rescue the third president from the lingering charge of atheism. The clergy knew nothing of his personal beliefs, Randall avowed. Retaining "the dogmatism and contentiousness of the Puritan," northern Congregationalists and Episcopalians had reacted impulsively to the southerner's honest doubt. As a profound thinker, Jefferson had problems with a skewed history shoddily studied and routinely mishandled by unquestioning religious practitioners.

So keen was he on getting the message across that Randall devoted the final chapter of his three-volume biography to the retrieval of a Christian Thomas Jefferson. He went so far as to certify (all evidence to the contrary) Jefferson's "belief in the efficacy of prayer." From here, Randall declared that the kindly Jefferson never in his life sought to tell another human being what he or she should think about God's existence.[4]

The so-called Jefferson Bible, the president's cut-and-paste version of the gospels, only became public at the end of the nineteenth century, when a descendant released the document to the Smithsonian. For his own private use, Jefferson had trimmed the books of Matthew, Luke, Mark, and John to include only the rational, intelligible, and deistic. His Jesus was a man of extraordinary humility who bore a sublime moral message. Period.

In *Thomas Jefferson: World Citizen,* Elbert Thomas preached a literal Jefferson, who examined religion as a humanist who thought a lot about tolerance and intolerance. Thomas wrote: "I have no desire to probe into Jefferson's soul in an attempt to expose any secret which he would not have revealed himself." He then proceeded to divide the moral world into competing choices: to invest one's passion in revelation or in social responsibility. Because Jefferson was no absolutist, he pursued the latter. He was a Christian moralist, regardless of what he believed in. And finally, wrote the Mormon senator, "none but a religious man could so prize the right of freedom of worship."[5]

There are outstanding questions about Jefferson's motives in his cutting-and-pasting hobby. (In his 2013 valedictory address to graduates at the University of Virginia, the political satirist Stephen Colbert dubbed Jefferson "Old Bible-slicer.") But Jefferson cannot be portrayed as a formal Christian any more than he can be dismissed as thoroughly atheistic. Dispirited by loose use of historical knowledge and invention of holy language, he referred to the Trinity as "an unintelligible proposition." He was most persuaded by a book written by a famous friend, the ironically named Joseph Priestley. One of the foremost scientists of the age and a Unitarian thinker, Priestley, in his *Corruptions of Christianity,* sought to expose—and we'll adopt Jefferson's word—the "charlatanism" of centuries of interpretation of the life of Jesus.[6]

Nevertheless, the simple fact that Jefferson devoted time in his retirement to a "religious" project sparked renewed interest at the dawn of the twentieth century, when a Virginia-born Iowa congressman named John Fletcher Lacey found a new, more reverent Jefferson in the cut-and-paste text on deposit at the Smithsonian. He arranged for a sizable run of a facsimile edition, and made it available to members of Congress. It was easy in any age to cherry-pick Jefferson quotes and "prove" him pious. The "Jefferson Bible," a new approach to the private man, made it much easier to embrace as a Christian one whom the "priests" abhorred.

Though he did attend Episcopal services in the neighborhood of Monticello, the only denomination that could legitimately claim Jefferson was the Unitarian, owing to its dual emphasis on reason and scientific inquiry. "There is not a young man now living, who will not die a Unitarian," Jefferson wrote, a bit too self-assuredly. As much as he believed in what he termed "rational republicanism," the Unitarian coincided with what he saw as "rational" religion. Reason was required to protect society from the rise of fanaticism.[7]

Christianity was secure enough that it needed no bolstering from Jefferson. As a result, his connection to the principle of church-state separation was how Jefferson's religious sentiment was most often expressed in the twentieth century. The *New York Times* reported in 1953 that an 1808 letter from President Jefferson to a hopeful churchman was on display at Princeton University, where the modern edition of the *Papers of Thomas Jefferson* was being assembled. The gentlemen in question, a New York clergyman, was urging the president, on behalf of several of his "clerical brethren," to propose a day for "Fasting, Humiliation, and Prayer." Jefferson replied just as soon as he received the pastor's appeal, and clarified his position: "I consider the government of the US. as interdicted by the Constitution from intermeddling with religious institutions, their doctrines, discipline, or exercises." Prayer was a religious exercise, he said, which a religious society could direct howsoever it chose. The Constitution was crystal-clear about this: he had "civil powers" alone. As a private man, Jefferson said, he would be pleased to convey his thoughts in a private letter; but as a public man, a president, he would continue to keep mum.[8]

Thus, one hundred years after Randall's over-the-top defense, the Jefferson who was under scrutiny did not have to be a Christian of one sort or another. In 1960, a minor crisis was settled at the U.S. Post Office when a new "Thomas Jefferson Credo" stamp featured only a portion of his most stirring quote in its design. Bowing to pressure, the government reinstated "over the mind of man" to the line that read,

"I have sworn eternal hostility against every form of tyranny." It just didn't capture Jefferson without "over the mind of man." Note that the words "upon the altar of God" appeared in neither version.[9]

Not inconsequentially, the Supreme Court addressed the issue of prayer in public schools in the early 1960s, and ruled by a 6 to 1 vote that it was unconstitutional for any state to endorse the ritual, even if individual students could opt out from it. In 1969, the liberal theologian Reinhold Niebuhr worried in print that President Nixon's coziness with the evangelist Billy Graham represented a dangerous turn, when the charismatic preacher held regular religious services in the White House. Thomas Jefferson and his fellow founders had placed their ban on a nationally established religion at the top of the Bill of Rights, Niebuhr attested, because they understood that "a combination of religious sanctity and political power represents a heady mixture for status quo conservatism."[10]

At the risk of sounding a bit peremptory, making a conventional Christian out of Thomas Jefferson is a foolish exercise. To prove the point, then, it is necessary to foreground the recent reappropriation of Jefferson as an ally of "Christian nation" enthusiasts who hold that the United States was founded by truly pious Christians. Why it matters just how "Christian" the founders were (so long as they did not mock faith, which they did not) is unclear. But since President Reagan's years in office, it has mattered to some a great deal. There are more than a few on the Right who remain invested in making Jefferson's religious views wholly compatible with their own ardent vision of conservative Protestantism. For them, the past must be reclaimed; it must conform to the ideological aims of the present; it must shine its formative light along a linear path from the national Genesis to today, in order to satisfy an anxiety-ridden sensibility.

IF PRESIDENT Reagan's small-government doctrine found a putative partner in Jefferson, Reagan's Christian "base" eventually found in Jefferson a credible Christian. This is doubly interesting: first, Jefferson is not the easiest of the founders to squeeze into a particularistic Christian mold; second, he viewed Jesus as a past actor whose essence was recast and, in the process, corrupted, whereas Reagan was a dramatic actor (and theatrical politician) who has proven as plastic as the historical Jefferson or the historical Jesus.

Pressing the flesh when he ran for office, Reagan carried himself as both a Hollywood star and a Bible-reading born-again Christian. He was able to shine symbolically as the jaunty messenger of simpler times. The sensation he caused magnified with his death, when the results of decisions he made became clouded and warm feelings took over again. He was a storied figure, "conjured up narratively," as the Finnish scholar Jan Hanska has shown, and cast as "a 'political messiah' to return hope and prosperity to America again." To white middle-class America, it was not difficult to fathom: he could be the answer to prayers. If his policies did not truly benefit those who needed help, his narrative did not suffer. He was taken to be honest, which was enough.[11]

Republicans' attachment to him bordered on piety. Like religion itself, Reagan was insistently shaped by an existing need "out there" to restore a lost sense of community, to rebuild the strength that accrued in belonging to an imagined force for good. His legend says that he brought down the evil Soviet empire. Some years after his death, at the Reagan Library in Simi Valley, California, the author of a religious biography of Reagan felt he was touching a relic when he inspected the original text of the "Evil Empire" speech. "That inked-up speech copy was an awakening," he wrote in the preface to his book. "Reagan's hand was all over it—deleting a word here, inserting whole new pages there."

His biographer found Reagan to be, like Jefferson, a man whose religiosity was something he did not care to share. Yet Reagan could often be found emphasizing, in public addresses over the years, sentiments on the order of that he had once given at a high school graduation in New Jersey: "No nation which has outgrown its God has ever lived to write additional pages of history. This nation is in need of a spiritual awakening and a reaffirmation of trust in God."

Reagan was, the biographer said,

> the antithesis of the deist. The deist believes that God created humanity, the earth, and the universe, and then essentially adopted a laissez-faire policy, stepping aside to allow human nature to take its course. Thomas Jefferson is generally accepted to have been a deist, but among American presidents he is a notable exception: most have perceived God's hand in daily events throughout the world, the nation, and their lives.

As a political speaker, Reagan loved Jefferson for placing the pursuit of happiness in the hands of independent, hardworking individuals. But there was, apparently, little to be gained from Jefferson's ambiguous treatment of religion.[12]

Reagan's God had a plan for Reagan's America. "There is a plan, somehow a divine plan for all of us," he said at the National Prayer Breakfast in 1982. "I know now that whatever days are left to me, belong to Him. I also believe that this blessed land was set apart in a very special way. Our forebears came not for gold, but mainly in search of God." If Jefferson sought to convey a melodic energy in language, Reagan led with what soothed and grew ecstatic. Both excelled at what the Scottish Hugh Blair, a master of rhetoric in Jefferson's time, termed "beauties" of speech, which could be delivered without exceeding the most simple style. "A writer of genius conceives his subject strongly," Blair wrote. "His imagination is filled and impressed with it."[13]

Reagan's words were compelling, even when they were written by others, because he owned them when he spoke them. The words had a bright quality to them. They only rang hollow to the people who didn't vote for him, who saw him as a cipher, a leader with "big" ideas who yet posed too few questions to his expert advisers. Still, his strength was not accidental.

Whether he believed it all or not, Reagan was the narrator of a story about a highly desirable, albeit mythic America. "God's chosen country" was a key element in the story he told. America's story fed his story—and vice versa. Both as an actor and as president he was known to require the rewriting of scripts, aiming to get the words just right. The core message was always an untainted love of country. "Well, I guess maybe I'm old-fashioned," he actually said, "but I don't think you can love America too much." (You can replace the word *America* with *God* and it would mean much the same.)[14]

Reagan took on the role of steady optimist, and played that role regardless. How much his actual religious faith directed him hardly matters. What matters is that he made God and America stauncher public allies than they had been for a very long time—arguably since the Revolution itself, when a euphoric literature delivered millennial expectations to the new nation.

It was nineteen years after his momentous defeat of Federalism that Jefferson, in retirement, told the political story of his "Revolution of 1800," a phoenix rising from the ashes of monarchical self-immolation. Reagan's "Revolution" announced itself right away, declaring, in effect, that the American people had a giant soul. Time, Inc. helped the cause along in February 1981 with its "American Renewal" special issue, planned to coincide with Reagan's entry into office. The magazine delivered its message by gently assuring "that the U.S. has a strong and beneficial role to play in the world." (Jefferson's version of this had been to call the new nation "the world's best hope.") With its accustomed firmness and journalistic muscle, *Time* proudly acknowledged its resolution to promote "the American secular religion." In 1981, you could say such things without sounding dogmatic.[15]

Reagan, for his part, did not mind conflating secular and literal religious enthusiasm, applying his honed skills as an actor speaking to the camera. Whereas his predecessor, the born-again Christian Jimmy Carter, kept his personal faith from being politicized, Reagan fanned the flames of religious conservatism. In 1983, for instance, he spoke at a convention of religious broadcasters, and said: "The First Amendment was not written to protect people and their laws from religious values; it was written to protect those values from government tyranny."[16]

All modern presidents say, "God bless America," but when Reagan said it, it had a more insistent ring. That is why the religious Right found their footing with Reagan. His sense of history as a teachable script led him as president to speak about how moved he was on looking at a painting of George Washington falling to his knees and praying in the snow at Valley Forge. The problem with Reagan's conviction, in this instance, is that the Valley Forge moment was contrived in later years. It was Reagan who was snowed by the picture of American history he refused to doubt. As many Americans followed the president's lead, interest in Jefferson's Christian credentials (along with those of his fellow "founding fathers") rose again.[17]

As one would expect, the Reagan script alarmed traditional humanists, who as readily turned to Jefferson for an antidote. "It would perturb him greatly," wrote Betty McCollister in the *New York Times* in 1983, "to learn that he, with the other Founding Fathers, stands accused of having established the Christian religion in the United States, and that certain segments of the Christian community, with President Reagan's acquiescence, seem to be nudging this country toward theocracy." She underscored what Jefferson himself had professed when he rejected the "arcane dogmas" of those, over time, who had perverted the original message of Jesus: "I am a Christian in the only sense [Jesus] wished anyone to be," Jefferson wrote definitively of himself. He identified with the moral reformer's doctrines "in preference to all others," admiring him for "every human excellence and believing he never claimed any other." Jefferson's Jesus was great, just not divine. As McCollister explained, the founders had *"providently* wrought" a Constitution that established a secular government. Hers was a wake-up call, warning against those in public life who would automatically read the preceding words as: *"providentially* wrought" (italics added).[18]

* * *

THERE HAD been rumblings of a religious counterthrust even before Reagan came into office, prompted by fears that secularists were out to erase God from history. The argument was that religion was the principal source of public morality, and that the proscription against prayer in public schools was producing much harm: a generation was coming of age that lacked the right values. Violence, crime, and a rise in unwed motherhood were all the result of godless public education.

Danbury, Connecticut, Baptists were the favored recipients of President Jefferson's now famous 1802 letter pronouncing his conviction that "a wall of separation" divided church and state. In the Reagan years, the Baptist preacher Jerry Falwell of Lynchburg, Virginia, leader of the Moral Majority, took up the charge to tear down that wall. Falwell's Liberty University acquired its university status in 1984, the year George Orwell had made notorious.

After the Reagan presidency, organizations large and small continued to take shape that were designed to give evangelicals a political home and to pressure lawmakers to adopt conservative social policies. A fight over the perceived threat to "traditional values" brought particular attention to the Christian Coalition, formed by conservative TV personality Pat Robertson in 1989. Robertson had run for president in 1988, an act of defiance that stirred the Christian Right.

The "born again" movement of evangelical Protestants, largely southern-directed, grew in strength during and after the Clinton years. Another organization that came to prominence was the Family Research Council. Its president, beginning in 2003, was former Louisiana state representative Tony Perkins, a Southern Baptist who had graduated from Falwell's Liberty University. Perkins had his own settled view on the meaning of Jefferson's church-state dynamic. In 1997, while a state officeholder and concurrently chief organizer of the Baton Rouge chapter of the Christian Coalition, he insisted that Jefferson's take on the separation of church and state had been widely misunderstood. The state was prohibited from involvement in church activities, Perkins affirmed, but the other side of the equation was inapplicable: the church was free to shape government.[19]

Social conservatives loved hearing such pronouncements. The other side had had its day. There were those like Isaac Asimov, the acclaimed science fiction writer and rationalist, who sensed what was happening and who warned at the end of his life, in 1992, that student-directed Bible clubs sprouting in public schools were a bad sign. Secularists had been so long dominant that they were not effectively organized. They did not even know how to begin to reteach what seemed intuitive. Undeterred in the face of the religious upsurge, one colleague of Asimov's at the American Humanist Association decided to celebrate Jefferson's 1993 bicentennial by promoting a competing organization on campuses, dubbed "Thomas Jefferson Societies"; each was to be dedicated to "the philosophies of this enlightened founding father of our democracy," who preferred the calm exercise of reason to the parroting exhortations of proselytizing zealots.[20]

Thomas Jefferson Societies went nowhere, as the religiously inspired—those who would come to be called "values voters"—kept on coming. When his position as a spokesman for social conservatism was secure, Tony Perkins drew new inspiration from the founders. He tapped the 1797 Farewell Address of President Washington (authored largely by Alexander Hamilton), in which the first president had said: "Of all dispositions and habits which lead to political prosperity, religion and morality are indispensable supports." For Perkins, these words provided solid evidence that the religious commitment of a grateful nation flowed from the national father.

That was just the start. Compiling textual evidence, Perkins took a generic statement, a palliative, from Jefferson's 1805 second inaugural address, and gave it special weight. As he embarked on a second term, Jefferson had said: "I shall need, too, the favor of that being in whose hands we are, who led our fathers, as Israel of old, from their native land and planted them in a country flowing with all the necessaries and comforts of life, who has covered our infancy with his providence and our riper years with his wisdom and power." Perkins (or his editor) capitalized "Being" and "His," though Jefferson did not. The modern man of faith was so confident in his interpretation of the second inaugural address that he made it a companion to the argument in favor of American exceptionalism. "Jefferson believed that God had led 'our fathers' and blessed the nation's birth and growth," Perkins held, ending his essay assertively: "That America is exceptional is beyond dispute. That real faith in the true God has helped make us so is also undeniable."[21]

Perkins conveniently left out the paragraph in Jefferson's draft that discussed religion in other than the boilerplate language that took no effort (and that his audience expected). "In matters of religion," Jefferson explained two-thirds of the way through his address, "I have considered that its free exercise is placed by the constitution independent of the powers of the general government. I have therefore undertaken, on no occasion, to prescribe the religious exercises suited to it;

but have left them, as the constitution found them, under the direction and discipline of state or church authorities acknowledged by the several religious societies." This language was consistent with what he had told the Danbury Baptists. It was consistent, too, with his 1800 letter to Dr. Rush spelling out why those who claimed that he hated Christianity actually had nothing to fear from him.[22]

For greater clarity, we should recur as well to Jefferson's first inaugural address, when the incoming president put on a spirited performance of tremendous import at a moment of heightened political anxiety:

> Enlightened by a benign religion, professed, indeed, and practiced in various forms, yet all of them inculcating honesty, truth, temperance, gratitude, and the love of man; acknowledging and adoring an overruling Providence, which by all its dispensations proves that it delights in the happiness of man here and his greater happiness hereafter—with all these blessings, what more is necessary to make us a happy and a prosperous people? Still one thing more, fellow-citizens—a wise and frugal Government.

What was Jefferson's aim here? To soothe. Not to proselytize. The "benignity" he associated with religious life required state and church to remain separate. "Wise" government was moderate, to facilitate private comforts. With good and tolerant neighbors, communities would thrive, and happiness would extend from the individual into society. Government was content, he went on to say, in leaving citizens "free to regulate their own pursuits of industry and improvement. . . . This is the sum of good government, and this is necessary to close the circle of our felicities." To Jefferson, God's design was not a president's to define, and "felicities" were the outgrowth of freedom from any institutional imposition.

A lack of nuance in their literalism has plagued modern religious conservatives. With greater care and objectivity than the likes of Tony Perkins have mustered, the historian Eran Shalev has explored the position of a biblical script in the thinking of founding-era Americans. He shows that just as they drew upon the ennobling example of Greek and Roman history to ground their republic in a moral universe understood by educated readers, they created "the American Israel" in order to reach out beyond the elite: "While Americans, in Thomas Paine's words, might have had it in their power to start the world over again, they chose to create it in the shadow of ancient worlds long departed . . . to dress up the new in the old and familiar." Jefferson romanticized a golden age of Anglo-Saxon freedom from political co-ercion in his *Summary View of the Rights of British America* (1774), and Revolutionary polemicists conjured George Washington as the Moses or Solomon for a new age—eighteenth-century tracts put their au-thors' rhetorical skills to the test. With dramatic political purposes, they copied the cadence of the King James Version and "republican-ized the Bible."

The implications of Shalev's research are clear: hyperreligious lan-guage at the time of the founding was aimed at "rallying the troops," that is, both citizen-soldiers and civilians en masse whose political al-legiance had to be won. Shalev calls this prescriptive vocabulary "pseu-dobiblicism," and it focused almost exclusively on the Old, not the New, Testament. When we look at the individuals concerned, Wash-ington, in his abundant correspondence, did not mention the name Jesus; Jefferson valued Jesus for his "human" attributes only. Address-ing the issue of Washington's faith, Jefferson himself said he had heard both from Dr. Rush and the New Yorker Gouverneur Morris, a Wash-ington intimate, that the First of Men, even as he injected a religious vocabulary in public statements, was not a Christian by any definition. Once America was on its feet and democratic institutions began to take root, biblical sentiment delivered in the ornate language of the King James Bible took its leave of national politics and returned to vil-lage pulpits—though posterity would believe what it wanted.[23]

As part of "pseudobiblicism," Americans responded to the Siren sound of "Divine Providence," an extremely common trope in writ-ings of the Revolutionary era and beyond. But that script did little more than serve mellifluously what we nowadays call "civil religion." It was not an American invention, either, having been employed by the English to reckon themselves a divinely blessed people. As the scholar of early American religion Gregg L. Frazer, a practicing Chris-tian, readily attests, the concept of Divine Providence had no Chris-tian content. It was a convenient turn of phrase, clearly comforting and altogether simple to process. It was used extensively in schoolchil-dren's textbooks as well as in popular histories. While anyone could read Christianity into presidential addresses, this did not by any means indicate that religion was regarded as more than a Revolutionary prop to aid in securing political union, social stability, and peace of mind. For a host of evangelicals, however, Jefferson's religion would come to bear a heavy weight in the snowballing "Christian nation" debate at the turn of a new millennium.[24]

EACH ONE of the ambitious conservative advocacy groups began with its own special concern. As president of the Family Research Council, Tony Perkins was most outspoken in his group's opposition to gay rights, appearing often on cable news. Increasingly political in his public statements and writings after President Obama took office, he took umbrage at the Democrat's record on religious freedom, arguing in 2012 that the Affordable Care Act, or Obamacare, had extreme provisions offensive to religious interests, to wit, requiring employers such as religious hospitals and religious universities to provide sterilizations and contraceptives ("including some that can cause abortions"). Said Perkins: "Thomas Jefferson would have considered this to be tyranny of the worst kind." Nothing in the Jefferson record even faintly suggests that he would opt to elevate church doctrine over the individual conscience. What is Jeffersonian in allowing a Catholic hospital the right to impose its religious views and practices on a non-Catholic employee?[25]

In their production of outlandish conspiracy theories, Protestant evangelical groups became strange but predictable bedfellows of the Tea Party. In 2009, with the election of President Obama, the Christian activist Ralph Reed founded the Faith and Freedom Coalition precisely to bring religious conservatives together with Republican renegades. In the 1980s, as a graduate student at Emory University in Atlanta, the boyish Reed was raised up by Pat Robertson and made principal spokesman for Robertson's Christian Coalition. In the mid-1990s, owing to his success in bringing out the Christian conservative vote, he was featured on the cover of *Time.* Then, after unsuccessful bids for political office, sidelined temporarily following the scandalous revelation of his close financial ties to the imprisoned lobbyist Jack Abramoff, Reed resurrected himself.

His Faith and Freedom Coalition ran with the official motto "Restoring America's Greatness & Founding Principles." Among its advertised purposes, the group advanced the need to limit government, lower taxes, and support "profamily" (antigay, anti-abortion) legislation. Reed exhorted pastors to tell the churchgoing public how they should vote, and he highlighted the need to protect conservatives from the "bigotry and discrimination" issuing from a cadre of bloodthirsty secularists. The preceding were all policies meant to reflect America's "founding principles." But bitterness and bile were not "founding principles" any more than blurring the boundary between secularist and atheist was. Reed's alarmism was, in fact, just what Jefferson was reacting against in 1800 when he called out religious conservatives who would exercise "tyranny over the mind" in a republic devoted to the pursuit of reason (along with happiness).[26]

It is admittedly difficult to enter the mind of someone who professes that the greatest threat to America in the twenty-first century is secularism, let alone to ascertain what Jefferson represents to such an individual. Nevertheless, we must try. In *A Nation Like No Other* (2011), Newt Gingrich was appealing to a prospective conservative electorate when he warned against the secular threat: "Our entire American system of government is premised upon a deeply religious ideal," he guaranteed his readers. America's motto "All men are created equal" was—and of this he had no doubt—"a profound religious principle that recognizes God as the ultimate authority over any government." With this impression as his point of embarkation, Gingrich singled out the only force that could subvert a God-centered, God-committed family- and community-based republic: it was the "radical secularists," and they were bringing about "an America that openly rejects faith and the faithful." Here, Gingrich ignores the obvious: His "God" is not the deistic God that Jefferson and his peers were invoking.

Every fanatical movement needs an enemy to confront. Those whom Gingrich termed "radical secularists" would ruin America by converting it into "utilitarian culture," a term he did not care to explain other than to state, counterintuitively, that the *secularists'* creed would create economic disparity. In contradistinction to his model of a Christian culture, secularism, he said, "elevates the powerful and crushes the weak."

Were secularists the real troublemakers here? As Speaker of the House in the mid-1990s, Gingrich was known for such questionably "Christian" measures as tax breaks for the rich, financial favors for large corporations, and attacks on social programs and health and safety standards in the workplace. He was reprimanded for personal ethics violations and consequently lost his speakership. Nevertheless, as he laid out his vision in *A Nation Like No Other,* he kept piling on glib, disingenuous criticism of the antireligious threat. Radical secularists, he charged, liked to harp on past social ills that white churchgoing Christians were supposedly guilty of condoning. Calling this condemnation a misreading of history, Gingrich aimed to prove that it was Christianity that made government self-correcting—after all, he said, it took a Baptist minister (the Reverend Martin Luther King) to come along and speak out against racial injustice. Naturally, Gingrich did not contend with the fact that many proslavery apologists of the 1850s were deeply religious men; nor did he devote ink to a consideration of why the religious convictions of the southern white majority did not instruct them to champion civil rights as soon as Dr. King's movement began to gain ground. Instead, we are meant to understand that it is the "radical secularists" who seek "to undermine the moral legitimacy of America's religious heritage."

The Gingrich formula has been to affect deep thought, but to substitute for conscientious inquiry the gaudiness of ostentatious ambiguity. What could he have meant by the intended insult to secularism in associating it with "utilitarian culture"? The Protestant ethic itself, so long a source of national strength and consistency, is every bit as utilitarian as constitutional secularism. Defining moral standards for others was easier for Gingrich than explaining his own journey; for he was divorced from as many houses of worship as wives. Raised Lutheran, for decades a Southern Baptist, he has been, since 2009, a proud Catholic.

In 2011–12, the Gingrich method allowed professedly Christian southern whites to embrace long-discredited forms of prejudice and rewrite history once again. In a Gingrich-authorized world, it was possible to rationalize, as in the early 1960s, that the Declaration of Independence ensured the right to segregated housing. A Corpus Christi, Texas, newspaper had lectured outsiders at the time that the phrase "all men are created equal" did not mean that all were intellectually equal, nor did it imply that there should be equality of education among blacks and whites. Fearing that inequality was "eroding the moral foundation" of the United States, the 1963 report of the secular Commission on Civil Rights directly confronted that moribund ideology. Such independent, government-protected activism on behalf of social equality reminds us that Christianity was not and is not the only (or even the principal) historical force operating on the nation's moral identity.

But the shameless presidential hopeful of 2012 feared no contradiction. Gingrich went on to blame radical secularists for the failure of schools to preach the importance of the Great Awakening in colonial history, explaining that it was "religious convictions that motivated those first Americans to risk everything" to secure their freedom and independence. The Awakening "shaped the American character," he assured. More than any boycott of British goods, more than secular interests, those few short years of religious upheaval in the 1740s "cemented a deep and immoveable belief that ultimate authority rested with God alone, that God—not government—gave man his rights."

Gingrich was in campaign mode. While radical secularists "claimed to support religious neutrality," he charged, their "real agenda" was quite the opposite, and their "dogmatic intolerance" of people of faith a matter of deep concern. It was they who were the insidious "sect" undermining liberty. "Worse still," the Georgia politico exclaimed, "in flagrant violation of the anti-establishment clause, today the judiciary is effectively establishing this radical secularist religion as the official religion of the federal government." On the basis of this argument, the historical Jefferson falls neatly into Gingrich's definition of "radical secularist"; for the clerics who felt threatened by his prospective presidency reduced his political beliefs to godlessness. He would "get rid of religion and the clergy," rang out one representative voice, that of Reverend William Linn of New York.

The one Jefferson quote in Gingrich's combative book comes in defense of family values as bound up in faith: "The happiness of the domestic fireside is the first boon of Heaven," wrote Jefferson to a cabinet secretary in 1813, "and it is well it is so, since it is that which is the lot of the mass of mankind." This is not a statement one can read a lot into. Suffice it to say that Gingrich was one southerner whose preachings evaded the two key elements of a Jeffersonian religious sensibility: a humbling awe before grand nature's organization; and an embrace of that justice and goodness Jesus taught. We can pretty much guess where Jefferson would place Newton Leroy Gingrich on his list of must-read authors: "I rarely waste time in reading on theological subjects, as mangled by our Pseudo-Christians," Jefferson wrote impatiently in 1816.[27]

IN 2010, the nation's attention was drawn to the Texas Board of Education, when it made sweeping changes to the state's secondary school social studies curriculum. For years, the Lone Star State had paid a premium to the big publishers in order to get religious conservatives' message across, erasing, in the process, much of the history of New Deal programs; other states, less proactive, ended up conceding to Texas domination over the nation's public school textbooks. In consequence of editorial decisions made after the election of Barack Obama, greater importance was assigned to the Right's victories of the 1980s and 1990s. Falwell's Moral Majority was included in the social studies curriculum, as was principled opposition to the Equal Rights Amendment, Newt Gingrich's political agenda, the 1994 "Contract With America," and, incongruously, the National Rifle Association.

In 2010, the Texas Board of Education took particular aim at

Thomas Jefferson, whose historical role, they concluded, deserved to be minimized in public school pedagogy for one simple reason: his reputation for questioning the values of religious conservatives. The name "Ronald Reagan" was inserted on more pages, while Jefferson's was summarily dismissed from the long-favored list of influential philosophers (along with religious skeptics such as Voltaire), and supplanted by Thomas Aquinas and John Calvin, two men who were obviously less uncomfortable with the marriage of church and state. "History has already been skewed," said one elected board member, who was trained not as an educator but as a dentist. "Academia is skewed too far to the left." The designation "Enlightenment" was no longer to be used in the context of eighteenth-century intellectualism, and the oft-abused "capitalism" was replaced with the friendlier "free enterprise system."

According to the blog of the liberal commentator Bill Moyers, one liberal education board member wanted students to be asked to discuss the reasons why religious freedom had to be protected, and why the founders did not show preference to one particular religion. A conservative countered that the premise was wrong, that the founders "didn't intend for separation of church and state." After minimal debate, the liberal's motion was rejected, and the text amended to say that church-state separation was not critical to the First Amendment. It bears mentioning that no historians sat on the Texas Board of Education.[28]

This was a low point in Jefferson's posthumous career as a patriotic symbol. The Internet did not help, either. Along with the earlier-mentioned inaccurate Jefferson quotes found in cyberspace and fact-checked by Monticello's research department, various other spurious attributions have emerged, each put forward as a "smoking gun" to confirm the founder's anti-Christian bias. Some were twisted versions of things Jefferson actually wrote, while others were obvious fabrications, to wit: "Christianity is the most perverted system that ever shone on man."

While Jefferson's critics in the Texas schoolbook business were seeing to it that this most unreliable founder was kept from polluting children's minds with ungodly thoughts, a handful of highly influential social conservatives were taking pains to rebrand Jefferson as a respectful worshipper of Christ who wanted nothing so much as to educate Americans to the world's only perfect religion. The historian of religion Edwin S. Gaustad had laid the groundwork in his less than rigorously researched book *Sworn on the Altar of God* (1996), in which he asserted that Jefferson was more open to revealed religion than previously thought. With such pronouncements as "Jefferson assumed an ordered, theocentric world," he reclaimed the questioning founder for the cause of religion. Unlike "aloof, passionless" deists, Jefferson "believed that God continued to create and sustain the world moment by moment," and he was "comfortable with the general notion of immortality." At the end of the book, Gaustad suggested readers ponder the best way to incorporate Jefferson into America's overall religious profile: "The question now posed is to what degree Jefferson himself survives as a kind of 'grand church' to which a large cross-section of citizens can rally." Jefferson, who called himself a sect of one, would probably have found Gaustad's idea more absurd than actually irritating.[29]

If historians, as a sect, are occasionally prone to overreading, a susceptible religious public, open to "signs" from God, can be downright unresisting in its hopes of locating meaning in evidence compiled for them by one of the faithful. Meet the "self-taught" historian David Barton. In the early twenty-first century, there was arguably no one who received as much attention in conservative circles for his investment in religion and the founding. Large numbers rallied round, as Barton, a native Texan, published *The Jefferson Lies* in 2012. Helping him boast his historical discoveries before a credulous audience of many millions was the easily agitated, wildly popular radio and television personality Glenn Beck, a man who never made it past high school and called Barton his "mentor," "one of the most important voices in America."

The Jefferson Lies caused a stir when it was first released, and sold quite well. With great fanfare, Barton connected the sensational "lie" that Jefferson had fathered Sally Hemings's children to the equally unpalatable "lie" that Jefferson was less than a Christian or had ever advocated "a secular public square." If the lion's share of the book advances a religious interpretation of American history, its author's opening chapter is a crude reiteration of the "Why Randolph Jefferson actually did it" line of thinking. After exonerating brother Thomas from the insulting charge of having had sex with his servant, the author proceeds to argue, with the same selective reading of the few sources that appealed to him, that Jefferson was emphatically not a racist but instead a "lifelong unwavering advocate for emancipation."[30]

Here and throughout, Barton decried the systematic belittling of great men, a sinister enterprise conducted by unpatriotic deconstructionists (his term) who had succeeded (so far) in brainwashing the public at large. Eagerly affirming Tony Perkins's message that "real faith in the true God" was what made America exceptional, and the Gingrich dictum that "our entire American system of government is premised upon a deeply religious ideal," Barton avowed that the "greatest casualty" of deconstructionism was "American exceptionalism—the belief that America is blessed and enjoys unprecedented stability, prosperity, and liberty as a result of . . . God-given inalienable rights, individualism, limited government," and so on. After several decades of battering, American exceptionalism was now "no longer recognized, understood, or venerated." It was incumbent on religious conservatives to take back Thomas Jefferson.[31]

Among Barton's more inflammatory statements was the following:

> Jefferson was not a secularist, deist, or atheist. He never wavered
> from his belief that God actively intervened in the affairs of men. He
> thus regularly prayed, believing that God would answer his prayers
> for his family, his country, the unity of the Christian church, and the
> end of slavery.[32]

He intimately associated Jefferson with the leaders of a spiritual movement, circa 1810, known as the "Christian Connection," simply because it had a presence in central Virginia. Barton on Jefferson: "The greatest influence on his personal religious views was the religious disposition of the community around him." It is difficult to imagine a more ludicrous take on the mind of Jefferson: no evangelical minister could ever have talked him into anything; he was certainly not a passive "mirror that accurately reflected the spiritual condition of his cherished central Virginia," as Barton would have it. Besides, the most noteworthy promoter of the movement in question was a Presbyterian minister from Pennsylvania, and Jefferson reserved some of his harshest words for the stern Presbyterians, whose denominational structure, like the Anglican, uncomfortably resembled a political structure. For Barton, though, nothing of merit in Jefferson's writings undermined the founder's "strong conviction in a personal God Who answers prayers and intervenes in the affairs of mankind and before Whom every individual would stand to be judged."[33]

Like the dishonest Gingrich or the misguided Perkins, the incendiary Barton would not be worth addressing in depth were it not for the influence he held as a self-promoting foot soldier in the culture wars. Could he possibly not know how flawed his history was? It would seem unlikely. For his statistical authority on the majority of slave owners' alleged tendency to avoid having sex with their slaves, he inexcusably drew upon a proslavery writer of the 1850s. For his conviction that Jefferson was the close friend of a little-known Virginia evangelical named James O'Kelly (though they never corresponded), he gave weight to an unsubstantiated story that was current in Christian circles in the early twentieth century. Such examples indicate how far the modern crusader will go to defend an idealized image.

Barton identified as the closest to an impeccable source for the truth about Jefferson the three-volume biography produced by Henry S. Randall in 1858—with the illogical explanation that a work authorized by Jefferson's grandchildren had to be superior. While precious itself as a historical artifact, and useful and rich in anecdote, Randall's *Life of Jefferson* is so deeply biased that it requires very close, prudent, skeptical reading, which a methodologically deficient propagandist such as Barton evidently could not comprehend. He began his project, instead, with the now well-established conservative premise: that America's progenitors cannot be diminished in stature or shown as morally blemished without mutilating the perfect purpose for which the United States of America was brought into existence.

Like the campaigning Gingrich, the indoctrinator Barton stoked the fire of reaction in 2012, and in the process served to cheapen the study of history. Even his publisher agreed, pulling the book from retail shelves after an independent investigation called its arguments into question. A carefully researched book by a pair of intellectually honest evangelical scholars (a psychologist and a political scientist) soon after emerged, shredding Barton's arguments. It was called *Getting Jefferson Right*.[34]

Though *The Jefferson Lies* was taken out of circulation, its author continued to deny that he had made any significant misstatements or had misconstrued evidence—yet he had gone so far as to claim that the vast majority of delegates to the Constitutional Convention were evangelicals. Visibly shaken by *Getting Jefferson Right*, whose authors he had previously held in esteem, Barton went on Glenn Beck television to defend himself.

Beck had always loved props, and Barton, equipped with founding-era artifacts he had collected, pulled out an 1803 newspaper that was, for him, a piece of sacred evidence from the Christian nation. It was proof positive that President Jefferson had used federal funds to send missionaries to an Indian tribe. Never mind that the Kaskaskia people, not Jefferson nor his administration, had asked for a missionary presence—as the authors of *Getting Jefferson Right* had clarified. Never mind that the Indians had enjoyed long and friendly ties to Catholic French

Canada. Barton had his Christian version of DNA in the antique paper, which he twisted so as to imply that the Indians' Catholicism fed into Jefferson's master plan to evangelize all the tribes. "Pardon me for reading out of context," said Beck, preciously, before querying how it was that Jefferson was able to resist the prevailing anti-Catholicism. "Jefferson really wanted to help the Catholic Church," returned his guest, automatically—for even the vaguest expression of Christianity warmed his heart. "He's one of the biggest pro-Jesus guys out there," Barton declared of Jefferson.

The author's show-and-tell went on for a good quarter hour. Beck, who insisted that his friend was the target of a leftist witch hunt, looked on agog, as Barton insisted that secularizing historians had all got Jefferson's religion wrong. Jefferson did not really aim to excise miracles from his cut-and-paste "Gospels of Jesus," though to the undiscerning eye it might have looked that way. So Barton turned next to his 1904 edition of the so-called Jefferson Bible, printed for Congress at the instigation of the Iowa legislator who had expressed astonishment on spying the Smithsonian's newly acquired treasure. Channeling the third president as if he had first anointed the Iowan as his apostle and now deputized Barton as a latter-day detective meant to spread the Word of "Jefferson's Bible," the discredited author fought to enlighten his viewers: "Jefferson says, *This is what every citizen needs to know.*'" The host was hanging on his every word. Opening the century-old volume, Beck sat transfixed. No less an authority than the Government Printing Office had issued the 1904 Jefferson Bible. Different times, then: the big, bad federal government was not yet overrun by those who hated Christians.

Barton, the mild-mannered, televangelist founder-worshipper, had spoken. Beck's suspicions were confirmed. Before dark modernity set in, the United States was indisputably a Christian nation. And Jefferson, despite all you've heard, was the first to hoist God's flag.

Though his book was pulled, Barton's fan base among conservatives in both houses of Congress refused to abandon him. "I'm not in a position to opine on academic disputes between historians," Senator Ted Cruz of Texas told Politico.com in September 2013. "But I can tell you that David Barton is a good man, a courageous leader and a friend. . . . David's historical research has helped millions rediscover the founding principles of our nation and the incredible sacrifices that men and women of faith made to bequeath to us the freest and most prosperous nation."[35]

***

ACCORDING to the historian of religion John Fea of Messiah College, the "Christian Nation" view requires belief in five principles: (1) that God shapes human history directly; (2) that the Christian nation created in 1776 had a morally related prehistory in the experience of Pilgrims, Puritans, and their ilk; (3) that the signers of the Declaration and framers of the Constitution were alike committed Christians; (4) that the Constitution is grounded in truths presented in the Bible; and (5) that modern secularists—"revisionists"—have purposefully acted to undercut the Christian narrative and its crucial role in U.S. history. Fitting Jefferson into the "Christian Nation" box takes considerable work.[36]

The red-white-and-blue charade manifest by Glenn Beck—a man part doomsayer, part faith healer—has clear eighteenth-century roots in the magical thinking promoted by popular prophets. It must be more than simple coincidence that Beck first began to appear regularly on conservative Fox News in January 2009, the same month that Barack Obama took the oath of office. Others at the network focused on the Left's "infatuation" with Obama but were, at least temporarily, constrained by their journalistic personae; and Beck, unplugged, off-the-cuff, found a niche. He had bluntly told Roger Ailes, the network's chief executive, "I believe we are in dire trouble, and I will never shut up." Ailes replied that he saw Obama's election as "the Alamo," and thereupon gave Beck free rein, for a time.[37]

The parallel between Presidents Jefferson and Obama is notable for the disturbing presence they personified to a fear-directed community of interests: two transformative figures on the national political stage both accused of bearing ill will toward Christianity. Religious conservatives, two centuries apart, boiled over in their rush to demonize a secular leader they felt threatened the power structure. In 1801, an itinerant preacher from Maine wrote to congratulate Jefferson on his accession to the presidency: "Many declare you an Atheist; but be it so, I much rather a liberal Atheist should govern the people, than a bigoted Saint, who knows not God." No poll was conducted at election time to determine the percentage of Americans who thought Jefferson an atheist; but in 2013, 20 percent of Republicans seriously entertained the belief that Barack Obama was, literally, the Antichrist.[38]

Was there a lesson here? Beck's association with David Barton serves as a reminder that significant numbers of the religious Right have never really been interested in history. They have drawn on Jefferson and his fellow founders in order to advance a coercive agenda. Far more than other conservative groups, religious conservatives aim for a kind of social control that can only be solidified by gaining control over the historical narrative. In denying the substance of intellectual arguments—ignoring, for example, Jefferson's actual embrace of the right of conscience—politicized evangelicals of the present generation have instead sought to change the world by refashioning democracy's muse into the man they prefer him to be: righteous, as they define righteous; devout, as they define devout.

As is often the case, public debate says more about the debaters than about Jefferson. The college-educated men we call "founding fathers" were steeped in the physical sciences as much as they were students of political philosophy. Of course, they were not unfamiliar with the inside of a church. But any reference to "nature's God" or to "Providence" in the hallowed texts to which they signed their names emphatically did not indicate a retreat from rational argument or their cession of any earthly power to unseen forces.

To those history purists who double as founder fundamentalists, however, our world would come apart if America's creation were somehow withdrawn from God's unceasing protection. After September 11, 2001, pressure built to strengthen that understanding. Among the professed patriots elected to state legislatures after the ghastly and disorienting terrorist attacks of that date, the history purists were quick to call attention to the threat of tyranny posed by Islamic (Sharia) law in the heartland of America. Sharia law? One might wonder how such a disengagement from reality is possible; but in attempting to make sense of a world that had seemingly changed forever, tyranny had a new first name. It was not monarchical, as it was for Jefferson; it was not Nazi, as it was for Roosevelt; nor Communist, as it was before 1990; it was now Islamic.

To founder fundamentalists, the first Muslim congressman, Keith Ellison of Minnesota, crossed a line when he took his oath in 2007, and took the symbolic step of being sworn in on Thomas Jefferson's copy of the Koran, circa 1765, now owned by the Library of Congress. Jefferson's Bible was one thing; Jefferson's Koran was something entirely different. In the so-called war on terror, Muslim had become another synonym for un-American. Ellison's act was not only not enough for redemption; it was perceived by the Right as an obnoxious stunt.[39]

There is a certain irony in this episode. Founder fundamentalists, whether or not they doubled as Christian fundamentalists, behaved in much the same way as those they detested in the Muslim world who accepted the infallibility of the early lawgivers of their religion. Fundamentalists, by definition, perceive their faith as the only true faith. Not only are good and evil clear-cut; tradition is be codified, properly interpreted, and applied broadly by high priests. Whether we are talking about patriotic excess or the politicization of an old religion, the underlying compulsion is similar. Usually without knowing it, true believers wish to escape history when they fail to acknowledge history's real complexity.[40]

AS THE legal scholar Andrew Koppelman recently explained, polemical conservatives and die-hard liberals both have history to hang their hats on. God is directly invoked in the Declaration of Independence, and public prayers and other ceremonial expressions of religiosity were routine. But God is strictly left out of the federal Constitution. As president, Jefferson refused to issue national days of fast or thanksgiving; and the Danbury Baptist letter is quite explicit. "Both sides are right," says Koppelman, clarifying how public religion evolved. In colonial times, prayer and Bible worship were thought generic enough not to threaten the viability of one or another social group; yet as early as the Revolution, "Christ" was already being left out of public pronouncements.

As time passed, the acceptable possibilities for belief and nonbelief changed. Christian morals remained teachable, but the Bible, when read in schools, had to be presented without religious commentary. It was only in 1890, when it outlawed Mormon polygamy, that the Supreme Court called the United States "a Christian nation." The mid-twentieth century introduced what Koppelman calls "nonsectarian monotheism." In the Cold War, as passions rose in opposition to Soviet atheism, Congress added "under God" to the Pledge of Allegiance. But the High Court also ended Bible reading in public schools and updated the Establishment Clause to honor nontheistic religion, thus restricting what generically Judeo-Christian symbols could be seen in public places. Ever since, at every level of society, arguments have continued in trying to draw lines and make certain that no religious community will enjoy preferential treatment. "In God We Trust" remains on our national currency because its function is regarded as purely ceremonial.

How to be friendly to religion without offending secular viewpoints? Though an ingenious architect as well as a constitutional thinker, Jefferson did not feel compelled to give the specific proportions of his "wall of separation"; keeping religion personal was all he really cared about. Perhaps it is in deference to Jefferson's deistic perspective that we are left with "ceremonial Deism," as Koppelman describes a culture "in which many people feel that their religious beliefs are somehow associated with patriotism."[41]

Jefferson wrote to his nephew Peter Carr at the time of the Constitutional Convention, in the Enlightenment spirit: "Question with boldness even the existence of a god; because, if there be one, he must more approve the homage of reason, than that of blindfolded fear." Ronald Reagan spoke at a prayer breakfast in Dallas 197 years later to an audience sure to be swept away by his performative skill: "If we ever forget that we are a nation under God, then we will be a nation gone under."

The difference in tone between these two offerings could hardly be greater. It is not that Jefferson would have dismissed Reagan's hyperbolic pandering, because Jefferson himself invoked godly providence in boilerplate pronouncements designed to rally the people. The difference, then, comes in the eighteenth-century man's refusal to brook unscientific nonsense; and the twentieth-century man's conflation of Americanness and godliness. Reagan intensified the patriotic script for which presidents are known, and urged the faithful to commune with every bracing myth about God and country that Hollywood ever inspired.[42]

In Jefferson's rational religion, the most modern educational tools had to come first. For him—for any Jeffersonian—truth lies in reason, not in blind faith. As such, the authors of the Old Testament were primitive thinkers, and theirs a text that spoke in religious tones only to fellow primitives. The Word of God? A Jeffersonian questions faith as a scientist might, asking: Why should a parishioner be praised as a "godly" man, simply for suspending his critical judgment and buying into whatever iteration of biblical history a narrowly educated preacher has mangled? When it's easier "just to believe," or when emotional consensus is reached without a proposition being tested by questioning souls, then humanity suffers. Jefferson could only detest a situation in which political requirements fused with those of sectarian religion.

Religion was something different to him. If God was to be deduced, it could only occur by studying the constitution of life and the marvelous combinations of symmetry and diversity contained on Earth and visible across the skies. A "rational" inference about the divine in nature can perhaps be drawn, a Jeffersonian would propose; but beyond that, the mystery would have to remain unsolved until the post-corporeal incarnation, or sensory impersonation, was attained. Jefferson did not use the word *heaven* when he speculated about an afterlife. It was, always, "the future state."

A NATIONAL poll taken in 2007 found that only 45 percent of respondents would cast their vote for a "well-qualified" presidential candidate nominated by their preferred party, if that person was an atheist. And whereas 94 percent would vote for a generic African American, 92 percent for a Jewish candidate, 88 percent for a woman, 72 percent for a Mormon, and 55 percent for a gay American, the acknowledged atheist fared most poorly. A separate survey found that 40 percent rated atheists as "not at all" in accord with their personal vision of social stability. Muslims scored significantly higher than atheists. Nearly half of those surveyed said they would be disturbed if their son or daughter wished to marry an atheist. Unless attitudes have changed since 2007, atheists still appear to be regarded as a most unsound element in American society.[43]

The "secular threat" in Washington is, practically speaking, insignificant, and it is a poll-tested fact that the vast majority of Americans profess belief in one or another form of God. Aside from the calls to prayer many presidencies are prone to issuing, government in the modern age tends to be scrupulous in projecting the nonsectarian monotheism that Jefferson (i.e., the public Jefferson) validated. On a somewhat deeper level, Jefferson as a secular visionary did not see scientific study and religious life as pursuits that were in any way antithetical the supreme intelligence in nature was to be uncovered collaboratively.

Nor, importantly, did he find it politically necessary to offset Protestant enthusiasm. The evangelicals he knew did not seek to impose on government. They would not have, say, force-fed their nonscientific faith to nonevangelicals by rendering an issue such as fetal rights a prime directive in voting. Early republican evangelicals merely wanted to practice freely and attain equality with the older, previously favored sects.

That, then, is where we have seen the most change. In our lifetimes, evangelicals have been unabashedly aiming to exercise greater power over the national mind, one family at a time. They operate on the belief that those who are hostile to religion are steadily rising in society and would, if they could, have all individuals conform to programs that are godless and government-run. This attitude—that heretics endanger the state—is a throwback to McCarthyism, when anyone questioning orthodoxy was deemed disloyal to the larger American essence. You don't want to be insufficiently God-fearing, and you don't want to doubt American exceptionalism.

Outspoken evangelical organizations such as "Focus on the Family" counter secular influence by promoting moral standards derived from the "biblical worldview" they glean. The most forward of their number promote an agenda that involves "praying through" daily troubles, getting behind abstinence education, and "impressing" God's Word on the young. Men are judged to have a natural inclination to seek adventure and take risks; it is, therefore, the job of fathers to teach sons to perform their God-granted role in the world in the right way. A praying patriarch at home is needed; not a distant, preying government contemptuous of religion.[44]

Admittedly, our government today, formed as it was to be unemotional, is far from successful using its Jefferson-like rational religion to keep the peace. Under a secular Constitution, government has little choice in the language it uses to communicate spiritually. It tries to be respectful to all, to moderate what cannot otherwise be balanced. But it tends to be ineffective where sensationalizing preachers and apocalyptic ranters have found enough sheep to form a flock. "God" talk from the White House is not aimed at the "crazies," then, but at the fictive family of "middle America," the sons and daughters who enlist in the armed services and believe in the American dream. To the extent that they even exist, they are Norman Rockwell's offspring.

They are Democrats and Republicans alike. We see them on Sunday after church, pursuing happiness as a moral community—which is just how Jefferson meant for his famous phrase to be understood. The difference lies between two types: churchgoers who quietly lend their support to food banks, and ultraconservatives who claim for evangelical religion the mantle of moral policeman. The latter crowd is highly intolerant, even vengeful, as it rails against the innumerable temptations that freely operate in the public sphere.

In a free society, any who seek self-protection can wall themselves off if they choose. The problem arises when, to justify a need for social control, one who wields religion as a weapon paints government as an encroaching outside force, tactless, bureaucratic, and dehumanizing, untrusted even when it comes bearing financial assistance. At such times, all government has in its spiritual arsenal to defend itself is the symbolic aura of a muted religiosity spoken in tones of solemn commitment after natural disasters; and presidents who say, "May God lead us through . . . May God protect . . . May God bless the United States of America."

What we see in action here is, more or less, a continuation of Jefferson's solution. Rational religion, the government's "ceremonial Deism," responds to the pull of secularism while giving a gift to people of faith. It counteracts the extravagance of those who just can't get enough religion, and who remain suspect of every smart federal program; it can never win them over, though; and if it retreats a single inch from its "God" language, it is bound to offend the millions schooled in conspiracy, who are apt to cry "Socialism!"

In the draft of a letter he wrote early in his retirement to a Virginia Presbyterian (who would later become a Baptist), Jefferson summed up his mind quite neatly. "Every religion consists of moral precepts, & of dogmas," he observed. "In the first they all agree. . . . In their particular dogmas all differ." While all agreed that murder, theft, and deceit were good "thou shall nots," ritual aspects of religious practice varied widely, as did the character of each group's "metaphysical speculations"—all of which were "totally unconnected with morality, & unimportant to the legitimate objects of society. Yet," Jefferson continued, "these are the questions on which have hung the bitter schisms of Nazarenes, Socinians, Arians, Athanasians in former times, & now of Trinitarians, Unitarians, Catholics, Lutherans, Calvinists, Methodists, Baptists, Quakers E^{t}c. Among the Mahometans we are told that thousands fell victims to the dispute whether the first or second toe of Mahomet was longest; & what blood, how many human lives have the words 'this do in remembrance of me' [Luke 22:19] cost the Christian world!"

In the version of the letter he ultimately sent, Jefferson opted to police his prose, because he did not know the recipient personally and feared any wider distribution. He did not wish to expose what he saw as organized religion's absurd precepts. So he removed the reference to "metaphysical speculations," deleted the names of the Christian sects and their "bitter schisms," and even softened his critique of the violence borne of religious differences.

Yet because he retained his original draft of the letter, we can see his mind at work: "We all agree in the obligation of the moral precepts of Jesus: but we schismatize & lose ourselves in subtleties about his nature, his conception maculate or immaculate, whether he was a god or not a god, . . . whether we are to use our own reason, or the reason of others, in the opinions we form. . . . It is time then to become sensible how insoluble these questions are by minds like ours, how unimportant, & how mischievous." This is what he wanted to say, but couldn't without taking the risk that his reasoned view would embarrass and anger the conventionally religious.

To sum up Jefferson's long-held assessment of religion, it was this: Morals, well-taught, make the world a better place. Dogmas, aggressively promoted, inhibit the honest pursuit of knowledge. Believe what you want. Just try not to be stupid, and don't let others think for you. If there is a God, no human can affect to know his mind, so what good is there in trying to enforce belief?[45]

But among more and more on the religious Right, that is not an acceptable description of Jefferson's mode of thinking. To be cherished by today's religious conservative, an American founder must have loved God and "family values" in a way that mirrors the conservative movement's priorities. So their history-conscious spokespersons superimpose on leading men past an unchanging value of disciplined devotion to God and a purity of character learned from the example of fathers and forefathers. To remain in the pantheon, a Jefferson or a Washington has to be seen to have exhibited the right values; selective quotations accomplish this need to reclaim and refashion.

It's all about saving the problematic Jefferson, and of making it blasphemy to call Washington a deist. What proselytizers such as Tony Perkins and David Barton have refused to understand, of course, is that while Jefferson felt strongly about the positive moral effects of religious teachings, he had stronger feelings when it came to the power-engrossing resolve of any representative of a religion who sought to impose his views on others, anywhere. "It cannot be a religious duty to erect the standard of uniformity," Jefferson wrote, quintessentially.[46]

In advocating for education, he tended to be most forthcoming about his attachment to the pursuit of truth. In the report of 1818 setting forth the operating principles behind his as yet unconstructed University of Virginia, Jefferson advertised how he felt about the long train of abuses perpetrated by politically entitled religious leaders. He reproved the power-engrossing moves of those who would lead their flock backward to conformity. This too-sanguine child of the Enlightenment assumed that his generation had put a stop to the political triumph of ignorance:

And how much more encouraging to the achievements of science and improvement is this, than the desponding view that the condition of man cannot be ameliorated, that what has been must ever be, and that to secure ourselves where we are, we must tread with awful reverence in the footsteps of our fathers. This doctrine is the genuine fruit of the alliance between Church and State; the tenants of which, finding themselves but too well in their present condition, oppose all advances which might unmask their usurpations, and monopolies of honors, wealth, and power, and fear every change, as endangering the comforts they now hold. Nor must we omit to mention, among the benefits of education, the incalculable advantage of training up able counsellors to administer the affairs of our country in all its departments, legislative, executive and judiciary, and to bear their proper share in the councils of our national government; nothing more than education advancing the prosperity, the power, and the happiness of a nation.[47]

Jefferson was condemning the grasping self-promoter and his need for willing dupes. He was discrediting the doctrinarian whose inflexible rules encourage a tame conformity. It was, in short, religious imposture that Thomas Jefferson spiritedly scorned when he swore his eternal hostility to tyranny over the mind of man.

7

"HISTORY BECOMES FABLE"

Yesterday's Future

IN 1814, as the attorney William Wirt was at work on his full-scale biography of the elusive Patrick Henry, Jefferson wrote to him at length, bemoaning the mismanagement of history by those who presumed much with too little information at hand. "Hence history becomes fable instead of fact," said the former president, then past seventy. "The great outlines may be true, but the incidents and colouring are according to the faith or fancy of the writer." Nine years later, in his eightieth year, he wrote to Associate Justice William Johnson, whom he had appointed to the U.S. Supreme Court: "History may distort truth, and will distort it for a time, by the superior efforts at justification of those who are conscious of needing it most."[1]

Of all that Jefferson wrote over the course of a lifetime, these separate remarks best capture the running theme of the foregoing chapters. With temporal distance comes temporal distortion. Our national origins story is constantly being renegotiated and reshaped, a societal impulse that shows no sign of abating. Let us at least acknowledge that Thomas Jefferson would relate to very few of the claims made in his name over the three-quarters of a century since his Tidal Basin memorial was built.

To the extent that we wish to trace our essence, our collective identity, to morally secure beginnings, we live in the past—a past that is imperfectly known. The Revolutionaries we honor did not speak in a unified voice, though it certainly feels good to imagine that they did; patriotic pretense, while nothing criminal, needs to be offset. Those who seize upon an "original meaning" should recognize that they have a problem in ventriloquizing the founders: useful fictions have substituted for serious inquiry. Despite "superior efforts at justification," as Jefferson so aptly put it, our ventriloquists (either inadvertently or willfully) distort historical truth by assigning to that magical date of July 4, 1776, a ready awareness of embryonic national greatness. The power of rationalization explains an irony of history: the record is wont to supply contradictory evidence for many of our most hallowed assumptions.

WHY JEFFERSON? In our retrospective yearning, no one else among the Revolutionaries possesses the combined intellectualism and inspirational vocabulary that he does. In the five "Presidential Experts Polls" conducted by Siena College over the period 1982–2010, Jefferson has always ranked among the top five presidents overall, neck and neck with Washington; he and Madison are ranked one and two, respectively, in intelligence. In the category of "communication ability," he comes in first, winning by a landslide. Washington led an army, but it is not he who lights the way backward. Jefferson is the eternal flame.[2]

This is just what he wanted, actually. In Jefferson's mind, the only possible alternative to his republican vision for America was "consolidated" government, a regime in which the privileged few lorded over the many, and bankers sucked the system dry. Jefferson was always pulling for meritocracy, theorizing the good that expanded opportunities and porous social boundaries would yield. The whole idea of corrupt nepotism, of eldest sons having the inside track in building political dynasties, smacked of the effete social order that America was meant to have replaced.

Jefferson anointed himself the victor in a "Revolution of 1800" that reversed the trend he saw toward a restrictive government that subverted individual rights. By this logic, he would not have minded being thought of as democracy's muse, symbol of humane change; in contrast, his predecessor Adams, no fan of popular politics, spent most of his posthumous career as the heroic Revolutionary who proved a failure as chief executive.

History shows that defining oneself in opposition to an unpopular predecessor is key to the enduring reputations of those we might call "storied" presidents. The political scientist Stephen Skowronek has produced one such study, and writes: "Presidents who traditionally appear on lists of America's most effective political leaders—Thomas Jefferson, Andrew Jackson, Abraham Lincoln, and FDR—were, like Reagan, opposition leaders standing steadfast against already discredited political regimes." (Skowronek was writing just before the election of the charismatic Barack Obama, who succeeded an obviously discredited president as well.) "What they shared," he says, "was a moment in a political sequence in which presidential authority is at its most compelling."[3]

As the beneficiaries of political strife, these presidents (or their reputation crafters) could always claim that they came into office as the result of a popular upsurge, the fruit of political democracy. What this means is that the stories told about our republic involve the implicit understanding that America's destiny is preordained and progressive. On the other hand, the conservative impulse is to identify a golden age of "founding fathers," with prophets (especially Jefferson) who dubbed America's message of hope the harbinger of a better world. Making our assessments all the more confused is the historian's contention that the collective founders were never truly married to their vaunted rhetoric. To call the Americans a people *capable* of self-government did not imply that they would regularly *exercise* self-government. Even the sanguine Jefferson had occasional doubts.

Modern commentators tend to designate as a Jeffersonian one who finds it easy to identify with what is casually styled "the American Dream." A Jeffersonian vocabulary enlarges the meaning of "independence"; it is, most broadly, about finding fulfillment. It can justify libertarian selfhood as automatically as it registers the improved chances granted by FDR's New Deal and LBJ's Great Society. It is about the public good.

To the neo-Jeffersonian modern liberal, a society that fails to adequately educate its citizens, or a government that enacts laws to protect and reward only those who have amassed wealth and power, is institutionally corrupt. To the neo-Jeffersonian modern conservative, the "self-made man" succeeds with hard work and a sound head and heart; the deserving are able to catch their lucky break. Whereas Jefferson would never have said that those born to privilege deserve what they have, he did not approve government handouts as a substitute for private philanthropy. He can be twisted to suit varying agendas.

Jeffersonianism as an ideal goes through its ups and downs. Without sounding ridiculous, politicians will say things like, "Every new immigrant has the same access to the American Dream as one whose ancestors came over on the *Mayflower*." But Jeffersonianism's fading features are regularly lamented, too, when every generation poses that fearful question: "Can the American Dream be saved?" Either way, Jeffersonianism presupposes the authority and the viability of the Dream.[4]

Frustrated with the machinery of the modern world, we recur to that picture of health and hope enshrined in Jeffersonian optimism. As a young nation, America was "the world's best hope," Jefferson told an adoring public. The phrase is still irresistible, but not so easy to extrapolate. Jefferson's mind was shaped by conditions that prevailed in an agrarian age. But now, as the family farm is gobbled up, as an overreliance on fossil fuels, the presence of nuclear waste, and the as yet undetermined consequences of global warming all beset us, his words have been emptied of their original meaning; time and nature have caused his own award-winning invention, the "mouldboard plough of least resistance," to oxidize, to rust away. And in spite of all that, we moderns want to find Jefferson useful.

More evenhandedly than most, in promoting his documentary *Thomas Jefferson,* the filmmaker Ken Burns remarked: "We are all in some way or another the descendants of Thomas Jefferson, for good or for ill." Somehow, at key moments, the politically minded choose to forget that Jefferson couldn't solve the most intractable problems of his own time; instead, they unearth a morally supportive quote and grant it universal power. He is made the definer of essential American values.

We decided long ago to call our republic a representative democracy, wanting to believe that the electoral system in place makes it possible to overcome the gross inequality that ensures built-in limits to democratic uplift. Similarly, "Jeffersonian democracy" is the term we generally give to a measure of political openness and emotional contentment. Our failure to give real substance to the phrase "pursuit of happiness" (though we love its sound) in the context of modern political expectations should caution us that we are conceptually crippled in trying to fix a Jefferson for our times.

Visit Monticello. Stand in the parlor and look up at the decorative molding, repainted; or look around at the blue-tinted china, the oil paintings brought over from Europe, the burnt whale-oil lamps, the faded, brittle, leather-bound books. And what of the mute, melancholy feeling you get when you peer into any of his weathered mirrors? The life-breath on the mirror is frozen. He is long ago and far away. We reproduce the drama of him, but not as well as we imagine. Our problem with Jefferson is that there are simply too many of him, and they are all ghosts.

In adopting a Jefferson for our time, we mock ourselves. His words are decontextualized in order that he have something important and reaffirming to tell each living generation. He is not a Republican. He is not a Democrat. But if we still hope to determine whether it is today's

Republican or today's Democrat who is closer to capturing the historical Jefferson, we need pose this two-part question: What was more critical to him, (*a*) an unintrusive federal government, prevented from reaching into the affairs of individuals and families, a government that implicitly supports entrepreneurial energy; or (*b*) a sensitive federal government, responsive to all of its citizens, especially the most vulnerable, a government that applies every means at its disposal to protect the American people against unjust concentrations of power? There really isn't an answer to the question, because, once again, Jefferson lived in an unreachable past.

TO LIBERALS, history is a cautionary tale justifying the need for creative change. To conservatives, it is a cautionary tale justifying the need to monitor change lest it diminish the inherited values of a hallowed past. How one embraces Jefferson is all a matter of emphasis.

In the late summer of 2012, in the middle of a heated presidential campaign, Dick Armey of Texas, former House majority leader, appeared on MSNBC's *Hardball* with the contentious host Chris Matthews. At that time the chairman of the Tea Party organization FreedomWorks, and a onetime economics professor with libertarian convictions, Armey called on America to recover its founders' principles. He lavished praise on Jefferson, Madison, and their peers for creating "the greatest government in the history of the world." Insisting that the Constitution was put in place to guarantee that government serve the people, he added that only the modern Republican Party aimed to "return to that structure" the founders had created. Republicans alone, he said, "understand the miracle of America."[5]

Calling America a "miracle" nation, as Dick Armey did, is not just an example of civil religion. It is a reminder of the partisan purposes to which language is put. Both Republicans and Democrats simplify memory in order to justify an ideology. In referring to the American Revolution, they'll say, for example, "the colonists felt," as though "the colonists" embodied a collective mind. Or it's "the citizens of our republic" and "the American people," as though citizens, en masse, have ever agreed on anything. "The founders," or patriarchally, "our founding fathers," conjures something akin to a biblical sensibility. It is entirely normal to collectivize past opinion. But it is of limited value when one hopes to capture historical truth.

Jefferson stands for a vocabulary of virtue. In all he wrote, he joined politics to moral principle, which renders him equally useful to the Left and the Right. Jefferson the liberal indulged in studies that allowed him to fantasize the perfectibility of man. Believing that the combination of education and environment shaped a people, he maintained a strong conviction that nature led humanity on the path toward greater justice. This, in turn, gave him confidence in the future of self-government. While accepting that the United States would remain a society composed of "two classes, the laboring & the learned," he believed in expanding and improving public education until it was effective in combating injustice and inequality.[6]

Jefferson the conservative was always afraid of losing freedom to a resurgent "monarchical" party. He was afraid, too, that the political North was growing into an economic behemoth (the early republican equivalent of what is meant these days by the designation "Wall Street"). The agrarian South, with its draining humidity, logistical disadvantages, and cankerous slavery, watched its once considerable position in national assemblies dissolve but for the bluster. In taking it upon himself to embellish the precapitalist imagery shoring up his American Dream, Jefferson contributed at the same time to the political predicament that his generation, collectively speaking, was ill-equipped to solve: There were masses of nonwhites whose pain and frustration could only be denied through the construction of a narrative in which they appeared happiest when managed by enlightened white men.

No one ever decried tyranny over the mind of man better, and yet Jefferson could not admit that the South he loved was losing the battle of ideas. From his productive perch atop Monticello, this is almost understandable. The University of Virginia of his creation, with its classical forms and inviting lawn, combined the salutary rural air and an expansive library. America could be inventive without skyscrapers, strong and isolated from harmful foreign influences without a defense budget in the billions or trillions of dollars.

Even today, portions of the South remain a world apart. In unhealthy ways tied to the past, it is oblivious, when it wants to be, to the social and economic progress of the North and Northwest; oblivious, when it wants to be, to its own stagnant, trailing vision. With regard to sectional attributes alone, then, our Jeffersons (both liberal and conservative personae) are relevant in the twenty-first century. Liberals want to see him as a force for honest and open, intellectually advanced, participatory democracy. Conservatives want him to be a sentinel against big government and the subordination of the states and suppression of individual rights. An illusive Jefferson defends the "American way of life," whether it is northern- or southern-accented, and whether it is of a progressive or nostalgic character.[7]

LET US shift slightly, and examine the human dimension of Jefferson's legacy. Americans, we recognize, are a people whose ideals are often in conflict with their impulses. As a self-righteous breed of obsessive voyeurs, they regularly do what is forbidden to them. Since the medium of television first took over home life, the nation's history has consisted of a series of morality plays in which suspicions are aired, crimes are reported and solved, and the tiresome sexual indiscretions of public figures are held out like catnip. We cannot help, sometimes, looking to the past with the same sense of prurience and intrigue.

Less pervasive owing only to limitations in technology, scandal was a part of daily life in eighteenth-century London and in Jefferson's America, too. The original revelation, in 1802, of Jefferson and his "African Venus" Sally Hemings certainly fit the bill. Chastity and innocence were removed from America's story, with manners soon to follow. This, we find, is what freedom and democracy bring that is not spelled out in the Constitution.

A different sort of backward glimpse at celebrity culture reveals a passion for veneration that rejects the base, voyeuristic impulse. Modern patriots have transformed a select few of the nation's founders into superior beings; they have assured themselves that the Revolution yielded a bumper crop of genius to be harvested annually through commemorative ritual and happily consumed in hack journalism and popular history.

It must be read ironically, then, that in the view of history he embraced, Jefferson fully expected posterity to outdo the vaunted achievements of his generation. To a favored French correspondent, he expressed confidence that future generations would become progressively better at seeking truth: "Altho' I do not, with some enthusiasts, believe that the human condition will ever advance to such a state of perfection as that there shall no longer be pain or vice in the world, yet I believe it susceptible to much improvement, and, most of all, in matters of government and religion; and that the diffusion of knoledge among the people is to be the instrument by which it is to be effected." It is further irony that he was certain about his countrymen's ability to resist politicizing religion. We must accept that the modern voter is not the well-informed citizen that Jefferson projected.[8]

As a prognosticator, he has had a very mixed record. First and foremost, he probably did not anticipate just how thoroughly Americans would come to deplore his lifelong engagement with slavery. They have largely excused (with insufficient cause) the likes of George Washington, while singling out the master of Monticello. But if Jefferson failed to protect himself on that score, he correctly foretold how revered the founders of the republic would be, and he ordered his private papers in such a way that his positive philosophy of human betterment would make it possible for the best Jefferson to be preserved in memory. It was pure luck that the Declaration of Independence he penned became the nation's most precious, most morally assertive text—and he certainly did not resist capitalizing on that historic happenstance. Jefferson seized every opportunity to convey the very process of its creation, annotating and explaining his several drafts. He tabulated, set in columns, indexed, and preserved with clear intent.[9]

It makes sense that we honor Jefferson for the role he played in Philadelphia. It is a bit puzzling, though, that while we hold him peculiarly accountable for his and his peers' failure to live up to *our* liberal expectations of racial harmony, we do not mock him for excess optimism with regard to the "natural" human tendency in favor of social justice and rational decision making. After all, he naively recommended the obliteration of contractual obligations at the conclusion of each generation, and the calling of national constitutional conventions on a regular basis to prevent the past from dictating to the present.

These days, we don't so much mind his utopian moments. Conservatives used to mind. They felt the same disgust Theodore Roosevelt voiced about Jefferson's defense of the blood spilling that fed the socially destructive French Revolution. The more "reasonable" intellectual perspective, they said, was that of the discriminating John Adams or of Edmund Burke in *Reflections of the Revolution in France.*

Traditionally, the Right has held that soft, idealistic democrats were never as good as the sophisticated mandarins who embraced policy as realists—a way of thinking that radical twenty-first-century Tea Partiers overturned by exaggerating the evils of federal programs seeking to balance practical enterprise with social justice. Conspiracy-driven grassroots activists thus rewrote the script of conservative intellectuals who scorned social groups they saw as "unreasoning," such as the Woodstock generation; for conservatism has always remained suspect of those on the fringe who angrily demand "freedom" without specifying limits. That said, most on the Right have been able to salvage Jefferson by seeing him strictly as a champion of small government.[10]

A problem inherent in Jefferson's latest incarnation, then, concerns the lack of an accepted definition of political freedom. To be a conservative is to place capitalist innovation ahead of government-initiated and government-directed institutions. This is one way to project how democratic forces best operate in a free society. Liberals are more open to federal experiment, federal regulation, and the monitoring of private industry. Theirs represents a second theory of balanced democracy in action. When differences in learned perspectives are so fundamental, debates over policy direction are perfectly understandable.

There is the intellectual landscape, and then there is the emotional. Representations of threats to liberty animated the unifying Patriots of the 1770s who needed to excite an otherwise passive citizenry to enlist in a campaign that was likely to benefit a class of people other than themselves. Representations of threats to liberty also animated secessionist fire-eaters in the years immediately leading to the Civil War. But winning people over is not the same as proving that America manifests Jeffersonian democracy when the interests of the wealthiest— they with the most to lose—come first. Self-invested leaders coax and cajole, wave their arms and sound alarms, and practice sleight of hand. In the 1850s, nonslaveholding southern whites were told that the abolition of slavery threatened *their* honor, *their* social positions—as if common men were the ones who mattered most. It has always been thus. Public sentiment is a mostly unreliable measure of the common good.

We know this because freedom is less easily visualized through language than is tyranny. In America, anticommunism (or anti-Islam) is an easy sell when dressed up in apocalyptic garb, proving merely that propaganda is as dangerous in a democracy as it is, more blatantly, in a closed theistic (Iranian) or atheistic (Soviet) society. When Jefferson stood for president, he invented the term "monocrats" to describe high Federalists who he feared were open to monarchism in America. Conservatives who opposed him resorted to labeling him a dangerous atheist who would dismantle organized religion. As the Confederacy was taking shape after 1860, any unsatisfied southern politician who resisted ratifying the new government's constitution was nothing short of an "abolitionist." Democracies, like tyrannies, are kept alive by a manipulation of language and exaggeration of the threat posed by any who challenge the urgent consensus.[11]

When political speech is so easily turned into demagogic sound bites, how secure is political liberty? Jefferson wondered, too. As an inveterate optimist, he stood for "rational" religion and "rational" liberty. Yet, in office, he fiercely criticized newspapers for having become "polluted vehicles." Political liberty, for Jefferson, required informed opinion shapers to rise above base posturing. At the same time, he averred that political liberty did not exist unless those who exercised the franchise understood their own best interests. "It takes time to persuade men to do even what is for their own good," he wrote at the start of the Washington administration, in 1790. The electronic media of today afford us a global view, made instantaneous via satellite link; yet the problems Jefferson identified continue to afflict us.[12]

The opposition media during Jefferson's presidency mocked him for his bookishness. When he was termed a "philosopher," it was to assail his recurrence to theory and an ostensible lack of engagement with the world outside his head. In a similar vein, President Obama, with degrees from Columbia and Harvard, was called a snob; a health-care plan that promised profits for big private insurance companies became "socialism" and creeping despotism. Branded "radical" by his overstressed opponents, Obama may have sought to continue liberal programs built on incremental change and conditioned by their successes or failures as social experiments. But to the emergent Tea Party, the freedom Obama sought to take away from them, once reclaimed through less government, would somehow, magically, maximize personal gain for the aggrieved, whose cause was incongruously underwritten by a handful of the richest men in America.

A portion of our disaffected citizens can justly be called Jeffersonian (or Old Republican, as the same element was known in the early nineteenth century). These are the folks who feel left behind in a decisively changing world. Small-town and rural populations are those most likely to hang on to models of a bygone order—especially the strongminded men they looked up to when young, such as a grandfather who fought in World War II. The sense of community was different when these men spoke with authority and made ends meet. Estranged from big government and distant from corporate boardrooms, the dreamers who remain attached to Jeffersonian simplicity resent all that intensifies feelings of powerlessness and that produces psychic confusion. At different times, the black president, gay marriage, and Mexican immigration have all qualified as dangers. Old Republicans want to nail shut Pandora's box, guard against intruders, and reconstitute the homogeneity that at one time felt protective.

SO, WHAT shall we do with "Jeffersonian democracy," the synthetic term we love to apply to the best imaginable America?

The historical Jefferson put his honorable ideals on paper, but as an elected public official he was often unable or unwilling to put into practice the ideals that history prefers to attach to him. As chief executive, he rationalized his decision to acquire a vast North American territory from Napoleon without consulting Congress. The Louisiana

Purchase was a prudent but extraconstitutional action that Jefferson recognized as such. He asked to be judged by his patriotic motives. After gaining majorities in both houses of Congress, the partisan president sought to create a vacancy on the Supreme Court by impeaching a Federalist jurist who had insulted his political agenda. Then, when his former vice president, as a private citizen, sought to acquire land from the Spanish through filibuster, Jefferson judged him a traitor, put him on trial for his life, and improperly coached the prosecution. In some instances, he was all-or-nothing in his demands.

He ended his second term with the self-inflicted national economic wound that was the Embargo—yet another piece of evidence demonstrating that Jefferson refused to reach any accommodation with his northern political opposition. The Embargo was a policy that proved oppressive as well as impractical. While meant to cripple Britain without resort to war, it was widely seen as an anticommercial measure designed out of spite by a Virginia agrarian who ordered gunships to the Canadian border to interdict desperate New England smugglers.[13]

So, let us not forget: Jefferson had an agenda. He believed (rightly, as things turned out) that the Federalist Party would disappear from the national landscape, and he wanted to hurry it along the road to oblivion. He lived to see the hated party fade away. But, in the process, he revealed his own inflexibility, a certain cold-bloodedness, a refusal to grapple with personal obsessions, and a dangerous sense of determinism.

Was the Federalist Party bad for America? Was the party of Jefferson and Madison better? We of a later age do not have to decide between the two, unless we perceive that our present is conditioned, positively or negatively, by the conclusions we draw about that long-ago-dissolved moment. To make "Federalist" equal to modern elitism or modern conservatism, to make "Jeffersonian democracy" the equivalent of modern liberalism, are false equivalencies.

Some are simply content to ignore outcomes and celebrate the "greatest generation" in general terms. The episodes from Jefferson's presidency related above reveal the complexity of history, without which myths of courage and grandeur would remain uncontested. Sadly, the critical efforts of professional historians appear parochial in the collective mind of a public (and elected politicians) more likely to be fed on storied biography, through which the nation's founding is conveyed as the work of a handful of great thinkers. The false belief that self-interest was absent from the conduct of politics in early America has led to rapturous statements about American exceptional-

ism, a heaven-directed "founding moment," and a "greatest generation" of world historical significance.

Enlisting Jefferson in a modern political party excerpts a very small
part of him for provisional purposes. The failure to approach the Jefferson image realistically, historically, is a reflection of what George
Santayana once called our "poetic ineptitude" in dealing with human
nature. In commemorating the lives of the principal founders, citizens
are only asked to regard the ideas and acts that belong on monuments.
Similarly, the "if-Jefferson-were-alive-today" mind-set unconsciously
fills in gaps in reasoning. Whenever partisan interests are engaged, history becomes creatively twisted and insufficiently reflective, perhaps
for the same reason that campaign promises are rarely kept. This is
one way to interpret Santayana's "poetic ineptitude." It is a short-
sighted approach to the study of the past, of course. But it persists.[14]

Distortion of the historical Jefferson partakes of the psychology
that moves the so-called marketplace of ideas. That marketplace is
susceptible to an intense (and at its worst, monopolistic) mind game
of artful manipulation, whereby spurious notions can result in a sea
change in popular belief. The marketplace of ideas is often despotic.
People will believe what they want to believe, whether or not that belief is rational.

ONE OF the joys in studying history is that as one escapes the artificial confinement of dates, noteworthy events, and election results,
what's left is the perpetual problem of describing the rich, tormented
life of the mind of past actors. There is no neutrality in historical life.
Thus, it is hard to think of a leader who has consistently adhered to his
stated ideology or intent. Franklin D. Roosevelt became a Keynesian
only after he became president. Jefferson, the states'-rights advocate,
imposed an across-the-board trade embargo, a thoroughgoing invasion of private citizens' economic freedoms. His small-government
ideology yielded to the Louisiana Purchase, unprecedented in scale.
Like Reagan, Jefferson was an enemy of government spending who
ran up substantial amounts of debt.

Regarding Jefferson's applicability to modern ideologies, let us acknowledge that the "best" Jefferson is magnetic. But we must never
lose sight of the fact that no one can bring him—lock, stock, and bar-
rel—into our time. We cannot know whether he would have approved
the methods of FDR in combating the Great Depression with grand
federal programs. FDR had little doubt that his behavior was Jeffer-

sonian. The same is true for every conservative who uses Jefferson's script to rail against big government. On the one hand, the historical Jefferson would be a hard sell with regard to extensive federal regulatory power, but no American power broker exasperated him more than the self-involved "stock-jobber," whose whole being, it seemed to Jefferson, consisted in unexpurgated exploitation. How would he have gone about rectifying the ever-widening gap between the wealthiest class of citizens and everyone else? There's no answer.

Jefferson is easily criticized for his complicity in the perpetuation of American slavery. We know why we judge him for his lack of vision and lack of action; much has been written on this subject. The explanation for history's refusal to criticize him for his excess optimism is far less controversial, and far less the subject of discussion, but the answer is equally obvious: The language of optimism is every politician's ally, to the extent that it is the willingly deceived voter's instrument of faith. Jefferson's amiable optimism lingers with us like a theology. Americans wish to believe they have been created in the image of their political maker, who envisioned for them a bright future, free from excessive government restraint and full of individual opportunity.

To borrow Hannah Spahn's conceptual category, we live with Jefferson in sentimentally constructed time, and we long for comforting examples of its blessings to nourish our common spirit. We seek to reconcile the instructive past with a relatively disorganized present. As Jefferson, the "emotive" founder, was constantly trying to tell us, we converse with our conscience when we converse with the past.[15]

One problem this book has exposed is modern politicians' overreliance on a view of history built on axioms rather than good evidence. Their intellectual laziness makes them dangerously inaccurate spokesmen for historical truth. That laziness has led to oversimplified claims about the founders as prophets whose ideas must remain sacrosanct. When one reaches this point in a political argument, it is hard to challenge the sole acceptable interpretation of the founders' creed without being branded unpatriotic. Therein lies the danger—therein lies tyranny over the mind.

IN THIS study of the fluctuating Jefferson image, one of our barometers has been the novelist John Dos Passos, who turned to the founding generation for advice in the 1950s and 1960s. Moving from the Far Left to the Far Right, he ran up against the same wall and posed a question that eventually looms before all mature students of American history:

The American author John Dos Passos (1896–1970) took a curious political journey over the course of his lifetime. A staunch leftist in the 1920s, he had gravitated to Goldwater conservatism by the 1960s. Yet in all those years he never stopped loving Thomas Jefferson, making him the focal point of two books. The scraps on which he jotted his notes show that Dos Passos often struggled with some form of the question, "Where would Jefferson stand, if he were alive today?" (Courtesy of Special Collections, University of Virginia Library)

"What does it all boil down to? I keep asking myself: Which of their grand notions still really move men's lives today?"

Writing *The Head and Heart of Thomas Jefferson* and *Shackles of Power: Three Jeffersonian Decades,* Dos Passos consulted a variety of primary and secondary sources and took thousands of pages of notes. In the process, he became nearly obsessed with that other predictable question. It is scrawled in his pocket memo pads and appears amid cross outs on typed drafts in his private papers. Most of the time, it isn't even a complete sentence. It just says: "If Thomas Jefferson were alive today, he . . . ," and then Dos Passos pauses to see if he is able to arrive at a worthy predicate.

Ambiguity is written all over the record keeper's undisciplined pages. "If Jefferson were alive today," Dos Passos tried one day in 1956, "I imagine the first thing he would do [would be to] call a convention to readjust our methods of government to the needs of present day society." And a few lines later, "education his cure all." Then something about "income tax." Skipping down the page: "Thomas Jefferson still survives today. His radical spirit. . . ," followed by empty space. Onto another undated, unfinished page: "Jefferson's political thought really applies today. . . . [I]n simple terms what did he believe" No period. No question mark. More ambiguity.

Only in the context of everything else Dos Passos is writing in these years do such scribblings become concrete. Ardent in his anticommunism, he was convinced that a central government's encroachment in areas better served by masters of industry—the knee-jerk expansion of government bureaucracy that the New Deal initiated—augured ill for that element of Jeffersonianism Dos Passos believed could still be usefully, healthily adapted to modern society: the principle that individual enterprise produced an independent citizenry.

The educated voter was the one who thought and acted as the Revolutionaries had in calling out an unrepresentative government. Jefferson's greatest value to posterity, Dos Passos intuited, rested with his anti-authoritarian voice. Picking apart a 1787 letter that traveled from Paris to Virginia, Dos Passos noted: "Jefferson's mind had been working on the question: what are governments for?" And the key takeaway was this: "that man was an institution building animal. The revolutionist of today became the vested interests of tomorrow. No class of men not even men who had devoted their lives to the cause of individual liberty . . . could be trusted with authority over their fellows." The new King George III would be homegrown.

Dos Passos directed his attention where Jefferson had, toward the ideal individualist, the informed voter who was savvy enough to make "wiser choices" than those who permanently surrendered political power to "an entrenched governing class." Left or Right, it hardly seems to matter: the obsessive Jeffersonian of the mid-twentieth century found himself caught in the same predicament that so many other social commentators have since faced. Repeating a phrase of Jefferson's from the 1787 letter, Dos Passos bemoaned: "One can't help wonder sometimes, whether, in spite of the universal diffusion of mass communication and mass education today, Jefferson would have considered us 'capable' of the 'attention' needed to preserve our liberties."

Educating for the future, Jefferson wanted a honing of judgment, believing such a plan practicable—a word he particularly liked. John Dos Passos felt the same. He drew up a simple maxim for modern times, which he interpolated from his study of Jefferson: "A good citizen is a man who knows how to make decisions well." Talent soared where free to climb. It worked in the private sector: this was why the political novelist had come to decry federal paternalism and government controls.[16]

Perhaps Dos Passos did not reckon sufficiently with the fact that Jefferson's grand method for nurturing republicanism was as much a pipe dream in Jefferson's day as in the twentieth or twenty-first century. Finding citizens well enough educated to distinguish effectively between just solutions and unequal distribution, good ideas and bad, required a degree of insight, and foresight, that was (and is) unfortunately rather rare.

As imaginative as he was in describing the human condition, Jefferson serves to inspire belief more than he prescribes solutions. Those who quote Jefferson in the dark and out of context to advance their causes do not acknowledge the weight of the problem: disengagement from the doable is a serious side effect of founder worship.

As the conscience of his nation, as democracy's muse, the post-modern Jefferson had/has no means to overcome the lust for power that directs the loudest and most public of those who campaign for office or profit from their connections to officeholders. Those who soar are not necessarily the most talented or the most deserving. Democracy has not moved toward meritocracy. If big government did not accomplish Jefferson's dream of a society capable of intelligent, mindful reform, surely small government has come no closer.

AT THIS moment in history, it would appear that the most eager readers of founding-era biography are conservative in their tastes. Or perhaps it is more accurate to say that a conserving impulse emerges in most of those who seek some kind of meaning by harkening back to the political thinkers and political actors who were present at the creation of a nation that came to dominate world affairs over the course of its first two centuries of independent nationhood. To relish a formative idea (republicanism) and reach back to a formative essence is, on some level, to desire a world that is stable and familiar. A conservative penchant is for fixed examples of a supremely well-educated leadership corps. The ennobled founder is associated with a government well run, and, consequently, he becomes a vehicle in the cause of clarifying unchanging values.

Whither Thomas Jefferson? It remains to be seen whether the liberalizing trend among the rising generation of Millennials will translate into a more Rooseveltian Jefferson, or whether Jefferson will even matter. The pessimist looks about and sees that the rapid digitalization of historical texts has done little to improve historical focus, if we judge by the minimal use of digital archives outside the discipline of history. Political "now-ness" is intensified in the so-called Information Age, while a considerable amount of technological innovation is channeled into lax amusement. So, Jefferson's fate may rest in the hands of people for whom the early American experience is increasingly irrelevant.[17]

As well, a general suspicion of past authority has ramped up in recent decades. Even to label a time the "Age of Jefferson" is shorthand that may not endure. But this is how we organize history in our minds: as continuity versus discontinuity. As the French philosopher of history Paul Ricoeur put it, historical time is "neither cyclic nor linear, but amorphous." How we link one episode to another is subjective; how we visualize and order time, and declare its coherence, is entirely arbitrary.[18]

It is hard, nonetheless, to imagine nationhood without recourse to historical studies. We constantly give the past new (psychic) life through the medium of the present, and there is no reason to think the impulse to do so will fade for any length of time. The Jefferson Memorial is as visible and central as any Washington, D.C., site. It bespeaks Jefferson's survival. Beyond documentary evidence of his political existence, the statuesque reminder of his value is of a similar order of magnitude as Lincoln's memorial, from which freedom has been rung at key moments.

The founders' "pastness" cannot be disconnected from our present need to reconstitute them. Who would wish to be untethered from them? The prospect of forgetting them makes patriotic Americans afraid. A founding paradigm marries us to a collective purpose and assures us of a collective life and livelihood.

Jefferson is, therefore, symbolic of a larger passion for a past that possesses internal coherence and continued vitality. As he was an inventive thinker and writer, his American progeny, up to now, anyway, finds him to be a primordial resource through which to assert a national existential consciousness. In spite of physical absence, in spite of temporal distance, he is still democracy's doorkeeper. And in spite of his partisan identity, he retains unifying attributes. In protecting the populist ideals that buttress democracy, and in representing the power of the Word as the main tool of that democracy, he is—he wasn't in his own time, but he is in posthumous incarnations—a guardian of constructive engagement, without which, we nowadays presume, republican government cannot thrive.

That's how John Dos Passos saw Jefferson more than a half century ago: as a benefactor, as the country's conscience, as the bold spirit of resilience during times in the nation's life when it was too easy to despair. His Jefferson embodied contemplation and expectation:

> Man learns slowly but he does learn. We can hope that, in spite of the dizzy technological spiral we can learn enough about our industrial society, get it under control, before it destroys us. In that emergency we will turn back to the record of Jefferson's generation, as a great storehouse of information on the art of politics, which in the best sense of the word, is the art of adapting a society to human needs.[19]

In the end, our task must be to historicize Jefferson, not elevate or dethrone him. We wallow in wishful thinking when we call him up to rescue us from ourselves. The world's instantaneity distances us from pure Jeffersonian solutions, now more than ever.

Not only has modern America been confused over what to make of Thomas Jefferson. One can easily argue that the world does not know what to do with history at all. Generation by generation, with every uncomfortable disjunction, and ever in search of a moral lesson, people invent a usable past. We err drastically in trying to acquire a practical understanding of present objects by making historical experience less indeterminate than it actually is.

There are multiple Jeffersons because there is never one solitary history. We are unlikely to find a Jefferson we all like and keep his flame burning. But that's all right. We owe it to ourselves not to homogenize the first "greatest generation"; nor should we ever hope to rescind the part of the past we dislike.

ACKNOWLEDGMENTS

It has been twenty years since Dick Holway agreed to publish my doctoral dissertation, and I am delighted to retain him as an editor and friend after all this time. The good people on Sprigg Lane do great work, and I wish to commend Anna Kariel, Mark Mones, and Mark Saunders in particular. Copy editor Susan Murray gave the manuscript a thorough scrubbing, and I thank her, too.

In and beyond Charlottesville, there is a thriving community of Jefferson scholars who comprise a lively critical public. The staff at the University of Virginia Libraries and International Center for Jefferson Studies were tremendously obliging over the course of my research, and in Jefferson's extended neighborhood I have enjoyed productive conversations with Barbara Oberg and James P. McClure, John Stagg, Andrew O'Shaughnessy, Jack Robertson, Susan Stein, J. Jefferson Looney, Lisa Francavilla, Anna Berkes, and Coy Barefoot. I owe a special debt to Daniel P. Jordan for his insights and his wisdom.

It is a comfort to know that I can turn for advice to top Jefferson scholars Frank Cogliano, Cinder Stanton, Annette Gordon-Reed, and my longtime advisor Peter Onuf. The body of work of each has remained within easy reach throughout this project. I appreciate, too, the good ideas and collegial enthusiasm of James H. Angel Jr., J. Christoph Hanckel, Maurizio Valsania, Amy Greenberg, Alexis McCrossen, David Waldstreicher, Douglas Egerton and Leigh Fought, Stacey Robertson and Tom Thurston, Ira Herbst and Heather Karp, Gibril Cole, Aaron Sheehan-Dean, Reza Pirbhai, Andrew N. Wegmann, Spencer McBride, and Terry Wagner. And for graciously providing unique and valuable information, sincere thanks to Stephen Plotkin of the John F. Kennedy Presidential Library, Steven Hochman of the Carter Center, and Peter Robinson of the Hoover Institution.

My son Josh has rooted for this book from the beginning, and my partner, Nancy Isenberg, has provided intellectual nourishment and critical support, as always. For many years, our dear friends Matthew Dennis and Elizabeth Reis, accomplished historians, have pored over our work, made constructive comments, and helped infuse good, positive energy into all we write. It is to these caring friends that this book is dedicated.

APPENDIX

Excerpts from President Ronald Reagan's Address at the University of Virginia, December 16, 1988

One of my staff mentioned that Thomas Jefferson's favorite recreation was horseback riding, and I said he was a wise man. [Laughter] And another member of the staff said that Thomas Jefferson thought the White House was a noble edifice, and I said he was a man of refined taste. [Laughter] And a third member noted that, after retiring as president, Thomas Jefferson, in his seventies, didn't sit back and rest, but founded the University of Virginia. And I said: There's always an overachiever which makes it hard for the rest of us. [Laughter]

But no speaker can come to these grounds or see the Lawn without appreciating the symmetry not just of the architecture but of the mind that created it. The man to whom that mind belonged is known to you as Mr. Jefferson. And I think the familiarity of that term is justified. His influence here is everywhere. And yet, while those of you at UVA are fortunate to have before you physical reminders of the power of your founder's intellect and imagination, it should be remembered that all you do here, indeed, all of higher education in America, bears signs, too, of his transforming genius. The pursuit of science, the study of the great works, the value of free inquiry, in short, the very idea of living the life of the mind—yes, these formative and abiding principles of higher education in America had their first and firmest advocate, and their greatest embodiment, in a tall, fair-headed, friendly man who watched this university take form from the mountainside where he lived, the university whose founding he called a crowning achievement to a long and well-spent life.

Well, you're not alone in feeling his presence. Presidents know about this, too. You've heard many times that during the first year of his presidency, John F. Kennedy said to a group of Nobel laureates in the State Dining Room of the White House that there had not been such a collection of talent, in that place, since Jefferson dined there alone. [Laughter] And directly down the lawn and across the Ellipse from the White House are those ordered, classic lines of the Jefferson Memorial and the eyes of the 19-foot statue that gaze directly into the White House, a reminder to any of us who might occupy that mansion of the quality of mind and generosity of heart that once abided there and has so rarely been seen there again.

But it's not just students and presidents, it is every American—indeed, every human life ever touched by the daring idea of self-government—that Mr. Jefferson has influenced. Yes, Mr. Jefferson was obliged to admit that all previous attempts at popular government had proven themselves failures. But he believed that here on this continent, as one of his commentators put it, "Here was virgin soil, an abundance of land, no degrading poverty, a brave and intelligent people which had just vindicated its title to independence after a long struggle with the mightiest of European powers."* Well, here was another chance, an opportunity for enlightened government, government based on the principles of reason and tolerance, government that left to the people the fruits of their labor and the pursuit of their own definition of happiness in the form of commerce or education or religion. And so, it's no wonder he asked that his epitaph read simply: "Here was born [Reagan misspoke: he meant "buried"] Thomas Jefferson, author of the Declaration of Independence, of the Statute of Virginia for Religious Freedom, and Father of the University of Virginia.'"

Well, as that epitaph shows, for all his learning and bookishness, Mr. Jefferson was a practical man, a man who made things, things like a university, a state government, a national government. In founding and sustaining these institutions, he wanted them to be based on the same symmetry, the same balance of mind and faith in human creativity evidenced in the Lawn. He had known personal tragedy. He knew how disorderly a place the world could be. Indeed, as a leader of a rebellion, he was himself an architect, if you will, of disorder. But he also believed that man had received from God a precious gift of enlightenment: the gift of reason, a gift that could extract from the chaos of life meaning, truth, order.

Just as we see in his architecture, the balancing of circular with linear, of rotunda with pillar, we see in his works of government the

* The commentator was the New York attorney James C. Carter, speaking in June 1898 at a building dedication at the University of Virginia.

same disposition toward balance, toward symmetry and harmony. He knew successful self-government meant bringing together disparate interests and concerns, balancing, for example, on the one hand, the legitimate duties of government, the maintenance of domestic order and protection from foreign menace, with government's tendency to preempt its citizens' rights, take the fruits of their labors, and reduce them ultimately to servitude. So he knew that governing meant balance, harmony. And he knew from personal experience the danger posed to such harmony by the voices of unreason, special privilege, partisanship, or intolerance.

And I do mean personal experience. You see, despite all of George Washington's warnings about the divisiveness of the partisan spirit, Federalists and Republicans were constantly at each other in those days. The Federalists of the Northeast had held power for a long time and were not anxious to relinquish it. Years later, a New York congressman honored the good old days when, as he put it, "a Federalist could knock a Republican down in the streets of New York and not be questioned about it."[†] [Laughter] The Federalists referred to Mr. Jefferson as—and here I quote—"a mean-spirited, low-lived fellow, raised wholly on hotcake made of coarse-ground southern corn, bacon, and hominy, with an occasional fricasseed bullfrog."[‡] [Laughter] Which, by the way, was the 1800 equivalent of what I believe is known here at UVA as a Gus Burger. [Laughter] And an editorial in the Federalist Connecticut *Courant* also announced that as soon as Mr. Jefferson was elected, "Murder, robbery, rape, and adultery and incest will be openly taught and practiced."[§] [Laughter]

Well, that was politics in 1800. So, you see, not all that much has changed. [Laughter] Actually, I've taken a moment for these brief reflections on Thomas Jefferson and his time precisely because there are such clear parallels to our own. We too have seen a new populism

---

[†] This line originates in a less-than-authoritative 1888 book, *The Story of New York,* whose author, Elbridge S. Brooks, openly mingled made-up characters with actual historical figures.

[‡] Monticello's Research Department has discovered this to be a spurious quote, dating to an 1879 collection of American folktales. President Reagan obviously could not include the words immediately preceding, which identified Jefferson as the child of "a half-breed Indian squaw and mulatto father."

[§] The *Courant*'s colorful, if slightly paranoid, opinion piece from which these words were drawn did not actually mention Jefferson by name, focusing instead on the numbers of Americans purportedly infected by French Jacobinism, and "capable of every deadly passion," who would welcome a civil war.

in America, not at all unlike that of Jefferson's time. We've seen the growth of a Jefferson-like populism that rejects the burden placed on the people by excessive regulation and taxation; that rejects the notion that judgeships should be used to further privately held beliefs not yet approved by the people; and finally, rejects, too, the notion that foreign policy must reflect only the rarefied concerns of Washington rather than the common sense of a people who can frequently see far more plainly dangers to their freedom and to our national well-being.

TRANSCRIBED FROM VIDEOTAPE HELD AT THE RONALD REAGAN PRESIDENTIAL LIBRARY

NOTES

Preface

1. See Matthew Dennis, *Red, White, and Blue Letter Days: An American Calendar* (Ithaca, NY: Cornell University Press, 2002), esp. chap. 4, on the "unheroic" Presidents' Day.

2. "49 Nobel Prize Winners Honored at White House," *New York Times*, Apr. 30, 1962 (henceforth cited as *NYT*); "Cognoscenti Come to Call," *Life*, May 11, 1962 (italics added). The *Times* article substituted "ate" for "dined," though typewritten notes, with handwritten edits in Kennedy's hand, use "dined"; this is the language that has descended to us, just as *Life* reported it.

3. Text of Kennedy's speech, *NYT*, Nov. 6, 1960; "Phrase from Jefferson Borrowed by Kennedy," *NYT*, Feb. 15, 1962; Thomas Jefferson (hereafter "TJ") to Lafayette, Dec. 26, 1820, Thomas Jefferson Papers, Library of Congress (henceforth cited as TJP-LC).

4. Andrew Burstein, *Jefferson's Secrets: Death and Desire at Monticello* (New York: Basic, 2005), chap. 8; Merrill D. Peterson, *The Jefferson Image in the American Mind* (1960; Charlottesville: University of Virginia Press, 1998); Francis D. Cogliano, *Thomas Jefferson: Reputation and Legacy* (Charlottesville: University of Virginia Press, 2006).

5. Michal Jan Rozbicki, *Culture and Liberty in the Age of the American Revolution* (Charlottesville: University of Virginia Press, 2011), 23. Rozbicki explains that early American rights discourse was bound up in understandings of individual liberty, security, and property that no longer govern. Thus, I try to keep the historical Jefferson in mind, even as I divert my eye to his modern interpreters; it is important to historicize such phenomena as the communication of culture and the limits of active expression if we are to understand and adhere to the primary obligations the discipline of history demands of its practitioners.

6. The falsification of history is a subject Jefferson addressed in a variety of ways himself, as he formulated his ideas of what a republic should be. His thoughts are neatly compressed in a letter penned in retirement to his old French friend Pierre Samuel du Pont de Nemours. The people were "competent to judge the facts occurring in ordinary life," Jefferson wrote, but not in those cases "requiring intelligence above the common level." Practical understanding was not

always intuited, and the same applied to the artful manipulation of language: "The human character" required "constant and immediate controul, to prevent its being biassed from right by seductions of self love." The entanglements of the ego (though, of course, he did not label it as such) were, in his view, productive of wrong ideas (see TJ to Du Pont de Nemours, Apr. 24, 1816, TJP-LC).

1 "Eternal Hostility Against Every Form of Tyranny"

1. Francis D. Cogliano establishes four stages in the history of Jefferson's posthumous reputation: from his death in 1826 to the Civil War, when states' rights, nullification, and slavery dominated; from 1865 to the 1920s, when Jefferson's reputation suffered; the Age of Roosevelt, when "the government sought to reach Jeffersonian ends by Hamiltonian means" (and in this, April 13, 1943, was a ceremonial watershed); and the "revisionist" period since the 1960s, as critical studies of Jefferson, undercutting New Deal hagiography, began to pour from the presses (see Cogliano, *Thomas Jefferson: Reputation and Legacy* [Charlottesville: University of Virginia Press, 2006], 5–14). Cogliano necessarily draws on the example of his predecessor in the study of Jefferson's historical reputation, Merrill D. Peterson, *The Jefferson Image in the American Mind* (1960; Charlottesville: University of Virginia Press, 1998).

2. TJ to Benjamin Rush, Sept. 23, 1800, in *Papers of Thomas Jefferson* (Princeton, NJ: Princeton University Press, 1950–), 32:168 (henceforth cited as *PTJ*); Peterson, *Jefferson Image,* 343–55; Brian Steele, "Remembering Jefferson in the 1920s: Claude Bowers and Albert Jay Nock," in "Jefferson's Lives," ed. Robert M. S. McDonald (unpublished manuscript); Peter J. Sehlinger and Holman Hamilton, *Spokesman for Democracy: Claude G. Bowers, 1878–1958* (Indianapolis: Indiana Historical Society, 2000), 114–17. On the Republicans' Hamilton preference from Theodore Roosevelt through the 1920s, and the impact of Bowers's book, see Stephen F. Knott, *Alexander Hamilton and the Persistence of Myth* (Lawrence: University Press of Kansas, 2002), chap. 5.

3. Claude G. Bowers, *Jefferson and Hamilton: The Struggle for Democracy in America* (Boston: Houghton Mifflin, 1925), 74, 90–93, 110–11, 140–51.

4. Sehlinger and Hamilton, *Spokesman for Democracy,* 131–37. In his foreword to the Sehlinger and Hamilton biography, Arthur Schlesinger Jr. ranked Bowers's 1928 speech with keynotes by Alben Barkley (1948) and Mario Cuomo (1984) as the "most effective political orations of the century" (ibid., x).

5. *Official Plan for the Nation-Wide Celebration of the 150th Anniversary of the Adoption of the Declaration of American Independence,* June 18, 1926 (Washington, D.C.: U.S. Government Printing Office, 1926).

6. Al Smith's acceptance of the Democratic nomination, Albany, NY, Aug. 22, 1928, American Presidency Project, University of California–Santa Barbara (henceforth cited as APP-UCSB), www.presidency.ucsb.edu; Sehlinger and Hamilton, *Spokesman for Democracy,* 137.

7. TJ to Joseph Priestley, Mar. 21, 1801, in *PTJ,* 33:394; "Campaign Address on Progressive Government at the Commonwealth Club," San Francisco, Calif., Sept. 23, 1932, in *The Public Papers and Addresses of Franklin D. Roosevelt* (New York: Random House, 1938), 742–49. FDR's Jefferson quotation is from a September

10, 1814, letter to Thomas Cooper, who was, like Priestley, a deeply learned English émigré. After saying, "We have no paupers," Roosevelt left out Jefferson's description of paupers, "the old and crippled among us, who possess nothing and have no families to take care of them, being too few to merit notice as a separate section of society, or to affect a general estimate." He most likely would have drawn this quotation from *The Writings of Thomas Jefferson,* ed. Andrew A. Lipscomb and Albert Ellery Bergh (Washington, D.C.: Thomas Jefferson Memorial Association, 1904), 14:182. This series was known as the Memorial Edition.

8. Rexford G. Tugwell, *The Democratic Roosevelt* (Garden City, NY: Doubleday, 1957), 96, 197.

9. Cordell Hull, *The Memoirs of Cordell Hull,* 2 vols. (New York: Macmillan, 1948), 1:173–75, 194–95. If his precise meaning is unclear in referring to Jeffersonian ideas that were "apt for quotation," Hull pronounced his Jeffersonianism more palpably in the early days of his administration of the State Department, when he advocated that "peoples everywhere . . . had to be kept educated, organized, and alert" to matters of their own general welfare. Addressing the Foreign Service in April 1933, he spoke for the president as well as himself in stressing that their objective while in office was "the constant pursuit of human liberties."

10. Ibid., 1:167–69, 197–98.

11. "Address at the Home of Thomas Jefferson, Monticello, Virginia," July 4, 1936, APP-UCSB, www.presidency.ucsb.edu/ws/?pid=15317.

12. Address at the Jackson Day Dinner, Jan. 8, 1938, *Public Papers and Addresses of Franklin D. Roosevelt* (New York: Macmillan, 1941), 37–42. On Jackson's foibles, see esp. Mark Cheathem, *Andrew Jackson, Southerner* (Baton Rouge: Louisiana State University Press, 2013); Andrew Burstein, *The Passions of Andrew Jackson* (New York: Knopf, 2003); and James C. Curtis, *Andrew Jackson and the Search for Vindication* (Boston: Little, Brown, 1976).

13. "Memorials to Thomas Jefferson and Alexander Hamilton" (HR-28468), 62nd Cong., 3rd sess., Jan. 29, 1913; Alan Havig, "Presidential Images, History, and Homage: Memorializing Theodore Roosevelt, 1919–1967, *American Quarterly* 30 (Autumn 1978): 514–32.

14. Press conference, Dec. 15, 1938, in *Public Papers and Addresses of Franklin D. Roosevelt* (1941), 605; Roosevelt to Edward M. House, Mar. 10, 1934, in *F.D.R., His Personal Letters, 1928–1945,* ed. Elliott Roosevelt (New York: Duell, Sloan and Pearce, 1950), 394.

15. *Report of the Thomas Jefferson Memorial Commission,* 75th Cong., 1st sess., H.R. Doc. No. 367 (1937); *Report of the Thomas Jefferson Memorial Commission,* 75th Cong., 3rd sess., H.R. Doc. No. 699 (1938).

16. Hugh Howard, *Dr. Kimball and Mr. Jefferson* (New York: Bloomsbury, 2006), 232–33, 240–43, 254; Marie Kimball, *Jefferson: The Road to Glory, 1743–1776* (New York: Coward-McCann, 1943); Elbert D. Thomas, *Thomas Jefferson, World Citizen* (New York: Modern Age, 1942), appendix VI, 266–71; Herbert E. Sloan, "The Frenchman and The Faculty Wife: Gilbert Chinard and Marie Goebel Kimball," in "Jefferson's Lives," ed. Robert M. S. McDonald (unpublished manuscript). With respect to the ladies who threatened to protect the cherry trees, Roosevelt quipped that he would employ crane operators to lift both the trees and the

women stubbornly clutching onto them, and deposit all elsewhere, safely (press conference of Dec. 15, 1938, in *Public Papers and Addresses of Franklin D. Roosevelt* [1941], 607; Conrad Black, *Franklin Delano Roosevelt: Champion of Freedom* [New York: PublicAffairs, 2003], 827–28).

17. Frederick J. Bradlee, "Thomas Jefferson Coolidge," in *Proceedings of the Massachusetts Historical Society* 72 (1957–60): 373–78.

18. Thomas, *Thomas Jefferson, World Citizen,* vii, 52, 133–34; Elbert Thomas obituary, *NYT,* Feb. 12, 1953.

19. Thomas, *Thomas Jefferson, World Citizen,* 194–97, 242–44.

20. Andrew Burstein, "Jefferson in Confucian Relief," *William and Mary Quarterly,* 3rd ser., 54 (Oct. 2007): 845–52; John Israel and Steven H. Hochman, "Discovering Jefferson in the People's Republic of China," *Virginia Quarterly Review* (Summer 1981): 401–19. Liu also compared Jefferson to the ancient Chinese poet T'ao-hua-shan, who preferred his tranquil home life to "fame and gain." Liu's portrait of Jefferson focused on moral consistency and humility, easily understood in opposition to behavior in official China, past or present: "He was a man of strict morals. As a public servant, he had no lust for power, still less any desire to use his office for his private interest. . . . He was honest and incorruptible, turning away any kind of bribery" (Liu Zuochang, "Thomas Jefferson and His Conception of Happiness," in *Thomas Jefferson and the Education of a Citizen,* ed. James Gilreath [Washington, D.C.: Library of Congress, 1999], quote at 300).

21. Kentuckian cited in William E. Leuchtenburg, *The White House Looks South* (Baton Rouge: Louisiana State University Press, 2005), 119.

22. Peterson, *Jefferson Image,* 355–76, quote at 360; Thomas, *Thomas Jefferson, World Citizen,* appendix III, 253–55. On June 27, 1936, a week before his Monticello speech, Roosevelt accepted renomination at the Democratic National Convention in Philadelphia. He invoked both Washington and Jefferson that day, reminding his hearers why the American Revolution was fought; it was, he said in the most liberal-democratic Jeffersonian mode, to place "the business of governing into the hands of the average man."

23. Wendell Willkie's acceptance speech, Aug. 17, 1940, APP-UCSB.

24. H.R. Rep. No. 1758, Mar. 12, 1940; and *Report of the United States Commission for the Celebration of the 200th Anniversary of the Birth of Thomas Jefferson,* Feb. 10, 1941. Regarding the use of the script of the Declaration of Independence during the New Deal and beyond, see Alexander Tsesis, *For Liberty and Equality: The Life and Times of the Declaration of Independence* (New York: Oxford University Press, 2012), chap. 15.

25. The Four Freedoms were set forth in FDR's State of the Union Address, Jan. 6, 1941. Fireside chat, Sept. 11, 1941, APP-UCSB; Claude G. Bowers, "Thomas Jefferson and South America," *Bulletin of the Pan American Union* (Apr. 1943): 190, reprinted in H.R. Doc. No. 37, pt. 4, 78th Cong., 1st sess., *U.S. Congressional Serial Set;* TJ to Jay, Aug. 23, 1785, in *PTJ,* 8:427.

26. "Memorial to Jefferson to Be Dedicated," Associated Press, Apr. 11, 1943.

27. *Thomas Jefferson Quiz Book,* comp. Edward Boykin, in Special Collections Library, University of Georgia, Athens, quote at 76; *Life,* March 8 and April 12,

1943. In *The Patriots*, Jefferson was played by Raymond E. Johnson, a popular radio soap-opera actor and series host.

28. Gerald W. Johnson, "Devil or Demi-God?," *Life*, Nov. 24, 1941. For an instructive study of Wilson and Jefferson, emphasizing race but also explaining their essential styles of argument and rationalization, see John Milton Cooper Jr., "American Sphinx," in *Jefferson, Lincoln, and Wilson: The American Dilemma of Race and Democracy*, ed. Cooper and Thomas J. Knock (Charlottesville: University of Virginia Press, 2010), 147–62.

29. In Merrill Peterson's trenchant characterization of Henry Adams: "He repeatedly called Jefferson a great man and his political creed the only workable starting point for American nationality. Yet he showed Jefferson casually abandoning his principles, creating none in their place, suffering the most humiliating defeats, drifting helplessly on the tide of circumstance" (Peterson, *Jefferson Image*, 283).

30. Hubert H. Humphrey, *The Political Philosophy of the New Deal* (Baton Rouge: Louisiana State University Press, 1970), 66–75, 119–20.

31. *Life*, May 19, 1941.

32. Undelivered address prepared for Jefferson Day, April 13, 1945, in *Public Papers and Addresses of Franklin D. Roosevelt, 1944–1945*, comp. Samuel I. Rosenman (New York: Harper, 1950), 613–16.

2 "His Mind Liberal and Accommodating"

1. Kyle Longley, *Senator Albert Gore, Sr.: Tennessee Maverick* (Baton Rouge: Louisiana State University Press, 2004), 72–73.

2. TJ to Kercheval, July 12, 1816, *The Writings of Thomas Jefferson*, ed. Paul Leicester Ford (New York: G. P. Putnam's Sons, 1899), 10:43.

3. Nathan Schachner, *Thomas Jefferson: A Biography* (New York: Appleton-Century-Crofts, 1951), 1:vii–viii; Encyclopedia of Science Fiction, www.sf-encyclopedia.com/.

4. Henry A. Wallace, "Thomas Jefferson's Farm Book: A Review Essay," *Agricultural History* 28 (Oct. 1954): 133–38; *The Eleanor Roosevelt Papers*, ed. Allida Black (Charlottesville: University of Virginia Press, 2012), 910–11.

5. "Remarks at a Supper for Democratic Senators and Representatives," Jan. 12, 1950, Public Papers of the Presidents of the United States, http://quod.lib.umich.edu; *Talking with Harry: Candid Conversations with President Harry S. Truman*, ed. Ralph E. Weber (Wilmington, DE: Scholarly Resources, 2001), 105; "Truman Pictures a Mme. President," *NYT*, Jan. 11, 1954.

6. Francis D. Cogliano, *Thomas Jefferson: Reputation and Legacy* (Charlottesville: University of Virginia Press, 2006), 86–92.

7. Harry S. Truman, "Address on the Occasion of the Publication of the First Volume of the Jefferson Papers," May 17, 1950, APP-UCSB.

8. In addition to Nathan Schachner's two-volume biography and Marie Kimball's ongoing work, the University of Virginia professor Dumas Malone published the first of his six magisterial volumes, *Jefferson the Virginian*. The entire set bears the title *Jefferson and His Time* (Boston: Little, Brown, 1948–80).

9. "Hollywood: Unmasking Informant T-10," *Time,* Sept. 9, 1985; Bernard F. Dick, *The President's Ladies: Jane Wyman and Nancy Davis* (Jackson: University Press of Mississippi, 2014), 88–89; "Reagan Played Informant Role for FBI in '40s," *Chicago Tribune,* Aug. 26, 1985. On Parnell Thomas's misdeeds, see www .politickernj.com/wallye/35228/story-j-parnell-thomas.

10. Dean Acheson, *Present at the Creation: My Years in the State Department* (New York: Norton, 1969), 364–70.

11. "President Extols Resigning Cabinet," *NYT,* Jan. 18, 1953.

12. Acheson to Truman, Feb. 10, 1953; Truman to Acheson, Mar. 6, 1953, and July 6, 1962, in *Affection and Trust: The Personal Correspondence of Harry S. Truman and Dean Acheson, 1953–1971* (New York: Knopf, 2010), 5, 10, 276.

13. *Talking with Harry,* ed. Weber, 104–5, 124–25.

14. Helen Cushman, oral history interview by William Moss, Dec. 7, 1980, Wellesley, MA, for the Robert F. Kennedy Oral History Program of the John F. Kennedy Library, Harvard University.

15. Arthur M. Schlesinger Jr., *Robert Kennedy and His Times* (Boston: Houghton Mifflin, 1978), 81–84; Burton Hersh, *Bobby and J. Edgar* (New York: Carroll and Graf, 2007), 128–29. Bobby and his new wife, Ethel, lived near, and belonged to, the Farmington Country Club, whose main building was designed by Jefferson in 1803 (see Lester David and Irene David, *Bobby Kennedy: The Making of a Folk Hero* [New York: Dodd Mead, 1986], 58).

16. McCarthy's friends tried to discourage him, saying: "Marshall has been built into such a great hero in the eyes of the people that you will destroy yourself politically." But McCarthy was bullheaded. He called Marshall's 1947 China mission one of "submission"; and he said that Marshall's adjunct, Acheson, exhibited loyalty first to Britain, and second to the Kremlin, with no feeling left for "the country of his birth." With Truman their "captive," U.S. policy consisted in appeasement of Moscow. America would thus become another of history's powerful empires "corrupted from within, enfeebled and deceived until they were unable to resist aggression" (Joseph R. McCarthy, *Retreat from Victory: The Story of George Catlett Marshall* [New York: Devin-Adair, 1954], 3, 69, 132, 164, 172).

17. "Portraits Shuffled in the White House," *NYT,* Feb. 13, 1953; "Stevenson Warns of Pitfalls Facing Republican Regime," *NYT,* Feb. 15, 1953.

18. "McCarthy Calls for Lie Tests in Tilt with Army," *New Orleans Times-Picayune,* Mar. 22, 1954.

19. Hallmark Hall of Fame episode accessed online at ctva.biz/US/Anthol ogy/Hallmark/HallOfFame_03_(1953–54). Helene Hanff was a struggling writer before achieving celebrity with *84, Charing Cross Road,* the charming record of her decades of correspondence with a London bookseller, later turned into a movie (Helene Hanff obituary, *NYT,* Apr. 11, 1997). Brooklyn-born Warner Anderson, concurrently playing a police lieutenant on a new cop show, portrayed Jefferson; he had previously appeared in such films as the submarine drama *Destination Tokyo* (1943) and played the court-martial judge in *The Caine Mutiny* (1954).

The "dangerous leftist influence" is epitomized in Augustin G. Rudd, *Bending the Twig: The Revolution in Education and Its Effect on Our Children* (Chicago: Heritage Foundation, 1957), which berated Charles Beard for his economic interpretation of the founding, faulted John Dewey for unleashing "collectivist" educational ideologues, and mourned that Washington and Jefferson were presented to high-schoolers merely as "large property owners and members of the ruling class" (quote at 79). The author, a *Mayflower* descendant, specifically recommended McCarthy's *Retreat from Victory*, along with *The United Nations: Planned Tyranny*, in his "Pests or Patriots," *American Mercury*, Dec. 1955, 152. In the same issue were the articles "Let's Put the Christ Back in Christmas" and "The Truth about Brain Washing."

20. "Truman Attacks Fake Crusaders," *NYT*, Nov. 11, 1953.

21. Arthur Herman, *Joseph McCarthy* (New York: Free Press, 2000), 298.

22. Schlesinger, *Robert Kennedy and His Times*, 105–6, 115. Schlesinger said that Bobby saw McCarthy as an "underdog," believed he was treated badly by the press, and thus continued to feel for him despite the methods he employed that had led Bobby to quit the committee. Bobby attended the disgraced senator's 1957 funeral in Appleton, Wisconsin (see David and David, *Bobby Kennedy*, 75–77).

23. Thomas Perkins Abernethy, "That Man Jefferson," review of *Jefferson Reader*, ed. Francis Coleman Rosenberger, *NYT*, Feb. 15, 1953.

24. "Douglas Warns U.S.," *NYT*, Nov. 4, 1957.

25. Column of Mar. 3, 1958, in *My Day by Eleanor Roosevelt: The Best of Eleanor Roosevelt's Acclaimed Newspaper Columns, 1936–1962*, ed. David Emblidge (New York: MJF, 2001), 258–59.

26. Arthur Schlesinger Jr., *Kennedy or Nixon: Does It Make Any Difference?* (New York: Macmillan, 1960), 2–5, 19, 35, 42–46.

27. Nixon nomination acceptance speech, July 28, 1960, APP-UCSB.

28. William C. Battle, oral interview by Guy Friddell, Feb. 17, 1965, John F. Kennedy Presidential Library. Like JFK, Battle was a PT boat commander in the Pacific during World War II. Kennedy later appointed him ambassador to Australia.

29. Sidney Hyman, "What Trendex for Lincoln?" *NYT*, Jan. 17, 1960.

30. Robert Dallek, *An Unfinished Life: John F. Kennedy, 1917–1963* (Boston: Little, Brown, 2003), 260.

31. Taylor Branch, *Parting the Waters: America in the King Years, 1954–63* (New York: Simon and Schuster, 1988), 344.

32. Dallek, *An Unfinished Life*, 325–27; Theodore C. Sorensen, *Kennedy* (New York: Harper and Row, 1965), 414–15; Caroline Kennedy statement made to Daniel P. Jordan, former executive director of the Thomas Jefferson Foundation at Monticello (in private communication with the author).

33. "The First Lady Brings History and Beauty to the White House," *Life*, Sept. 1, 1961.

34. William Voss Elder III, oral history interview by Ronald J. Grele, Dec. 15, 1965; and oral history interview with Esther Peters, July 14, 1964, both in John F. Kennedy Presidential Library; Craig Claiborne, "Thomas Jefferson Paved the Way for a French Chef in the White House," *NYT*, Apr. 10, 1961. Verdon left the White House in 1966, incensed that Lyndon and Lady Bird Johnson opted for "barbarities such as frozen vegetables" (Rene Verdon obituary, *San Francisco Chronicle*, Feb. 3, 2011).

According to Barbara Leaming, Jackie Kennedy used "historical cover" to justify purchases for the White House that actually reflected her personal taste (see
Leaming, *Mrs. Kennedy: The Missing History of the Kennedy Years* [London: Weiden-
feld and Nicolson, 2001], 45–47). For a more thoroughgoing study of Mrs. Kennedy and the White House Fine Arts Committee, see Barbara A. Perry, *Jacqueline
Kennedy: First Lady of the New Frontier* (Lawrence: University Press of Kansas,
2004).

35. "Jackson Ends Exile," *NYT,* Feb. 15, 1961; Eisenhower to Ralph Emerson
McGill, Oct. 7, 1960, in *Papers of Dwight D. Eisenhower,* ed. Louis Galambos et al.
(Baltimore: Johns Hopkins University Press, 2001), 2123–24; Karl Rove, interview
by Jonathan Rauch, in thebrowser.com and Salon.com, Sept. 10, 2012; "Campus
Conservatives," *Time,* Feb. 10, 1961. According to the magazine, the conservative
consensus held that unemployment "should be alleviated by charity," and that
children should "obey the Biblical command to honor parents" rather than place
that onus on the Social Security Administration. While some applauded the president's "Ask not what your country can do for you," regarding it as a conservative
call, others joined the new Young Americans for Freedom, which staged a march
on Washington in support of the House Committee on Un-American Activities.

36. Karl Rove, interview by Jonathan Rauch, in thebrowser.com and Salon.
com, Sept. 10, 2012; "Campus Conservatives," *Time,* Feb. 10, 1961.

37. *Pure Goldwater,* ed. John W. Dean and Barry M. Goldwater Jr. (New York:
Palgrave, 2008), 107.

38. *NYT,* Feb. 7, 1962; Dallek, *An Unfinished Life, 585.*

39. TJ to Charles Yancey, Jan. 7, 1816, in *Papers of Thomas Jefferson, Retirement
Series,* ed. J. Jefferson Looney et al. (Charlottesville: University of Virginia Press,
2004–), 9:330–31 (henceforth cited as *PTJ-R*). It would not have been a difficult
quote to find; it was a staple in John Bartlett's *Familiar Quotations,* a work regularly published and updated since the nineteenth century

40. Saul Padover, "Jefferson Still Survives . . . ," *NYT,* Apr. 8, 1962.

41. Anne Lincoln, oral history interview by Nancy Hogan, Feb. 9, 1965, John
F. Kennedy Presidential Library.

42. *Life,* May 11, 1962.

43. Cranston Jones, "Pride and Prejudices of the Master," *Life,* Apr. 27, 1959.

44. "We Hold These Truths . . . ," *NYT,* July 4, 1962.

45. "Jefferson Got Mad at the Press, Too, Mr. President," *Washington Post,* Jan.
20, 1963.

46. TJ to John Norvell, June 11, 1807, TJP-LC.

47. Andreas W. Daum, *Kennedy in Berlin* (Washington, D.C.: German Historical Institute, 2008), 156–59; Robert Oppenheimer, "A Talk in Chicago," *Bulletin of
the Atomic Scientists* (Oct. 1963): 4–6.

48. Walter Trohan, "Report from Washington," *Chicago Tribune,* Jan. 16, 1963.
Trohan was a giant in investigative reporting from early in the New Deal (which
he opposed) until his retirement in 1968. The first of his Jefferson quotes is from
the final section of the Kentucky Resolutions, Nov. 1798; the second, from a letter to Destutt de Tracy, Jan. 26, 1811; the third, to John Taylor of Caroline, June 4,
1798; the last, to William Ludlow, Sept. 6, 1824. Trohan did not take into account

that two of the four statements were made in protest against the illiberality of conservative Federalists who were centralizing their power.

49. John H. Glenn Jr., interview by Roberta Greene, June 30, 1969, Robert F. Kennedy Oral History Program, John F. Kennedy Library, Harvard University; Schlesinger, *Robert Kennedy and His Times,* 889.

50. In reply, Madison referred to the candidate's "polished manners" and "solid talents." The candidate, a Virginia judge, declined the appointment (TJ to Madison, May 13, 1825; Madison to TJ, Aug. 4, 1825, in *The Republic of Letters: The Correspondence between Thomas Jefferson and James Madison, 1776–1826,* ed. James Morton Smith [New York: Norton, 1994], 3:1937–40).

3 "We Confide in Our Own Strength"

1. Ralph Ketcham, *Individualism and Public Life: A Modern Dilemma* (New York: Basil Blackwell, 1987), 64–67, citing Reagan speech in *NYT,* Aug. 24, 1984.

2. Ronald Reagan, *The Notes: Ronald Reagan's Private Collection of Stories and Wisdom,* ed. Douglas Brinkley (New York: HarperCollins, 2011), 171.

3. Leonard W. Levy, *Jefferson and Civil Liberties: The Darker Side* (Cambridge: Harvard University Press, 1963), 158–65.

4. "Historian Assails Hamilton Action," *NYT,* Nov. 30, 1964. Major George Beckwith should be described in less sinister terms, as an unofficial envoy of the government in London, whom Jefferson refused to meet with in his official capacity. This does not make Hamilton's interference with Jefferson's department less obnoxious, but it does suggest Boyd's overreach (see Andrew Burstein and Nancy Isenberg, *Madison and Jefferson* [New York: Random House, 2010], 207–8; and Dumas Malone, *Jefferson and the Rights of Man* [Boston: Little, Brown, 1951], 272).

5. Levy, *Jefferson and Civil Liberties,* 17; *Washington Post,* Nov. 7, 1964.

6. "U.S. Honors Kennedy Sunday," *Chicago Tribune,* Nov. 20, 1964. The phrase, attributed to Secretary of War Edwin M. Stanton, is variously given as "belongs to the ages" and "belongs to the angels."

7. John Dos Passos, *The Shackles of Power: Three Jeffersonian Decades* (Garden City, NY: Doubleday, 1966); John Dos Passos, *The Head and Heart of Thomas Jefferson* (Garden City, NY: Doubleday, 1954); Virginia Spencer Carr, *Dos Passos: A Life* (Garden City, NY: Doubleday, 1984), 443–45, 475; White House press release, Apr. 28, 1962, John F. Kennedy Presidential Library; Marie Kimball, review of *The Head and the Heart of Thomas Jefferson,* by Dos Passos, *Pennsylvania Magazine of History and Biography* 78 (July 1954): 376–78. There were also some quite positive reviews of *The Shackles of Power: Saturday Review* took note of the author's view of Jefferson's "intellectual vitality and integrity" in promoting republican government; on May 8, 1966, the less erudite *Parade of Books* reported: "*The Shackles of Power* is a brilliant addition to historical works that now rather overshadow the contemporary fiction that brought Dos Passos fame in his youth" (John Dos Passos Papers, Special Collections, University of Virginia Library, Boxes 101, 119).

8. Francis D. Cogliano, "Merrill D. Peterson and the Apostle of Freedom: *Thomas Jefferson and the New Nation,*" in "Jefferson's Lives," ed. Robert M. S. McDonald (unpublished manuscript); Todd Gitlin, *The Sixties: Years of Hope, Days of*

Rage (New York: Bantam, 1987), 208. On Blind Lemon Jefferson, see www.allmu sic.com/artist/jefferson-airplane.

9. Dr. Max Rafferty, "UC Agitators and Tom Jefferson," *Los Angeles Times*, May 3, 1965.

10. TJ to Short, Nov. 28, 1814, TJP-LC; Robert Dallek, *Flawed Giant: Lyndon Johnson and His Times* (New York: Oxford University Press, 1998), 449. Jefferson elaborated in the letter that war must be a last resort: "All men know that War is a losing game to both parties." Still, his defense of America's motives is disingenu- ous, as the ambition to absorb Canada was an unspoken goal of those, including President Madison, who acquiesced to war in 1812 (see Burstein and Isenberg, *Madison and Jefferson*, chaps. 13 and 14).

11. Brock Brower, "Where Have All the Leaders Gone?" *Life*, Oct. 8, 1971.

12. Robert Dallek, *Nixon and Kissinger: Partners in Power* (New York: Harper- Collins, 2007), 206.

13. Richard Nixon, *In the Arena: A Memoir of Victory, Defeat, and Renewal* (New York: Simon and Schuster, 1990), 308; Richard Nixon, *1999: Victory without War* (New York: Simon and Schuster, 1988), 308–9. The "favorite" Jefferson quote is actually a close paraphrase: "We have no interests nor passions different from those of our fellow citizens. We have the same object, the success of representa- tive government. *Nor are we acting for ourselves alone, but for the whole human race.* The event of our experiment is to shew whether man can be trusted with self- government. The eyes of suffering humanity are fixed on us with anxiety as their only hope" (letter of July 6, 1802, italics added). Nixon got the gist of it right, and seems to have understood it in context. In her 1980 treatment of Nixon, Fawn M. Brodie incorrectly claimed this, Nixon's "favorite" quote, to have been a poor paraphrase of Thomas Paine (see Brodie, *Richard Nixon: The Shaping of His Char- acter* [New York: Norton, 1980], 118). It is worth adding of Nixon's engagement with history that at a press conference on September 16, 1971, he responded to a question about the uncertain democratic character of a South Vietnamese elec- tion by saying he was reading "a very interesting account" of the election of 1800, and that only 150,000 of the nation's 4 million people were then eligible to vote.

14. James Reston, "Mr. Nixon and Mr. Jefferson," *NYT*, Nov. 15, 1970.

15. John J. Sirica, *To Set the Record Straight: The Break-in, the Tapes, the Conspira- tors, the Pardon* (New York: Norton, 1979), 144–45, 238–39.

16. Stanley Cloud, "A Ghostly Conversation on the Meaning of Watergate," *Time*, Aug. 6, 1973.

17. "Va. Students to Counter Jefferson Birthday Rite," *Washington Post*, Apr. 12, 1969.

18. Hugh Sidey, "The Mandate to Live Well," *Time*, Apr. 15, 1974; Sidey, "The Consuming Pursuit of Power," *Time*, July 4, 1974.

19. Leon Friedman and William F. Levantrosser, eds., *Watergate and Afterward: The Legacy of Richard M. Nixon* (Westport, CT: Greenwood, 1992), 238–39.

20. On Jefferson in *1776*, see, for instance, Charles Champlin, "Our Founding Fathers in '1776,'" *Los Angeles Times*, Dec. 21, 1972; and "Monticello Recalls Jef- ferson the Man," *Chicago Tribune*, July 4, 1973.

21. Francis D. Cogliano, *Thomas Jefferson: Reputation and Legacy* (Charlottesville: University of Virginia Press, 2006), 171–75; Fawn Brodie, "Jefferson Biographers and the Psychology of Canonization," *Journal of Interdisciplinary History* 2 (Summer 1971): 155–71; Fawn M. Brodie, *Thomas Jefferson: An Intimate History* (New York: Bantam, 1974), 10–14, 614–16; Annette Gordon-Reed, "That Woman": Fawn Brodie's Intimate History of Thomas Jefferson," in "Jefferson's Lives," ed. Robert M. S. McDonald (unpublished manuscript).

22. Michael Kammen, *A Season of Youth: The American Revolution and the Historical Imagination* (Ithaca, NY: Cornell University Press, 1978), 91–94.

23. Both AP and UPI stories on the two-dollar bill, on April 13, 1976, were widely picked up; see also Louis Rukeyser, "The Two-Dollar Bill Is Back; Is 'Double-Dime' Next?," *Seattle Times*, Apr. 15, 1976. It was reissued in 1976, "for the sake of economy and convenience," and meant somehow to compensate for inflation. The two-dollar bill remains in circulation.

24. Library of Congress Annex, H.R. 11712, Mar. 4, 1976; Senate bill 2920, Apr. 13, 1976; *Thomas Jefferson Day*, House Report No. 94–979; Rep. Karth's remarks in the *Congressional Record* (henceforth cited as *CR*), House of Representatives, 94th Cong., 2nd sess., Apr. 13, 1976.

25. To understand the politics of Harry F. Byrd Jr. in connection with his father, Harry F. Byrd Sr., whose Senate seat he filled, see esp. Arthur Krock, "In the Nation: The Last Heir of Monticello," *NYT*, July 7, 1966.

26. *CR*, 94th Cong., 2nd sess., Apr. 13, 1976.

27. "Ford Warns New Citizens of Conformity," *NYT*, July 6, 1976; "Ford Welcomes New Citizens at Jefferson's Home," *Los Angeles Times*, July 6, 1976. (Many thousands around the country chose the bicentennial weekend to become citizens—more than seven thousand mainly Cuban refugees in Miami alone.) "Queen Visits Home of Author of American Independence," *Washington Post*, July 11, 1976. Speaking at the University of Virginia, Her Majesty wryly noted that she and George Washington had a common ancestor.

28. "What Is Happiness?" *NYT*, July 5, 1976.

29. Muskie speech in *CR*, Senate, 94th Cong., 2nd sess., July 2, 1976.

30. Peter Meyer, *James Earl Carter: The Man and the Myth* (Kansas City, MO: Sheed Andrews and McMeel, 1978), 18; Hugh Sidey, "Black Holes and Martian Valleys," *Time*, Apr. 10, 1978.

31. Douglas Brinkley, *The Unfinished Presidency: Jimmy Carter's Journey beyond the White House* (New York: Viking, 1998), 50; Jimmy Carter, *Keeping Faith: Memoirs of a President* (New York: Bantam, 1982), 21–23; Mary E. Stuckey, *Jimmy Carter, Human Rights, and the National Agenda* (College Station: Texas A&M Press, 2008), chap. 5, quote at 107; *Conversations with Carter*, ed. Don Richardson (Boulder, CO: Lynne Rienner, 1998), 146. Carter believed that LBJ "went to his grave convinced" that his southernness made him vulnerable to prejudice.

32. Statement of Steven Hochman in a private communication with the author, Feb. 6, 2014; Reagan to "Philip," undated, in Ronald Reagan, *Reagan: A Life in Letters*, ed. Kiron K. Skinner, Annelise Anderson, and Martin Anderson (New York: Free Press, 2003), 257–58.

33. www.presidency.ucsb.edu/ws/?pid=43130.

34. www.presidency.ucsb.edu/ws/?pid=38668.

35. Peggy Noonan, *What I Saw at the Revolution* (New York: Random House, 1990), 99.

36. Reagan, *The Notes*, xii, 16, 34–35, 109; comments by Peter Robinson, research fellow at the Hoover Institution, Stanford University, in a private communication with the author, Dec. 30, 2013.

37. To Thomas Cooper, on Nov. 20, 1802, Jefferson wrote: "A noiseless course, not meddling with the affairs of others, unattractive of notice, is a mark that society is going on in happiness. If we can prevent the government from wasting the labors of the people, under the pretence of taking care of them, they must become happy." To Samuel Kercheval, on June 12, 1816, Jefferson wrote: "I am not among those who fear the people. They, and not the rich, are our dependence for continued freedom. And to preserve their independence, we must not let our rulers load us with perpetual debt. We must make our election between *economy and liberty*, or *profusion and servitude*. If we run into such debts, as that we must be taxed in our meat and in our drink, in our necessaries and our comforts, in our labors and our amusements."

38. John McClaughry, "Jefferson's Vision," *NYT*, Apr. 13, 1982.

39. Ron Paul, interview, April 12, 1983. Edward Kennedy speech, April 18, 1983; Jesse Helms speech, May 19, 1983, both in *CR*, 98th Cong., 1st sess. The "tradition" was reported in Moncure Conway's book *Republican Superstitions as Illustrated in the Political History of America* (London: Henry S. King and Co., 1872), 47–48; it was told again in a Boston publication—"The Force Bill in the Senate," *To-day*, Dec. 25, 1890, 84. On March 1, 1994, Pat Leahy (D-VT) was reminded of the "famous colloquy" amid a Senate debate over the balanced budget amendment. And Senator Byrd's repetition of the story, on April 24, 2006, was accompanied by a reference to an 1871 letter from a constitutional law professor, Francis Lieber, to the Ohioan (and future president) James A. Garfield. Lieber recounted a story he had heard about Jefferson's visit to Mount Vernon, which found its way into Conway's book.

40. "Economic Bill of Rights" speech by Ronald Reagan, July 3, 1987, www.reagan.utexas.edu/archives/speeches/major.html.

41. Haynes Johnson, *Sleepwalking through History: America in the Reagan Years* (New York: Norton, 1991); John Patrick Diggins, *Ronald Reagan* (New York: Norton, 2007), quote at 51. See, for instance, Jefferson's description of the wards as a version of the townships of New England, "the wisest invention ever devised by the wit of man for the perfect exercise of self-government, and for its preservation" (TJ to Samuel Kercheval, June 12, 1816, in *The Writings of Thomas Jefferson*, ed. Paul Leicester Ford [New York: G. P. Putnam's Sons, 1899], 41).

42. See Andrew E. Busch, "Ronald Reagan's Public Philosophy: Strands of Jefferson and Hamilton," in *Ronald Reagan's America*, ed. Eric J. Schmertz et al. (Westport, CT: Greenwood, 1997), 1:41–52.

43. TJ to William Carmichael and William Short, June 30, 1793, in *PTJ*, 26:411.

44. Reagan, *The Notes*, 81; TJ to John B. Colvin (a Baltimore newspaper editor), Sept. 20, 1810, *PTJ-R*, 3:99–101; TJ to Samuel du Pont de Nemours, Jan. 18, 1802, *PTJ*, 36:391.

45. "A Reagan Farewell Address," *CQ Weekly,* Dec. 24, 1988; videotape of speech available at Ronald Reagan Presidential Library, Simi Valley, CA.

46. Reagan to "Philip," undated, in Reagan, *A Life in Letters,* 258.

47. Warren B. Rudman, *Combat: Twelve Years in the U.S. Senate* (New York: Random House, 1996), 64–68.

48. Lee Edwards, *The Essential Ronald Reagan: A Profile in Courage, Justice, and Wisdom* (Lanham, MD: Rowman and Littlefield, 2005), 145–46.

4 "The Boisterous Ocean of Political Passions"

1. Bill Clinton, *My Life* (New York: Knopf, 2004), 405–6.

2. "Clinton at Monticello as President-Elect," Federal News Service, Jan. 18, 1993 (via LexisNexis Academic); "Report of the Commissioners Appointed to Fix the Site of the University of Virginia," Aug. 4, 1818, Electronic Text Center, University of Virginia Library.

3. "Clinton's Journey from Monticello Carried Messages," *Morning Edition,* NPR, Jan. 18, 1993.

4. "Remarks of Bill Clinton at Ceremony to Mark the 250th Anniversary of Thomas Jefferson's Birthday," Federal News Service, Apr. 13, 1993. The Jefferson Memorial quote (1816) that Clinton used was not found in editions of *Bartlett's Familiar Quotations,* but has since been included in *The Yale Book of Quotations,* ed. Fred R. Shapiro (New Haven: Yale University Press, 2006), 395.

5. "The Cracks in Thomas Jefferson," *Economist,* Apr. 17, 1993; "Thomas Jefferson Commemoration Commission Act," July 23, 1992, accompanying House Report 5056.

6. Fouad Ajami, "Thomas Jefferson, Ultra All-American," *U.S. News & World Report,* Aug. 6, 1990 (these thoughts were expressed in the context of reviewing a new book, Robert W. Tucker and David C. Hendrickson, *Empire of Liberty: The Statecraft of Thomas Jefferson*).

7. "Notes on a Visit to Monticello on Sept. 20, 1991 of Dr. Zhelyu Zhelev, President of the Republic of Bulgaria," International Center for Jefferson Studies; conversation of the author with Daniel P. Jordan.

8. *CR,* 104th Cong., 2nd sess., Mar. 7, 1996.

9. *CR,* 103rd Cong., 2nd sess., House of Representatives, Mar. 16, 1994.

10. TJ to John Taylor, Nov. 26, 1798, in *PTJ,* 30:588–89; Andrew Burstein and Nancy Isenberg, *Madison and Jefferson* (New York: Random House, 2010), 523–29; Bob Smith statement, *CR,* 104th Cong., 1st sess., Feb. 3, 1995. Similar Jefferson imagery was repeated in the Senate three weeks later, on February 27, by first-term Texas Republican Kay Bailey Hutchison. She added one more Jefferson quip, this one from 1821: "There does not exist an engine so corruptive of the government and so demoralizing of the nation as a public debt. It will bring us more ruin at home than all of the enemies from abroad."

11. Robert J. Samuelson, "Corrupting the Constitution," *Newsweek,* Jan. 30, 1995; Paul Starr, "State of the Union? Someday, Paralyzed," *NYT,* Jan. 24, 1995.

12. Delay remarks, *CR,* 104th Cong., 2nd sess., July 9, 1996.

13. Leahy and Shelby remarks, *CR,* 105th Cong., 1st sess., Senate, Mar. 4, 1997.

14. Alan W. Bock, "Still Dangerous after All These Years," *Orange County Register*, Apr. 13, 1997.

15. Douglas Brown, "Gary Hart," *New Statesman*, Nov. 8, 1996; Gary Hart, *Restoration of the Republic: The Jeffersonian Ideal in 21st-Century America* (New York: Oxford University Press, 2002), quote at 220. Identifying "Jeffersonian Republicanism" in terms of each generation's need to invent its own, updated version of the founders' republic, Hart would entertain more local discretion in the area of education, and he looked favorably on town meetings and the Internet as forms of democratic expression. Perhaps the best way to describe Hart's program is to call it "rational Jeffersonianism."

16. For debate on congressional term limits, see *CR*, 105th Cong., 1st sess., Feb. 12, 1997; on the "Payment Protection Act," Owens remarks, *CR*, 105th Cong., 1st sess., Mar. 5, 1997; *CR*, 105th Cong., 1st sess., Mar. 30, 1998.

17. Conor Cruise O'Brien, "Thomas Jefferson: Radical and Racist," *Atlantic Monthly*, Oct. 1996, 53–74; Conor Cruise O'Brien, *The Long Affair: Thomas Jefferson and the French Revolution, 1785–1800* (Chicago: University of Chicago Press, 1996). O'Brien predicted that the "cult of Jefferson" would continue in the twenty-first century only as a white racist cult. Charlton Heston, "The Second Amendment: America's First Freedom," *Human Rights* (Fall 1999): 7. Heston's quote was drawn from Jefferson's early draft of a Virginia Constitution, prepared in the period following the adoption of the Declaration of Independence.

18. Cushing Strout, "Revising Jefferson's Portrait without a Fine Pencil," *Sewanee Review* 106 (Summer 1998): 505–11. The author, a literary scholar as well as intellectual historian, was an emeritus professor at Cornell University at the time of this review.

19. Lara M. Brown, "The Contemporary Presidency: The Greats and the Great Debate: President William J. Clinton's Use of Presidential Exemplars," *Presidential Studies Quarterly* 37 (March 2007): 124–38.

20. PBS interview with George Will, www.pbs.org/jefferson/archives/interviews/Will.htm.

21. From the debate of Oct. 17, 2000, at Washington University in St. Louis, www.debates.org/?page=october-17-2000-debate-transcript.

22. "Presidential Pinups," *National Journal* 34 (Feb. 16, 2002).

23. Culberson remarks, *CR*, 107th Cong., 1st sess., June 7, 2001.

24. *CR*, 107th Cong., 1st sess., Sept. 12, 2001; Jefferson to Jay, Sept. 23, 1785, in *PTJ*, 8:427.

25. Burstein and Isenberg, *Madison and Jefferson*, 401–5; Frank Lambert, *The Barbary Wars: American Independence in the Atlantic World* (New York: Hill and Wang, 2005); Robert J. Allison, *The Crescent Obscured: The United States and the Muslim World, 1776–1815* (New York: Oxford University Press, 1995); Stephen Cleveland Blyth, *History of the War between the United State and Tripoli and the Other Barbary Powers* (Salem, MA, 1806); Kevin J. Hayes, "How Jefferson Read the Qur'ān," *Early American Literature* 39 (2004): 247–61.

26. "Life, Liberty, and the Pursuit of Th. Jefferson," *Time*, July 5, 2004. The display text below the title: "HE DRAFTED THE DECLARATION, SPARKED A REVOLUTION AND BECAME ENSNARED IN A SEX SCANDAL WITH A SLAVE. . . ."

27. Andrew Burstein, *Jefferson's Secrets: Death and Desire at Monticello* (New York: Basic, 2005); Al Gore, *The Assault on Reason* (New York: Penguin, 2007), 12–14, 26–34.

28. "Remarks by the President and First Lady in Honor of Thomas Jefferson's 265th Birthday," Federal News Service, Apr. 14, 2008; "Remarks by George W. Bush at Monticello's 46th Annual Independence Day Celebration," Federal News Service, July 4, 2008; conversation with the protest organizer David Swanson, Charlottesville, May 30, 2013, and videotape of event; "Presidential Embrace" and "100-plus Give a Lesson in Free Speech," *Charlottesville Daily Progress,* July 5, 2008; "Independence Day: Monticello Gets Presidential Treatment," Charlottesville *Hook,* July 10–16, 2008; internal memos of July 7–9, 2008, International Center for Jefferson Studies, Monticello.

29. R. K. Ramazani and W. Scott Harrop, "Bush's War Betrays the Sage of Monticello's Vision for Liberty," *Richmond Times-Dispatch,* July 10, 2008.

30. Theda Skocpol and Vanessa Williamson, *The Tea Party and the Remaking of Republican Conservatism* (New York: Oxford University Press, 2012).

31. "Obama, Hollande, Renew Historic Bonds at Jefferson Shrine," Agence France Presse, Feb. 10, 2014; Margaret Talev, "Obama Gives Hollande Glimpse of French Influence on U.S.," bloomberg.com, Feb. 10, 2014. On February 11, welcoming Hollande to the White House, President Obama referred to France as America's oldest ally: "From a field in Yorktown to the beaches of Normandy . . . we owe our freedom to each other."

32. Associated Press, Feb. 10, 2007. Data on spurious Jefferson quotes provided by the Monticello research librarian Anna Berkes; see also www.monti cello.org/site/research-and-collections/tje/spurious-quotations.

33. Count of founder-related titles conducted by Professor W. Fitzhugh Brundage of the University of North Carolina–Chapel Hill, based on Library of Congress subject headings.

34. Barack Obama, interview by Matt Lauer on NBC's *Today* show, Feb. 1, 2009; Walter Russell Mead, "The Carter Syndrome," *Foreign Policy* (Jan/Feb 2010), www.foreignpolicy.com.

35. Ann Raver, "A Revolutionary with Seeds, Too," *NYT,* July 1, 2010; Kristen Hinman, "Thomas Jefferson, Founding Foodie," *American History* (Apr. 2011): 42–49; "Paulsen Receives 2010 Thomas Jefferson Award from Foodservice Distribution Industry," States News Service, June 29, 2010. The recipients that year were Erik Paulsen (R-Minnesota) and Ted Poe (R-Texas).

36. Josh Horwitz, "Thomas Jefferson and the 'Blood of Tyrants,'" *Huffington Post,* Sept. 1, 2009.

37. "Beck Claims Marines Were Created by Thomas Jefferson to Combat Islamic Pirates," Politifact.com, reprinted in *St. Petersburg Times,* Feb. 3, 2010; on Paine, Beck, and the Tea Party, see also Seth Cotlar, "Conclusion," in *Paine and Jefferson in the Age of Revolutions,* ed. Simon P. Newman and Peter S. Onuf (Charlottesville: University of Virginia Press, 2013), 277–96.

38. Sarah Palin, interview by Glenn Beck, Fox News, Jan. 13, 2010, www.fox news.com/story/2010/01/14/sarah-palin-on-glenn-beck/; "Sarah Palin Speaks at Tea Party Convention," Feb. 6, 2010, transcripts.cnn.com; Jada Yuan and Tali

Yahalom, "Sarah Palin Confronted Reporters at *Time* 100," *New York Magazine*, May 5, 2010, nymag.com/daily/intelligencer/2010/05/sarah_palin_confronted _reporte.html; Andrew Burstein and Nancy Isenberg, "Sarah Palin's Vacation from History," Salon.com, June 8, 2011. Whatever political savvy Palin possessed was matched by a defiant anti-intellectualism. A 2008 bumper sticker alluded to the orthographically challenged J. Danforth ("Dan") Quayle, George H. W. Bush's intellectually modest vice president, and proclaimed: "Sarah Palin Makes Dan Quayle Look Like Thomas Jefferson."

39. Burstein and Isenberg, "What They Really Mean by American Exceptionalism," Salon.com, Apr. 8, 2011.

40. Again, in July 2014, the Gingrich Foundation named Monticello its "Charity of the Month" (see www.gingrichproductions.com/2014/07/charity-of-the -month-thomas-jefferson-foundation).

41. Kevin Horrigan, "When Did Intellectualism, Education Become Bad Things?" *St. Louis Post-Dispatch*, Mar. 8, 2012.

42. www.youtube.com/watch?v=FXyQy71CRD4.

43. transcript.cnn.com/TRANSCRIPTS/1002/06/cnr.09.html.

44. Matthew Continetti, "The Two Faces of the Tea Party: Rick Santelli, Glenn Beck, and the Future of the Populist Insurgency," *Weekly Standard*, June 28, 2010; Rick Perlstein, "Beyond the Palin: Why the GOP Is Falling Out of Love with Gun-Toting, Churchgoing, Working-Class Whites," *Newsweek*, July 20, 2009.

45. "Michele Bachmann Salutes the Upside of Slavery," *Forbes*, July 8, 2011; "Congress Members Read Constitution Aloud," *NYT*, Jan. 7, 2011; "Constitution Read on House Floor, But It Wasn't So Simple," *Los Angeles Times*, Jan. 7, 2011.

46. Poe speeches in *CR*, 112th Cong., 1st sess., Mar. 8, 2011; *CR*, 112th Cong., 2nd sess., June 1, 2012; "Faux Thomas Jefferson Quote Cited by Rep. Poe," *Washington Post*, Aug. 17, 2012.

47. Quigley remarks, *CR*, 112th Cong., 1st sess., May 3, 2011.

48. In Glen Allen, Virginia, he said similarly: "Thomas Jefferson said it better than anybody else could when he wrote those words in the Declaration of Independence. It's the essence of the American idea" (Ryan speeches in Glen Allen, Virginia, Aug. 17, 2012, and in Roanoke, Virginia, Aug. 22, 2012, transcripts via LexisNexis Academic).

49. According to the organization's website, *"Rightful Liberty* means that neighbors keep their noses out of other neighbors' business, that neighbors *live and let live."* As for preparedness: "Every able-bodied Patriot of age within the Citadel will maintain one AR15 variant in 5.56mm NATO, at least 5 magazines and 1,000 rounds of ammunition" (www.iiicitadel.com). On the California-Oregon complaint against an insensitive Sacramento and equally oppressive Washington, see www.jeffersonstate.com; and Christopher Shay, "Second County Votes to Secede from California," Sept. 25, 2013, www.america.aljazeera.com; and the CBS Sunday Morning telecast of Nov. 3, 2013, www.youtube.com/watch?v=51Swv _mP9kY.

50. TJ to Charles Yancey, Jan. 6. 1816; TJ to Pierre Samuel du Pont de Nemours, Mar. 2, 1809, TJP-LC. In the case of Du Pont, Jefferson invited his old French friend to visit him in his incarnation as "the hermit of Monticello."

5 "Misery Enough, but No Poetry"

1. *CR,* 79th Cong., 1st sess., Oct. 18, 1945. Congresswoman Douglas was the first white member of the House to have African Americans on her staff.

2. Robin Blackburn, *The American Crucible: Slavery, Emancipation, and Human Rights* (New York: Verso, 2011); Nancy Isenberg, *Sex and Citizenship in Antebellum America* (Chapel Hill: University of North Carolina Press, 1997).

3. Article by Reverend David D. Vaughan, excerpted from *Kansas City (KS) Plaindealer,* Apr. 6, 1945; Elbert Thomas, *Thomas Jefferson, World Citizen* (New York: Modern Age, 1942), chap. 10, quote at 180. Kean's vindicating memorandum appears as an appendix in the book; Kean asserts that his ancestor "prepared the way for Lincoln's career" and that "Abraham Lincoln in 1865 consummated the task begun by Thomas Jefferson in 1769" (261, 265). In the feature column "Black Angles," also in 1945, a Little Rock newspaper promoted works on "Negro personalities" across the social spectrum. Monitoring other news outlets, the editor of "Black Angles" commended an Afrocentric publication out of Indianapolis in which quotes from Jefferson abounded—all attesting to the founder's abolitionist doctrines. These began with the fateful: "I tremble for my country when I reflect that God is just; that his justice cannot sleep forever" (from the same panel at the Jefferson Memorial). America's most definitive freedom lover had predicted in the 1780s that "the spirit of the master is abating, that of the slave rising" (see S. S. Taylor, "Black Angles," *Arkansas State Press,* Oct. 5, 1945).

4. *Notes on the State of Virginia,* ed. William Peden (Chapel Hill: University of North Carolina Press, 1955), Query 14 and 18; on the importance of Phillis Wheatley and Jefferson's willful misreading of her, see esp. David Waldstreicher, "The Wheatleyan Moment," *Early American Studies* 9 (Fall 2011): 522–51; and Andrew Burstein and Nancy Isenberg, *Madison and Jefferson* (New York: Random House, 2010), 230, 636; for fuller context, see Francis D. Cogliano, *Thomas Jefferson: Reputation and Legacy* (Charlottesville: University of Virginia Press, 2006), chap. 7.

5. Shane White, *Somewhat More Independent: The End of Slavery in New York City, 1770–1810* (Athens: University of Georgia Press, 1991), 81–86.

6. "Special Message to the Congress on Civil Rights," February 2, 1948, in *Public Papers of the Presidents of the United States,* January 1–December 31, 1948 (Washington, D.C.: U.S. Government Printing Office, 1964).

7. Hubert H. Humphrey, *The Education of a Public Man: My Life in Politics* (Garden City, NY: Doubleday, 1976), chap. 17 and 458–59n3. In the fall of 1945, as the troops—white, black, and Asian—were being transported home from service abroad, they all remained in segregated units. FDR had earlier vowed to black leaders that he would integrate the armed forces, but he ultimately could not deliver on his guarantee. Truman did so.

8. William E. Leuchtenburg, *The White House Looks South* (Baton Rouge: Louisiana State University Press, 2005), 182–89; *Arkansas State Press,* Dec. 3, 1948; Alexander S. Leidholdt, "Showdown on Mr. Jefferson's Lawn: Contesting Jim Crow during the University of Virginia's Protodesegregation," *Virginia Magazine of History and Biography* 112 (2014): 230–65; Gregory H. Swanson biography, www.virginia.edu/woodson/projects/kenan/swanson/swanson.html.

9. *CR*, Oct. 18, 1945 (Appendix); Helen Gahagan Douglas, *A Full Life* (Garden City, NY: Doubleday, 1982), 200–201, 212–14.

10. *Milwaukee Star*, Oct. 21, 1967, and June 26, 1968.

11. Statement by Daniel P. Jordan, Jan. 3–4, 2014, in private communication with the author.

12. David K. Shipler, *A Country of Strangers: Blacks and Whites in America* (New York: Knopf, 1997), 170–74; Lerone Bennett, "Thomas Jefferson's Negro Grandchildren," *Ebony*, Nov. 1954, 78–80; Pearl M. Graham, "Thomas Jefferson and Sally Hemings," *Journal of Negro History* 46 (Apr. 1961): 89–103. On the other side of the equation, Milton E. Flower's biography of the nineteenth-century New York journalist-biographer James Parton included in an appendix, in its entirety for the first time, the "Dusky Sally Story" as conveyed to Parton by Henry S. Randall (see Flower, *James Parton: The Father of Modern Biography* [Durham, NC: Duke University Press, 1951]). The historian Dumas Malone followed up with an appendix titled "The Miscegenation Legend" in the fourth of his six-volume *Jefferson and His Time* (see Malone, *Jefferson the President: First Term, 1801–1805* [Boston: Little, Brown, 1970], 494–98).

13. Boyd to Dos Passos, May 5, 1955, Papers of John Dos Passos, Special Collections, University of Virginia Library, Boxes 2 & 118. (See also Douglass Adair to Dos Passos, June 17, 1955, Box 2.) Dos Passos makes particular use of Flower's Parton documents.

14. Cooley oral history interview, Oct. 6, 1995, www.monticello.org/getting-word/people/robert-h-cooley-iii.

15. Stanton's research is most readily accessible in Lucia C. Stanton, *Those Who Labor for My Happiness: Slavery at Thomas Jefferson's Monticello* (Charlottesville: University of Virginia Press, 2012).

16. Annette Gordon-Reed, *Thomas Jefferson and Sally Hemings: An American Controversy* (Charlottesville: University of Virginia Press, 1997).

17. The Carr brothers explanation made sense insofar as Jefferson's two nephews were close in age to Sally, Jefferson thirty years her elder, and Jefferson's grandchildren waited until after the two Carrs were dead to finger them. Yet Jefferson's daughter Martha, who knew and interacted with Sally Hemings all her life, was unable to provide clarity for her own children. The one documented report of her making an effort to vindicate her father occurred when the mother of eleven tried to recollect the only one of Sally's several conceptions that she was certain had happened when her father was absent from Monticello. She wasn't saying what did happen, or who had fathered Sally Hemings's children (wouldn't she be at all curious?), but only assured the family of what didn't happen once. She may not have made a strong case, but neither did the oral histories absolutely convince. Furthermore, Fawn Brodie's distortions of eighteenth-century American English combined with overreaching Freudian readings to detract from her argument about cross-racial love. Until the advent of DNA, no one could claim to have built a rock-solid case, just as the emotional character of the Jefferson-Hemings relationship remains clouded even now, in that DNA does not go beyond the genetic explanation.

18. Until 1998, based on extant texts, I remained largely accepting of the Carr

brothers explanation. I was present during the February 1997 conversation at the White House, alongside Bob Cooley, and replied to the president's question in the Socratic mode: Could James Madison, who did not marry the celebrated Dolley Todd until he was in his forties, have been that elusive forty-year-old virgin? While the answer was unknowable, it was understood that many white southern boys first experienced sex with slaves; and Madison's passionate attachment to his wife, Dolley, suggests that he did not first discover sex as a middle-aged man. Of course, Madison's sex life did not carry the same interest as Jefferson's.

After this point, no longer quite so comfortable with the Jefferson-Randolph family explanation, I continued weighing the Jefferson-Hemings question, and awakened to the fact that in the artifacts they left behind, historical actors of the eighteenth century were generally not as forthcoming as inquiring modern minds would prefer—which fact continues to drive the work of scholars of gender and sexuality. For elaboration, see Andrew Burstein, *Jefferson's Secrets: Death and Desire at Monticello* (New York: Basic, 2005); and Andrew Burstein, "The Seductions of Thomas Jefferson," *Journal of the Early Republic* 19 (Fall 1999): 499–509.

19. Bill Clinton, *My Life* (New York: Knopf, 2004), 822.

20. Salon.com, Nov. 18, 1998. Hitchens's answer to the title question was: "They're both protected by a group of credulous historians." Burstein, Isenberg, and Gordon-Reed, "Three Perspectives on America's Jefferson Fixation."

21. Ann duCille, "Where in the World Is William Wells Brown? Thomas Jefferson, Sally Hemings, and the DNA of African-American Literary History," *American Literary History* 12 (Fall 2000): 443–62.

22. Barbara Chase-Riboud, *Sally Hemings: A Novel* (New York: Viking, 1979); Laura Dawkins, "'A Seeping Invisibility': Maternal Dispossession in Barbara Chase-Riboud's *Sally Hemings* and *The President's Daughter*," *Callaloo* 32 (Summer 2009): 792–808; Thandie Newton interview, Apr. 10, 2009, www.dailymail.co.uk. In 2000, as a direct result of the sensationalism over the DNA findings, *Sally Hemings: An American Scandal,* a television miniseries, aired on CBS, with Carmen Ejogo as Sally; Ejogo is the offspring of a Nigerian father and Scottish mother.

23. See Rachel F. Moran, *Interracial Intimacy: The Regulation of Race and Romance* (Chicago: University of Chicago Press, 2001), 44–47, quote at 47; Shipler, *A Country of Strangers,* 231.

24. See esp. Jared Sexton, *Amalgamation Schemes: Antiblackness and the Critique of Multiracialism* (Minneapolis: University of Minnesota Press, 2008).

25. Shipler, *A Country of Strangers,* chap. 4, quote at 243. On the long history of mixed-race politics, see Andrew N. Wegmann, "An American Color: Pigmentation, Culture, and Racial Identity in the Atlantic South, 1718–1865" (Ph.D. diss., Louisiana State University, forthcoming), chap. 2.

26. The "mighty near white" designation is that provided by Jefferson's slave Isaac, who was about two years older than Sally Hemings (see "Memoirs of a Monticello Slave," in *Jefferson at Monticello,*" ed. James A. Bear Jr. [Charlottesville: University Press of Virginia, 1967], 4).

27. Jones, *Race Mixing,* chaps. 4 and 5; David A. Rosenberg, "NY Review: Sally and Tom: The American Way," Backstage.com, Feb. 20, 2012. Ava Jenkins (Sally

Hemings) won the AUDELCO "best actress in a musical" award for "Excellence in Black Theater" (broadwayworld.com, Nov. 30, 2012).

28. Robert McG. Thomas Jr., "Robert Cooley 3d, 58, Lawyer Who Sought Link to Jefferson," obituary, *NYT,* Aug. 3, 1998.

29. Leef Smith, "A Monticello Homecoming for All," *Washington Post,* May 15; Leef Smith, "Jeffersons Split over Hemings Descendants," *Washington Post,* May 17, 1999; Michael Janofsky, "Jefferson Table Extended for Hemingses," *NYT,* May 17, 1999.

30. "Jefferson Heirs Plan Cemetery for Slave's Kin," Associated Press, Apr. 21, 2002.

31. Westerinen interview, www.monticello.org/getting-word/people/julia -jefferson-westerenin.

32. www.monticello.org/site/plantation-and-slavery/report-research-commit tee-thomas-jefferson-and-sally-hemings. For a complete and fair-minded summary of the atmosphere surrounding the Monticello Report and reactions to it (including the dissent of one of the committee members, White McKenzie Wallenborn, M.D.), see Cogliano, *Thomas Jefferson,* chap. 6.

33. The one dissenter was Professor Paul Rahe of Hillsdale College, who noted of Jefferson that "in his private, as in his public, life, there was, for all his brilliance and sagacity, something dishonest, something self-serving and self indulgent about the man." Note, too, that the *Monticello Report* of 2000 stated that "Randolph Jefferson and his sons are not known to have been at Monticello at the time of Eston Hemings's conception," a statement that differs from the Scholars Commission reference to an invitation to visit extended to Randolph.

34. See Joanne L. Yeck, *The Jefferson Brothers* (Dayton, OH: Greyden/Slate River Press, 2012). A decade after DNA testing, three books emerged in succession, each an extended rumination growing out of the 1998 findings. Annette Gordon-Reed's painstakingly researched *The Hemingses of Monticello* (New York: Norton, 2008) humanized the biracial families owned by Jefferson, and won the Pulitzer Prize in 2009. Clarence Walker's *Mongrel Nation: The America Begotten by Thomas Jefferson and Sally Hemings* (Charlottesville: University of Virginia Press, 2009) was a creative exercise in situating Jefferson-Hemings within the larger history of race mixing. As a successor to the TJHS-endorsed self-published book by Cynthia H. Burton, *Vindicating Jefferson: Fallacies, Omissions, and Contradictions in the Hemings Genealogical Research* (2006), William G. Hyland Jr.'s *In Defense of Thomas Jefferson: The Sally Hemings Scandal* (New York: Thomas Dunne, 2009) was an attorney's counterpoint to Gordon-Reed and the historians who were persuaded by DNA to reassess the issue. Hyland, it should be said, exhibited little curiosity about slavery or, for that matter, cultural history, and was apparently unaware that sexuality itself has a history. He shrugged off any need to understand assumptions and standards that pertained to Jefferson, his class, and his community. As a result, he isolated only certain kinds of evidence, mischaracterized whatever research did not suit his preconceptions, and wrote with the prosecutorial fervor favored by those who proudly declare themselves "Jefferson defenders." Like the TJHS, Hyland revealed himself intent on depriving the mature Jefferson of a sexual character.

35. www.tjheritage.org.

36. Eyler Robert Coates Sr., "Research Report on the Jefferson-Hemings Controversy: A Critical Analysis," in *The Jefferson-Hemings Myth: An American Travesty,* ed. Coates (Charlottesville: Jefferson Editions, 2001), 87. For Ellen Coolidge remarks, see Burstein, *Jefferson's Secrets,* 175–79.

37. Andrew Burstein, Nancy Isenberg, and Annette Gordon-Reed, "Three Perspectives on America's Jefferson Fixation," *Nation,* Nov. 30, 1998.

38. Historians have been commenting endlessly on the two aforementioned propositions since the appearance of Winthrop D. Jordan's seminal work on the subject, *White over Black: American Attitudes toward the Negro, 1555–1812* (Chapel Hill: University of North Carolina Press, 1968). For our purposes, let us simply borrow the words of Professor Gordon-Reed: "To own another human being, in a legal system that gave great deference to the rights of private property, meant that a master's use of a slave for work, or for sex, was really his business" (Gordon-Reed, *The Hemingses of Monticello,* 320). Her observation raises a thorny question: whether it can be considered consensual when any master has sex with any woman he legally owns—regardless of her bloodline, outward appearance, or other consideration. Furthermore, Americans tend to see race before they see class, and the long history of slavery and its aftermath makes this a perfectly logical approach. That is why the "upstairs-downstairs" relationship, though it may actually trump the black-and-white dynamic in historical reality, seems less interesting to those who speculate publicly about Jefferson and Hemings. Until cross-class associations carry the cultural weight of cross-color associations, Jefferson will remain emotionally mysterious in our efforts to comprehend the full nature of his relationship to the seamstress in his household. On the distinction drawn between white ("vanilla") sex and aggressive African sexuality, see Walker, *Mongrel Nation,* 39–42.

39. Walker, *Mongrel Nation,* 64–67. On the cruelly satirical treatment of Jefferson and race mixing, see esp. Elise Lemire, *"Miscegenation": Making Race in America* (Philadelphia: University of Pennsylvania Press, 2002), chap. 1.

40. This dutiful pose is constantly repeated. See, for instance, the two recent tomes by an Ivy League historian identified as "distinguished" and "authoritative"; Richard Beeman's titles express all: *Plain Honest Men: The Making of the American Constitution* (New York: Random House, 2009); *Our Lives, Our Fortunes and Our Sacred Honor: The Forging of American Independence, 1774–1776* (New York: Basic, 2013).

41. On the sexual environment and male prerogative, see Peter W. Bardaglio, *Reconstructing the Household: Families, Sex, and the Law in the Nineteenth-Century South* (Chapel Hill: University of North Carolina Press, 1995); G. J. Barker-Benfield, *The Horrors of the Half-Known Life* (New York: Harper and Row, 1976); Peter Wagner, *Eros Revived: Erotica of the Enlightenment in England and America* (London: David and Charles, 1988); Richard Godbeer, *Sexual Revolution in Early America* (Baltimore: Johns Hopkins University Press, 2002); Sharon Block, *Rape and Sexual Power in Early America* (Chapel Hill: University of North Carolina Press, 2006); Ruth H. Bloch, "Changing Conceptions of Sexuality and Romance in Eighteenth-Century America," *William and Mary Quarterly* 60 (Jan. 2003): 13–

42; and Andrew Burstein, "Jefferson in the Flesh," in *Seeing Jefferson Anew: In His Times and Ours,* ed. John B. Boles and Randal L. Hall (Charlottesville: University of Virginia Press, 2010), 172–94. The critique of patriarchal assumptions in Mary Wollstonecraft's writings in the 1790s both explicitly and implicitly took on men's treatment of women as weak, irrational beings—as objects of frivolous interest. Note, too, that in many elite families, women who had endured dangerous pregnancies sometimes tacitly accepted husbands' taking of mistresses.

We must not, then, assume that modern preoccupations about sex apply to Jefferson's America. The female body, like the female imagination, was regarded as subject to hysterical troubles; masturbation was seen as perverse, not a normal outlet for either men or women; procreative expectations were valued differently than they have come to be since; and power relations between husbands and wives, parents and children, etc., created both a domestic environment and social standards not comparable to ours—especially within the institution of slavery. The generation that succeeded Jefferson's began the shift toward Victorian sexual ethics. Like modern founder fundamentalists, they could not see that desire is almost always linked to possession, and that desire tends to be destabilizing to the ego—or to the national superego. In this regard, see also Michel Foucault, *The History of Sexuality: Vol. 1, An Introduction* (New York: Random House, 1978).

42. Toni Morrison interview, *Huffington Post,* May 16, 2008, www.huffington post.com/2008/05/08/toni-morrison-on-calling_n_100761.html. Interestingly, Garry Wills titled his 2003 study of Jefferson *Negro President,* owing to a very different set of circumstances than that which Toni Morrison's Bill Clinton or the literal African American Barack Obama had to face. Wills's book examined the "race card" surrounding the election of 1800, when Jefferson profited from the ⅗ clause that counted human property as part of each state's population in each census. By artificially inflating slave owners' power in this way, seats in the House of Representatives (and thus electoral votes) were apportioned to favor the South (see Wills, *Negro President: Jefferson and the Slave Power* [Boston: Houghton Mifflin, 2003]).

43. On this issue, see, in particular, Mark M. Smith, *How Race Is Made: Slavery, Segregation, and the Senses* (Chapel Hill: University of North Carolina Press, 2006).

44. Suzanne W. Jones, *Race Mixing: Southern Fiction since the Sixties* (Baltimore: Johns Hopkins University Press, 2004), 22–27, 137–47; Ernest Gaines, *A Lesson before Dying* (New York: Knopf, 1993), quote at 166–67. In an October 2013 interview, Gaines told me that he gave no thought to the historical Thomas Jefferson in contemplating the racial tensions he described in the novel; nor did the Jefferson-Hemings DNA study hold much meaning for him subsequently. For him, the Jefferson surname had long since been appropriated by his and other African American families—how others might respond to the not-so-hidden resonance of the name indicates the invisible, occasionally ironic, pull of history.

45. James C. Cobb, *Away Down South: A History of Southern Identity* (New York: Oxford University Press, 2005), 262–64.

46. For a thorough analysis of the Right's resistance to trends in multicultural education, see Gary B. Nash, Charlotte Crabtree, and Ross E. Dunn, *History on Trial: Culture Wars and the Teaching of the Past* (New York: Knopf, 1997).

47. Newt Gingrich, *A Nation Like No Other: Why American Exceptionalism Matters,* with Vince Haley (Washington, D.C.: Regnery, 2011), 6–11; Matthew Shelley, "Gingrich Calls Obama's Comments on Trayvon Martin Shooting 'Disgraceful,'" *National Journal,* Mar. 23, 2012. Trayvon Martin's killing was a reminder of how automatic it remained in the twenty-first century to suspect a black male of criminal activity, and to resort to violence—to "nip in the bud" some planned offense. The 1955 murder of the teenager Emmett Till, who looked at a white woman "the wrong way," may be a primitive version of the Trayvon Martin affair, but underlying assumptions of legitimacy and enforcement of authority over young black males were relatable. When George Zimmerman stood trial for the murder, his attorney quoted the highest authority he could find that would resonate with the jury, Thomas Jefferson, as he gave his final summation: "I consider trial by jury as the only anchor ever yet imagined by man, by which a government can be held to the principles of its constitution" (July 12, 2013).

On the dangers of accepting the conservative economic narrative that idealizes heroic entrepreneurship in a free market of winners and losers (ostensibly unconnected to race), see George Lakoff, *Whose Freedom? The Battle over America's Most Important Idea* (New York: Farrar, Straus and Giroux, 2006), esp. chap. 9.

Peter S. Onuf argues that "the solipsistic exceptionalism of our mythology" encourages a denial of the impulse to vanquish enemies by any means available; he traces the impulse both to Jefferson and the Revolution's convenient invention of "the people" through whom democracy lived and breathed. National self-preservation may well be what impels Gingrich, though his version of exceptionalism focuses on a kind of social regulation that did not have to be negotiated in Jefferson's time (see Onuf, "Thomas Jefferson and American Democracy," in *Seeing Jefferson Anew: In His Times and Ours,* ed. John B. Boles and Randal L. Hall (Charlottesville: University of Virginia Press, 2010), 13–39, quote at 33. On the whiteness of exceptionalism, see also Walker, *Mongrel Nation,* 6–7.

Among nonhistorians, interesting studies have been conducted showing that the politics of "inclusion" merely perpetuates the white-based standard for meaningful citizenship. The sociologist Barbara Trepagnier has examined the images and assumptions that help to preserve white cultural and economic dominance. She identifies the taxonomic character of American racism, for example, denoting the Gingrich type, with its emphasis on individual responsibility and denial of society's responsibility, as "symbolic racism" (see Trepagnier, *Silent Racism: How Well-Meaning White People Perpetuate the Racial Divide* [Boulder, CO: Paradigm, 2010]). Similarly, the political scientist Joel Olson writes of whiteness as a constraint on the meaning of freedom, requiring one to avoid being associated with a negative stereotype, that is, to avoid being classed with those of a degraded social status. Regardless of what federal law says, whiteness is the upper stratum of the social order and continues to denote privilege, or at least a reasonable expectation of privilege. In Jefferson's time, nonwhiteness (a $\frac{3}{16}$ or greater African bloodline) assumed property status under slavery. The abolition of slavery ended "master" as well as "slave," without depriving the former master of a cultural identity. Olson argues that abolishing the category of "white" in demography will perform a useful social function, and the negative valuation of "nonwhite" will be erased (see Olson, *The Abolition of White Democracy* [Minneapolis: University of Minnesota Press, 2004]).

48. In Schlesinger's words, "The American creed envisages a nation composed of individuals making their own choices and accountable to themselves, not a nation based on inviolable ethnic communities" (Arthur M. Schlesinger Jr., *The Disuniting of America: Reflections on a Multicultural Society* [New York: Norton, 1991], quotes at 19, 43, 134).

49. For a good treatment of the socioeconomic dilemmas of Jefferson's Virginia and its enduring impact, see Susan Dunn, *Dominion of Memories: Jefferson, Madison, and the Decline of Virginia* (New York: Basic, 2007).

50. On Jefferson as a Virginian, see esp. Ronald L. Hatzenbuehler, *"I Tremble for My Country": Thomas Jefferson and the Virginia Gentry* (Gainesville: University Press of Florida, 2006); and Burstein and Isenberg, *Madison and Jefferson*, passim. On southerners and slave-breeding discourse, see Marie Jenkins Schwartz, *Birthing a Slave: Motherhood and Medicine in the Antebellum South* (Cambridge: Harvard University Press, 2006); and Gregory D. Smithers, *Slave Breeding: Sex, Violence, and Memory in African American History* (Gainesville: University Press of Florida, 2012). On Jefferson's aggressive opposition to coercive centralized power, his defense of the rights of slave owners, and the South's ever-hardening ideology, see John Chester Miller, *The Wolf by the Ears: Thomas Jefferson and Slavery* (New York: Free Press, 1977), chap. 24; Peter S. Onuf, *Jefferson's Empire: The Language of American Nationhood* (Charlottesville: University of Virginia Press, 2000); Roger G. Kennedy, *Mr. Jefferson's Lost Cause: Land, Farmers, Slavery, and the Louisiana Purchase* (New York: Oxford University Press, 2003); Dunn, *Dominion of Memories*, chap. 9; and Jeremy J. Tewell, *A Self-Evident Lie: Southern Slavery and the Threat to American Freedom* (Kent, OH: Kent State University Press, 2013).

51. Cobb, *Away Down South*, chap. 10; Bebe Moore Campbell, *Your Blues Ain't Mine* (New York: Putnam's, 1992), 90. In general, see David R. Goldfield, *Black, White, and Southern: Race Relations and Southern Culture, 1940 to the Present* (Baton Rouge: Louisiana State University Press, 1990).

52. Jeffrey T. Kuhner, "Bush Recognizes Black Jefferson Kin; Scholars Doubt Slave Child Story," *Washington Times*, Apr. 13, 2001.

53. Brent Staples, "A Hemings Family Turns from Black, to White, to Black," *NYT*, Dec. 17, 2001; Brent Staples, "Lust across the Color Line and the Rise of the Black Elite," *NYT*, Apr. 10, 2005; "Jefferson Group Bars Slave's Descendants," *NYT*, May 6, 2002; Nathaniel Abeles, letter to the editor, *NYT*, May 28, 2002; Lucian K. Truscott IV, "The Reunion upon a Hill," *NYT*, July 10, 2003.

54. "Thomas Jefferson Descendants Work to Heal Family's Past," NPR, Nov. 11, 2010, transcript accessed via LexisNexis Academic, www.lexisnexis.com.

55. Numerous scholars have written on Jefferson's coolness regarding the personal implications of his investment in the institution of slavery. I will call attention to a few pertinent texts, not mentioned elsewhere in these notes, the most incisive recent commentary being Cassandra Pybus, "Thomas Jefferson and Slavery," in *A Companion to Thomas Jefferson*, ed. Francis D. Cogliano (Malden, MA: Wiley-Blackwell, 2012), 271–83; see also Onuf, *Jefferson's Empire*, chap. 5;

Onuf and Ari Helo, "Jefferson, Morality, and the Problem of Slavery," in *The Mind of Thomas Jefferson*, ed. Onuf (Charlottesville: University Press of Virginia, 2007), 236–70; Lucia Stanton, "The Other End of the Telescope: Jefferson through the Eyes of His Slaves," *William and Mary Quarterly* 57 (Jan. 2000): 139–52; and Paul Finkelman, *Slavery and the Founders: Race and Liberty in the Age of Jefferson* (Armonk, NY: M. E. Sharpe, 1996), chaps. 5 and 6.

Several brochures produced by the Smithsonian for the January–October 2012 exhibition were each titled, *Slavery at Jefferson's Monticello: Paradox of Liberty*. One brochure featured a section called "Life at Monticello: From A to Z," which included the provocative: "A is for [Slave] Auction," "H is for Hemingses," "P is for Passing," "R is for Resistance," and (to be completely up-to-date) "Y is for Y Chromosome." The exhibition was cosponsored by the National Museum of African American History and Culture.

56. Tess Taylor, *The Forage House* (Pasadena, CA: Red Hen Press, 2013).

57. T. E. King et al., "Thomas Jefferson's Y Chromosome Belongs to a Rare European Lineage," *American Journal of Physical Anthropology* (Apr. 2007): 584–89.

6 "Abortion to Their Hopes"

1. One of the most expressive of Jefferson's rants against his clerical detractors is his draft of "Essay on New England Religious Intolerance," ca. Jan. 10, 1816, in *PTJ-R*, 9:380–81. More generally, see Andrew Burstein, *Jefferson's Secrets: Death and Desire at Monticello* (New York: Basic, 2005), chap. 9.

2. TJ to Adams, Apr. 11, 1823, in *The Adams-Jefferson Letters: The Complete Correspondence between Abigail and John Adams and Thomas Jefferson*, ed. Lester J. Cappon (Chapel Hill: University of North Carolina Press, 1959), 591–94. In his study of America's tradition of relating religious ideas to its position in the world, the Cambridge University historian Andrew Preston writes of Jefferson that he "loathed institutional religion as a profane earthly artifice that came between humanity and the heavens and kept the people subservient to the clergy." And, he adds, the other men thought of as the principal founders felt little if any religious passion. The reason why American religion, generally, retained its viability as a component of republican liberty over time, then, was its diversity and relative resistance to the promotion of authoritarian, hierarchical relationships (see Andrew Preston, *Sword of the Spirit, Shield of Faith* [New York: Knopf, 2012], chap. 5, quote at 88).

3. TJ to Rush, Sept. 23, 1800, in *PTJ*, 32:168; Rush to TJ, Oct. 6, 1800, in *PTJ*, 32:205. For an excellent synthesis of the religious issue brought before the public in 1800, see Robert M. S. McDonald, "Was There a Religious Revolution of 1800?" in *The Revolution of 1800: Democracy, Race, and the New Republic*, ed. James Horn, Jan Ellen Lewis, and Peter S. Onuf (Charlottesville: University of Virginia Press, 2002), 173–98.

4. Henry S. Randall, *The Life of Thomas Jefferson* (New York: Derby and Jackson, 1858), 2:648–52, 3:553–61. For those who might seize upon a Jefferson statement without regard to its full context, Randall reminded the reader: "The

controversial language of any period can only be fairly judged by the customs and the spirit of that period" (ibid., 3:560).

5. Elbert Thomas, *Thomas Jefferson: World Citizen* (New York: Modern Age, 1942), chap. 2, quotes at 41, 56.

6. Colbert speech at www.youtube.com/watch?v=kNkxQKGex28. *Jefferson's Extracts from the Gospels*, ed. Dickinson W. Adams (Princeton, NJ: Princeton University Press, 1983); Burstein, *Jefferson's Secrets*, 253–55. In *The Religious Life of Thomas Jefferson* (Charlottesville: University Press of Virginia, 1984), Charles Sanford explains that the question is moot as to whether Jefferson should be called a theist or a deist, because in his time both indicated belief in a "great, unknown power behind the Creation," and both rejected Trinitarianism (91).

7. Merrill D. Peterson, *The Jefferson Image in the American Mind* (1960; Charlottesville, University Press of Virginia, 1998), 300–303; *Biographical Directory of the American Congress, 1774–1949* (Washington, D.C.: U.S. Government Printing Office, 1950), 1427–28.

8. Samuel Miller to TJ, Jan. 18, 1808; TJ to Miller, Jan. 23, 1808, TJP-LC; *NYT,* Apr. 12, 1953.

9. "Jefferson Words Added on Stamp," *NYT,* Feb. 8, 1960.

10. Edward B. Fiske, "Niebuhr Is Critical of President's Sunday Services," *NYT,* Aug. 7, 1969.

11. Jan Hanska, *Reagan's Mythical America: Storytelling as Political Leadership* (New York: Palgrave Macmillan, 2012), 26–32, 108–17. "Reagan's storytelling was tied to his own life story but even more it represented the past, present, and future of America," observes Hanska. What is interesting to the critic is how Reagan "blurred the boundaries of the internal and external elements of the story" (quotes at 26, 32).

12. Paul Kengor, *God and Ronald Reagan: A Spiritual Life* (New York: Regan-Books, 2004), quotes at x, 126, 129.

13. Remarks at Annual National Prayer Breakfast, Feb. 4, 1982, at www.presidency.ucsb.edu/ws/?pid=43075; Hugh Blair, *Lectures on Rhetoric and Belles Lettres* (1783; Philadelphia: Troutman and Hayes, 1852), Lecture XVIII.

14. Hanska, *Reagan's Mythical America*, 110.

15. *Time,* Feb. 23, 1981.

16. Reagan remarks, Annual Convention of National Religious Broadcasters, Jan. 31, 1983. Note, too, that on Jan. 27, 1987, in the bicentennial year of the Constitutional Convention, he concluded his State of the Union Address before a joint session of Congress: "Let's stop suppressing the spiritual core of our national being. Our nation could not have been conceived without divine help. Why is it that we can build a nation with our prayers, but we can't use a schoolroom for voluntary prayer? The 100th Congress of the United States should be remembered as the one that ended the expulsion of God from America's classrooms." Numerous websites contain extensive Reagan quotes and video clips pertaining to God, faith, and the Bible.

17. On the political ramifications of Reagan's religiosity, see Preston, *Sword of the Spirit, Shield of Faith,* chap. 29. On Reagan and Washington at Valley Forge, see John Fea, *Was America Founded as a Christian Nation?* (Louisville, KY: Westmin-

ster John Knox Press, 2011), chap. 11; for Fea's synthesis of Jefferson's views, see ibid., chap. 13.

18. Betty McCollister, "Keep Church and State Apart," *NYT*, May 8, 1983.

19. For expressions of Robertson's and Perkins's advocacies, and those of their followers, see Harry R. Jackson and Tony Perkins, *Personal Faith, Public Policy* (Lake Mary, FL: FrontLine, 2008), esp. chaps. 1 and 2; "Jefferson, Madison Went to Church inside Capitol," mobile.wnd.com/2014/03/jefferson-madison-went-to-church-inside-capitol/; www.rightwingwatch.org/content/christian-coalition; onepeoplesproject.com/index.php/en/rogues-gallery/16-p/1337-tony-perkins.

20. Sidney Goetz, "Commemorating Thomas Jefferson," *Humanist*, May 1, 1993.

21. Perkins statement from report of May/June 1997, www.publiceye.org.

22. Draft, Second Inaugural Address, TJP-LC.

23. Eran Shalev, *American Zion: The Old Testament as a Political Text from the Revolution to the Civil War* (New Haven: Yale University Press, 2013), 2, 99–104; Fea, *Was America Founded as a Christian Nation?*, 173–74.

24. Gregg L. Frazer, *The Religious Beliefs of America's Founders: Reason, Revelation, and Revolution* (Lawrence: University Press of Kansas, 2012), chap. 8; Fea, *Was America Founded as a Christian Nation?*, 7–12, 60–65. Frazer coins the term "theistic rationalism" to describe the common conception that appealed to the founders in the Age of Enlightenment; he writes, unmistakably, that while the founders were in no way "irreligious" or anti-Christian, "America was not founded as a Christian nation. . . . They meant to construct a purely secular state with no connection between the government and religion" (234). On the use of the concept of Providence for political ends, see Spencer McBride, "The Pulpit and the Nation: Clergymen, Political Culture, and the Creation of an American National Identity" (Ph.D. diss., Louisiana State University, 2014), chaps. 1 and 2.

25. "Tony Perkins: Obama Is No Champion of Religious Freedom," Jan. 7, 2013, www.charismanews.com.

26. See www.ffcoalition.com; Bill Moyers, "A Crash Course on Ralph Reed," *Huffington Post*, Oct. 30, 2012.

27. Newt Gingrich, *A Nation Like No Other: Why American Exceptionalism Matters*, with Vince Haley (New York: Regnery, 2011), 46, 74–97, 152. On the civil rights era correction to Gingrich's logic, see Alexander Tsesis, *For Liberty and Equality: The Life and Times of the Declaration of Independence* (New York: Oxford University Press, 2012), chap. 16, quote at 301–2. Reading, in this context, that Gingrich touts "freedom of conscience" as a mainstay of the U.S. political tradition, one might assume that a Muslim's God would satisfy his definition of properly God-centered government, until he qualifies, as follows: "One must recall just how deeply and fervently committed the Founders were not to an abstract notion of faith, but to a faith that was explicitly Christian. . . . The Founders' distinctively Christian faith is well documented, as is their conviction that government must be infused with Christian principles" (76). Linn pamphlet of 1800 cited in McBride, "The Pulpit and the Nation," chap. 6, "The Myth of the Christian President"; TJ to Francis Adrian Van de Kemp, July 30, 1816, in *Jefferson's Extracts from the Gospels*, ed. Dickinson W. Adams (Princeton, NJ: Princeton Uni-

versity Press, 1983), 375.

28. Gail Collins, "How Texas Inflicts Bad Textbooks on Us," *New York Review of Books*, June 21, 2012; "Messing with Texas Textbooks," June 29, 2012, www.billmoyers.com/content/messing-with-texas-textbooks; James C. McKinley, "Texas Conservatives Win Curriculum Change," *NYT*, Mar. 20, 2010.

29. Edwin S. Gaustad, *Sworn on the Altar of God: A Religious Biography of Thomas Jefferson* (Grand Rapids, MI: William B. Eerdmans, 1996), 34–36, 142–44, 212–15, 227–28. On historians' limited engagement with modern political concerns over church-state separation, see Francis D. Cogliano, *Thomas Jefferson: Reputation and Legacy* (Charlottesville: University of Virginia Press, 2006), 147–55.

30. David Barton, *The Jefferson Lies: Exposing the Myths You've Always Believed about Thomas Jefferson* (Nashville: Thomas Nelson, 2012), quote at 194. In Barton's reading, Randolph frequented the slave quarters and had an eye for black ladies, whereas elder brother Thomas (their owner) never joined in their frolic. And one descendant's oral history suggested that Randolph may have fathered "colored children" apart from Hemingses—this was Barton's best evidence. For him, only the Jefferson brother who openly enjoyed the society of slaves could have been Sally Hemings's sexual partner; he did not engage with the fact that the white Jefferson family ultimately fingered the Carr nephews (and not Uncle Randolph) with the same certainty that Barton and other conservatives now show in pointing an accusatory finger at Randolph.

31. Ibid., xix, 3. Lumping together various dangers perceived by the religious Right, Barton bemoaned modern feminists, who somehow profited by the Jefferson-Hemings DNA interpretation. For Barton, it was the feminists' contention that *"any* type of sexual relations between a male and a female constituted rape." Mr. Barton was annoyed by the "particular agendas," as he phrased it, of all who would abandon the great man theory of history as part of their anti-Christian reappraisal of American history and critique of American society.

32. Ibid., 196. In 2011, Barton also insisted that Thomas Paine had stated, "You've got to teach creation science in the public school classroom"—a clear anachronism as well as an absurd misreading of Paine's perspective on religion (see Chris Mooney, *The Republican Brain: The Science of Why They Deny Science— and Reality* [New York: Wiley and Sons, 2012], 205).

33. Barton, *The Jefferson Lies*, 170–77, 190–91.

34. Jennifer Schluessler, "Hard Truth for Author: Publisher Pulls 'The Jefferson Lies,'" *NYT*, Aug. 14, 2012; Warren Throckmorton and Michael Coulter, *Getting Jefferson Right: Fact Checking Claims about Our Third President* (Grove City, PA: Salem Grove Press, 2012). More generally, for his sources Barton relied on avid supporters of the politically conservative Scholars Commission; on avowedly Christian periodicals; on the Internet; on an uncritical reading of letters professional historians have pored over repeatedly; and on the subjective writings of a host of nineteenth- and early-twentieth-century popular works. In his footnote recommending appropriate works on Jefferson, he inexplicably identifies some historically unrefined, unremarkable, unoriginal nineteenth-century biographies in addition to Randall's, plus Dumas Malone's modern six-volume treatment (1948–80), the one superior—if, of course, worshipful—source he mentions.

Finding a protective text like Randall's allowed Barton (and others who seek only an untainted, unquestioned Jefferson) to take solace. But to embrace Randall as a kind of revealed scripture directing Jefferson studies is to say that there is minimal need to examine history at all.

35. David Barton on Glenn Beck TV, Aug. 18, 2012, video, http://glenn becksbooklist.com/2012/08/; Throckmorton and Coulter, *Getting Jefferson Right*, chap. 1; Ed Crews, "Jefferson's Secret Bible," *University of Virginia Magazine*, Spring 2012; Peter Montgomery/People for the American Way, "Exposing David Barton's Bunk," report of Apr. 2011, www.pfaw.org/rww-in-focus/barton-s -bunk-religious-right-historian-hits-the-big-time-tea-party-america. See also www .youtube.com/watch?v=lodtPJPB5vU; and Stephanie Simon, "Evangelical Historian Remains Key Ally of Right," politico.com, Sept. 13, 2013.

36. Fea, *Was America Founded as a Christian Nation?*, 59.

37. Beck interview reported in the *Los Angeles Times*, Mar. 6, 2009.

38. Susan Juster, *Doomsayers: Anglo-American Prophecy in the Age of Revolution* (Philadelphia: University of Pennsylvania Press, 2003); William Scales to Jefferson, May 5, 1801, in *PTJ*, 34:38–41; "One in Four Americans Think Obama May Be the Antichrist," www.theguardian.com, Apr. 2, 2013.

39. "Ellison to Take Oath on Thomas Jefferson's Quran," NPR, Jan. 3, 2007, transcript via LexisNexis Academic, www.lexisnexis.com; Denise A. Spellberg, *Thomas Jefferson's Qur'an: Islam and the Founders* (New York: Knopf, 2013). Developing the seventeenth- and eighteenth-century antecedents of anti-Islamic slurs and stereotypes, Spellberg devotes her afterword to a clear-headed discussion of the post-9/11 mind-set.

40. The foregoing observations were influenced by George Lakoff, *Whose Freedom? The Battle for America's Most Important Idea* (New York: Farrar, Straus, and Giroux, 2006), esp. chap. 10.

41. Andrew Koppelman, *Defending American Religious Neutrality* (Cambridge: Harvard University Press, 2013), 26–77, quotes at 28, 74. For another recent, extremely cogent evaluation of the establishment issue and the ongoing Christian nation debate, see John A. Ragosta, *Wellspring of Liberty: How Virginia's Religious Dissenters Helped Win the American Revolution and Secured Religious Liberty* (New York: Oxford University Press, 2010), esp. chap. 6; and McBride, "The Pulpit and the Nation."

42. TJ to Carr, Aug. 10, 1787, in *PTJ*, 12:15–17; Reagan remarks in Dallas, Aug. 23, 1984, www.reagan.utexas.edu/archives/speeches/1983/13183b.htm.

43. Tania Lombrozo, "Would You Vote for an Atheist? Tell the Truth," Nov. 13, 2012, www.npr.org.

44. www.focusonthefamily.com.

45. TJ to James Fishback, Sept. 27, 1809, in *PTJ-R*, 1:563–66.

46. Ibid., 1:564, 566.

47. "Report of the Commissioners Appointed to Fix the Site of the University of Virginia," Aug. 4, 1818, Electronic Text Center, University of Virginia Library.

7 "History Becomes Fable"

1. TJ to Wirt, Aug. 14, 1814; to Justice Johnson, June 12, 1823, TJP-LC. Although Wirt was a superior lawyer (and future attorney general), he himself got carried away in romancing Patrick Henry, as Jefferson came to affirm. Jefferson wished more of history's actors would produce firsthand accounts to aid biographers; but the perversion of history Jefferson most disliked was the five-volume "libel" authored by Chief Justice John Marshall, a biography of George Washington that portrayed Jefferson's political experience in ways Jefferson deeply resented.

2. For the poll, see www.siena.edu/pages/179.asp?item=2566. The two Roosevelts and Lincoln are at the top of the list, on the basis of rankings done by more than two hundred people identified as experts on the presidency; Lincoln, Washington, and John Adams are 1-2-3 in the category of "integrity," where Jefferson ranks #14; he is third in "imagination," behind Theodore Roosevelt and Lincoln. Eight of the top ten in "communication ability" are presidents who belong to the television age.

3. Stephen Skowronek, *Presidential Leadership in Political Time: Reprise and Reappraisal* (Lawrence: University Press of Kansas, 2008), 93.

4. See Lawrence R. Samuel, *The American Dream: A Cultural History* (Syracuse, NY: Syracuse University Press, 2012); and Robert Wuthnow, *American Mythos: Why Our Best Efforts to Be a Better Nation Fall Short* (Princeton, NJ: Princeton University Press, 2006), chap. 4. Even the myth has taken a shortcut, as Wuthnow, a sociologist, explains. Today's self-made tend to be media figures, and success "a matter of cultivating one's image, or of inventing and reinventing oneself, and not necessarily being a person of long-standing moral virtue" (122).

5. *Hardball*, Aug. 31, 2012. Armey's remarks are not surprising. His allies conceived of the founders in glowing terms for the same reason that many idealize both the U.S. Constitution and Holy Scripture as unimpeachable sources of authority: "A better day has gone before—if only we can restore it." Liberals point to fights over slavery and segregation and women's suffrage as examples of social progress that required generations before the law caught up with activists' desire to enact new standards of equal justice; going back and peeling away the founders' "genius" to find bigotry and narrow self-interest does not threaten liberals' sense of personal happiness or community safety: "A better day lies ahead—if we make it happen."

6. Maurizio Valsania, *Nature's Man: Thomas Jefferson's Philosophical Anthropology* (Charlottesville: University of Virginia Press, 2013), 100–103; Brian Steele, *Thomas Jefferson and American Nationhood* (New York: Cambridge University Press, 2012), chap. 3.

7. On the failure of the Jeffersonian era South to grow with the times, see Susan Dunn, *Dominion of Memories: Jefferson, Madison, and the Decline of Virginia* (New York: Basic, 2007). For an impressive interpretation of the South's cultural position in evolving notions of American nationhood, see Jennifer Rae Greeson, *Our South: Geographic Fantasy and the Rise of National Literature* (Cambridge: Harvard University Press, 2010).

8. TJ to Du Pont de Nemours, Apr. 24, 1816, TJP-LC.

9. For the history of the Declaration of Independence as a moral instrument, from 1776 to the modern era, see Alexander Tsesis, *For Liberty and Equality: The Life and Times of the Declaration of Independence* (New York: Oxford University Press, 2012); other useful interpretations of the document's life and meaning include Robert M. S. McDonald, "Jefferson's Changing Reputation as Author of the Declaration of Independence," *Journal of the Early Republic* 19 (Summer 1999): 169–95; and Jay Fliegelman, *Declaring Independence: Jefferson, Natural Language, and the Culture of Performance* (Stanford, CA: Stanford University Press, 1993).

10. Drew Maciag, *Edmund Burke in America: The Contested Career of the Father of Modern Conservatism* (Ithaca, NY: Cornell University Press, 2013), esp. chaps. 3, 7, and conclusion; Rachel Hope Cleves, *The Reign of Terror in America: Visions of Violence from Anti-Jacobinism to Antislavery* (New York: Cambridge University Press, 2009).

11. George Rable, *The Confederate Republic: A Revolution against Politics* (Chapel Hill: University of North Carolina Press, 1994), quote at 61.

12. TJ to John Norvell, June 11, 1807, TJP-LC; TJ to Charles Clay, Jan. 20, 1790, in *PTJ*, 16:129–30.

13. Andrew Burstein and Nancy Isenberg, *Madison and Jefferson* (New York: Random House, 2010), chaps. 11 and 12; Francis D. Cogliano, *Emperor of Liberty: Thomas Jefferson's Foreign Policy* (New Haven: Yale University Press, 2014).

14. From George Santayana, *Character and Opinion in the United States* (1920), chap. 6, in *Selected Critical Writings of George Santayana*, vol. 2, ed. Norman Henfrey (New York: Cambridge University Press, 1968).

15. Hannah Spahn, *Thomas Jefferson, Time, and History* (Charlottesville: University of Virginia Press, 2011), chap. 3.

16. John Dos Passos Papers, Special Collections, University of Virginia Library, various undated folders, in particular Box 119.

17. In one respect, Millennials give every appearance of bucking the trend, at work since the 1990s, of using Jefferson and his fellow founders in support of the "Christian nation" concept. On their increasing reluctance to affiliate with religious institutions or attribute the course of human events to divine attention, see Vern L. Bengston, "Generation Atheist," *Salon.com*, Nov. 4, 2013; and Vern L. Bengston, *Families and Faith* (New York: Oxford University Press, 2013); with regard to the deeper cultural disruptions taking place as the world of print yields to electronic forms of communication, and consciousness of history's importance recedes, see Sven Birkerts, *The Gutenberg Elegies* (New York: Faber and Faber, 2006).

18. Paul Ricoeur, *Memory, History, Forgetting* (Chicago: University of Chicago Press, 2004), 153–76, quote at 156.

19. Draft of an essay, "Jefferson Today," John Dos Passos Papers, Special Collections, University of Virginia Library, Box 119.

INDEX

Italicized page numbers refer to illustrations.

Gaines, Ernest J., 150, 238n44

Gaustad, Edwin S., 179

George III, King, 66

Gingrich, Newt: on exceptionalism, 114–15, 152; and government shutdown (1995), 96; quote on founders and marijuana, 116; and race, 153–54, 176–77; on religion and "radical secularists," 176–78, 181–82

Glass, Carter, 19

Glenn, John H., xi, 49, 134

Goldwater, Barry, 42–43

Gorbachev, Mikhail, 81–82, 131; at Monticello (1993), 89

Gordon-Reed, Annette, 133, 136, 145

Gore, Albert A., Jr., 85, 101, 106–7

Gore, Albert A., Sr., 27

Graham, Billy, 167

Great Awakening, 177

Griffin, John Howard, 135

Haley, Alex, 135

Hamilton, Alexander, 3, 4, 12, 18, 21, 27, 32, 34, 38, 58, 60, 78, 83, 101, 117, 172; Bowers's characterization of, 5, 24; Boyd charges with malfeasance, 53; Dos Passos characterizes, 54; fantasy conversation with TJ, 59; political persuasion of, 5–6, 9; as slave owner, 127; TR and Bill Clinton on, 100; worldview of updated, 111

Hand, Learned, 51

Hanff, Helene, 35, 222n19

Hanska, Jan, 168

Hart, Gary, 97, 230n15

Hayes, Rutherford B., 32

Heffley, Joel, 92

Helms, Jesse, 74

Hemings, Eston, 134, 141–44

Hemings, Madison, 70, 133, 140

Hemings, Sally, 62, 70, 99–100, 132–48, 154, 156–58, 161, 180, 199

Hemingway, Ernest, 54

Henry, Patrick, 193

Heston, Charlton, 99–100

Hitchens, Christopher, 134

Hochman, Steven, 68

Hollande, François, 109–10

Hoover, Herbert, 6–8, 10, 34, 38, 103

Horrigan, Kevin, 115

House, Colonel Edward, 5, 13

Hoyer, Steny, 91

Hull, Cordell, 5, 10, 219n9

Humphrey, Hubert H.: on integration, 129; on New Deal, 24–25; and 1968 election, 24

Hussein, Saddam, 89, 106

Iran-Contra affair, 79

Isenberg, Nancy, 134

Jackson, Andrew, 11, 38, 42, 194; chauvinism of, 111; as democratic exemplar, 12, 23, 32, 36, 68, 69; and Tea Party, 117, 120

Jarvis, William Charles, 130

Jay, John, 127

Jefferson, Martha ("Patty"), 62, 136

Jefferson, Randolph (TJ's brother), 142–43, 145, 180, 244n30

Jefferson, Thomas: agrarianism of, 28, 50, 83, 155–56, 198; and Benjamin Banneker, 127, 131; birthday marked, x–xi, 21, 25, 28, 44, 60, 63, 72, 88, 107, 125, 131, 157; class identity of, 11, 63, 88, 115; critique of sanctimonious clergy, 162–64, 178, 241n2; on debt, 63, 72, 83, 90–93, 96, 102, 105, 204; defines his Christianity, 170; deism of, 168, 176, 186–87, 242n6; directs Barbary Wars, 20, 104–5, 113, 118; on education, 7; Embargo policy of, 52, 56, 203, 204; evangelicals lay claim to, 179–85; on falsification of history, 217n6; first inaugural address of, ix, 58, 173; as force for humane democracy/social justice, 4, 6, 25, 32, 33, 130, 196; and freedom of conscience, x, 20, 69, 86, 163, 175, 185; and Sally Hemings, 62, 70, 99, 100, 132–47, 156, 158, 180, 199, 234n17; as icon of conservatives, 18, 48–49, 76–77, 90–93,

Jefferson, Thomas (*cont.*)